Che in Verse

aflame books

Edited by
Gavin O'Toole and Georgina Jiménez

Aflame Books
2 The Green
Laverstock
Wiltshire
SP1 1QS
United Kingdom
email: info@aflamebooks.com

ISBN: 9780955233951

Cover design by Peter Davidson of DVH Design, South Africa

Printed by Guangzhou Hengyuan Printing Co, China

For our children, Isabel, Nina and Caitlin

TABLE OF CONTENTS

Contents

Contents

12

Contents

PREFACE

Inevitably, to compile a collection of poetry and song of this kind requires being in contact with and accepting the help of many kind people, who have assisted us in finding material, reading and assessing it, searching for writers and publishers, researching references, and translating and editing the poems and songs themselves. We are lucky to have benefited in this endeavour from the enthusiastic help and support of a large number of individuals and — over and above those who have granted us permission to reproduce poems, songs or translations (see Acknowledgements) — we would like to thank those mentioned below as well as all those who helped us but who may not be mentioned here.

Our gratitude goes, first and foremost, to the Institute for the Study of the Americas (ISA) of the University of London, where one of the editors, Gavin O'Toole, was granted a Visiting Postdoctoral Fellowship to support the research that has culminated in this book. Without that institutional support, gaining the participation of so many poets and songwriters from across the world would have been immeasurably more difficult. We are thankful in particular to Professor James Dunkerley, Karen Perkins and Olga Jiménez of ISA. Second, our gratitude goes to all the poets and songwriters, their families or those who manage their creative efforts whose work is reproduced in this book. As will become clear from the *Introduction*, the commitment they have shown and the sacrifices so many of them have made for their art is recognised. We are also grateful to all our translators, and in particular those who went beyond the call of duty to help us: Alexandra Stanton, Yusuf Eradam, Simon Patton, and Brother Anthony of Taizé.

Many other people helped make this book possible and they are gratefully acknowledged from Page 324.

Gavin O'Toole and Georgina Jiménez
London, May 2007

INTRODUCTION

GAVIN O'TOOLE

The poems in this book speak eloquently of self-sacrifice — the sacrifice of a man and a small band of comrades for what they considered to be a noble cause — but also the sacrifices made by the poets and songwriters moved by this story and the injustice of the world in which it was acted out. Many of those poets and songwriters whose work is included paid a high price for their beliefs — and some paid dearly for writing about Ernesto "Che" Guevara, the Argentine-Cuban guerrilla who was executed in Bolivia on October 9 1967 and who is the subject of this collection.

The Turkish poets Metin Demirtaş and Arif Damar, for example, were arrested and prosecuted in Ankara in 1968 for the poems about Che Guevara that are reproduced in this anthology. At that time Turkey was considered in the anti-communist West as a bulwark against Soviet expansion into the Mediterranean, and Demirtaş and Damar were among a number of writers and publishers prosecuted. This was a period of leftwing unrest and the growing threat of military reaction during which, behind the constitutional government of Süleyman Demirel, the chiefs of staff pressed hard for tough action against militants.

Demirtaş was acquitted on July 12 1968 after more than a month of imprisonment during his trial. Notes of his defence counsel reveal that he challenged the verdict on his poem by a panel of experts and argued in favour of recognising Guevara not as a communist but as a great anti-imperialist, so linking him with Turkey's own tradition of nationalist struggle against the Ottoman Empire. Defence notes from his trial read:

> "… we must underline how wrong is the verdict of a jury [of consultants] who understand communism when in fact it is anti-imperialism that is at issue. To them, communism and anti-imperialism are identical. No doubt, communism is against imperialism, but

communism does not necessarily mean anti-imperialism... The Turkish Republic was born out of a war against foreign imperialistic aspirations ie. we, Turkish patriots, owe our existence to this war against imperialism...".[1]

Damar — one of the major poets of the 1940s socialist generation in Turkish literature — was no stranger to persecution: he was prosecuted or detained no less than four times for his poetry. In his defence during his 1968 trial in Ankara, which also resulted in his acquittal, he, too, made an impassioned plea for the court to recognise the importance of Guevara as a hero of anti-imperialism and, therefore, of direct relevance to Turkey. With some prescience, Damar said:

"One day, history will search for the reactions of intellectuals from different nations to this unfortunate death of Che Guevara. If history says Turks gave no response to this event, then our children in the future will be put to shame. By writing this poem, let alone commiting a crime, I believe I have paid my duty to my own people by not staying indifferent to his death. I wrote my poem in such a feeling for my own people here in Turkey. It is no propaganda."[2]

The words of these poets — and the repression or censorship endured by others such as the Indian K.G. Sankara Pillai for daring to write about Guevara — help to explain why, as the Soviet Latin Americanists Vera Kuteischikova and Lev Ospovat suggested in 1977, Che's exploits have become part of the poetic patrimony of the world.[3] Che Guevara is seen by the poets from across the world whose work is reproduced here as a source of inspiration standing uniquely above both the specific circumstances of his own individual experience and above other heroic figures from contemporary history. This suggests that he can be considered, as I shall argue below from an analysis of the verse reproduced in this collection, a *sui generis* martyr of a rare, universal kind arguably comparable in our experience only with Jesus Christ — a figure with whom poets frequently compare him.

This book brings together verses written by 135 poets and song-writers from 53 countries — many published for the first time in English — that are dedicated to, about, or make a telling reference to Che in an effort to explore the Guevara phenomenon through verse. It is our privilege to be able to republish these works and others that have not seen the light of day for many years in an era in which the political postures many of these poets adopted have almost been forgotten and are only, hesitantly, being rediscovered. The aim is to shed some light on what it is about this historical figure that has been of such enduring cultural appeal far beyond his homeland. Guevara is by no means the only storied Latin American hero who in death has transcended a national setting to become an international icon, but arguably he is the most important.[4] This book also gives us an opportunity to look briefly at the relationship Che Guevara himself had with poetry and his own writings, and it is to that we first turn.

Biographies of Guevara invariably make reference to his intellectual development and the avid reading habits he developed from childhood as a result of his asthmatic condition, which confined him to bed and forced him to spend long hours consuming literature. His parents instilled in him an interest in books but it is likely that his mother, Celia de la Serna y Llosa, was the most important influence upon his early intellectual development, overseeing his home-based education and nurturing his love of literature.[5] Poetry was in the family: Celia had been raised by her older sister, Carmen, who in 1928 married a communist poet and journalist, Cayetano Córdova Itúrburu.[6] Che's father, Ernesto Guevara Lynch, is depicted in biographies of his son more as an active than a studious man, and there is a celebrated account of him as a boy slapping the young Jorge Luis Borges after the latter had reported him to a teacher for not letting him study.[7] In his own writing about his son, Guevara Lynch makes reference to but does not dwell upon the young Ernesto's extensive reading matter.[8]

Like any boy, Ernesto Guevara loved reading adventure stories and those about travel, swallowing up the tales of Alexandre Dumas, Robert Louis Stevenson, Jack London, Jules Verne and Emilio Salgari and exploring the work of Miguel de Cervantes,

Anatole France, Horacio Quiroga and Giovanni Boccaccio. However, in a comprehensive survey of the extent to which literature shaped Che's personality, Kuteischikova and Ospovat argued that poetry was of particular interest to him.[9] His family became friendly with the exiled militant Spanish communist poet Rafael Alberti when Ernesto was about 11, and as a teenager he read Alberti's work and that of other poets linked to the Spanish Civil war such as Pablo Neruda, Antonio Machado, Miguel Hernández and Federico García Lorca.[10] Guevara's mother taught him French, and he began to read Charles Baudelaire in the original and, as a youth attending the Colegio Nacional Deán Funes of Córdoba, displayed a sophisticated level of cultural reading.[11] Taibo (1999) says that he also read the poetry of Paul Verlaine and, once his family had moved to Córdoba when he was 15, the work of the symbolist poet Stéphane Mallarmé, whose complex use of language suggests a sophisticated knowledge of French.[12] Anderson (1998) suggests that the teenage Ernesto showed a particular interest in the ribald, reciting bawdy verses to a blushing Dolores Moyano, a friend of his sister.[13] Accounts of Che Guevara's interest in poetry follow him in his peregrinations across Latin America. Taibo recounts that his friends often recalled him reciting poetry, in particular that of Neruda.[14] Alberto Granado refers frequently to Che dipping into poetry during their now famous motorcycle trip across Latin America, and said that he could recite verses of Neruda and José Martí from memory.[15] In Peru during the same trip, Guevara literally submerged himself in reading about history and archaeology.[16]

Later, in Guatemala, Guevara and the Peruvian Hilda Gadea — who would become his first wife — discovered a shared interest in poetry and she loaned him a book by her countryman, the radical César Vallejo.[17] Gadea also introduced Che to the work of the Spaniard León Felipe, whose poetry he came to know well and often quoted. Taibo recounts an anecdote by Che's friend Ricardo Rojo of a time in Mexico City when Guevara finally met Felipe in a café: that when both men crossed their legs during their conversation he could see that their shoes had been worn through to the soles.[18] In turn, Che Guevara gave Gadea a volume by the Uruguayan poet Juana de Ibarbourou, sometimes known as Juana de América, an early Latin American feminist.[19] An important poem by Ibarbourou, in which her feminism is very evident, ironically is titled "La Higuera" ("The Fig Tree"), the name of the village in Bolivia in which Che would later die. Ibarbourou's poetry, often erotic, also deals with the theme of death, expressing both an intense fear of oblivion but also playing with the notion of living on after death through plant life. Guevara and Gadea also shared an interest in Rudyard Kipling's *If*, one of the world's most reproduced poems evoking virtues of heroism and stoicism.[20]

During a trip to El Salvador in this period, Che was briefly picked up by the police for reciting radical poetry and talking about agrarian reform. Taibo recounts that he received a dressing down, and stern words of advice: stick to his love for poetry but avoid politics.[21] He moved on to Mexico where, from December 1955, he studied Russian at the Mexican-Soviet Institute of Cultural Relations in Tacubaya, Mexico City. It is likely he came into contact with Russian poetry and he expressed his interest in Soviet literature to Nikolai Leonov, a young Soviet diplomat studying Spanish who knew Raúl Castro. Che borrowed from Leonov the influential communist novel by Nikolai Ostrovsky, *How the Steel Was Tempered* and Boris Polevoi's socialist adventure novel *A Story About a Real Man*.[22] In his book, Ostrovsky, a socialist realist, exhorts his readers to sacrifice in fighting for the liberation of mankind. On the eve of leaving the country for Cuba, Che bought two books for a comrade Carlos Bermúdez: *Reports Written Under the Noose* by the Czech communist Julius Fucík, which brims with hope for a better, communist future, and *The Young Guard* by the Russian writer Alexander Alexandrovich Fadeyev, which recounts the exploits of guerrilla Komsomol fighters battling the Nazis.[23]

When the Cuban revolutionary war had begun, books accompanied Che Guevara into the field during the guerrilla campaign in the Sierra Maestra. He set aside time for reading and accounts suggest he often asked comrades to bring books from the city, including the poetry of Neruda, Goethe, the heretical John Milton and Luis de Góngora.[24] Witnesses recount that Guevara battled fatigue so that he could remain awake in order to read.[25] Kuteischikova and Ospovat reviewed the long list of books that can be found in accounts of Che Guevara's period in the Sierra Maestra, and say journalists who visited the guerrilla leaders in the hills noted his expansive reading tastes: Marx, Jean-Paul Sartre, Merleau-Ponti, the radical Spanish dramatist Ramón María del Valle-Inclán, Arnold Toynbee, Simone de Beauvoir. They quote an old peasant Chana Pérez: "He never left his backpack with his books. I also remember that when he had a book in his hands he became so calm, as if half absent, and his face looked kind, as if he was in another world."[26]

In the heady early days of the revolution after the military victory, Guevara also met or corresponded with several poets. In early January 1959, he received the Haitian René Depestre at the La Cabaña fortress in Havana and talked at length with him about poetry. On February 5 1959 he wrote to another poet, Pedro Revuelta, thanking him for verses and songs dedicated to him, and closed by sending a "… greeting from a revolutionary who never turned out to be a poet".[27] In his official positions within the new government, he demonstrated a strong inclination for universal ideas, counting among his friends or correspondents such illustrious intellectual figures as Sartre, De Beauvoir, René Dumont, Charles Bettelheim and Ernesto Sábato. In a homage to his Guatemalan friend and fellow revolutionary, Julio Roberto Cáceres Valle, "El Patojo", Che Guevara instinctively drew upon poetry, referring to, then quoting, the poetry of his *compañero*: "Old mutual friends in Mexico… brought me some poems he had written in a notebook and left there. They are the last verses of a revolutionary; they are, in addition, a love song to the revolution, to the homeland, and to a woman."[28] According to Castañeda (1997), the only child of Che Guevara's born out of wedlock that he would acknowledge was Omar Pérez, named after the Persian poet Omar Khayyám, a copy of whose work, the *Rubaiyat*, Che gave to Lilia Rosa Pérez, the boy's mother. Khayyám's poetry demonstrates a nihilistic preoccupation with mortality and transience. Ironically, Omar Pérez became a poet himself who served time in one of the labour camps for dissidents established by his own father.[29]

Later, during Che Guevara's famous stopover in Ireland in March 1965 — the last time he was seen in public outside Cuba —

he held long conversations with the Cuban poet and editor of the *Casa de las Américas* magazine, Roberto Fernández Retamar, who was returning from Paris on the same plane. Fernández Retamar had met Che several times in the company of other poets, such as Neruda and Nicolás Guillén, but during the unscheduled stopover at Shannon Airport gained the opportunity to talk at length with him.[30] In the second of two articles about this encounter, Fernández Retamar recalled that only later did he realise what some of the things they had discussed meant — for it would be in the week after their return to Cuba that Che Guevara decided to leave the island once and for all.[31] Shortly after they had landed, Fernández Retamar went to see Che to request back from him an anthology of poetry compiled by Federico de Onís Sánchez, the Spanish critic and writer, that he had lent the comandante to read on the plane. When the book was returned, Che Guevara's secretary told Fernández Retamar that he had been told to copy down one of the poems, but asked him to be discreet about this: the poem was "Farewell" by Neruda.

Kuteischikova and Ospovat suggest that Neruda had become an important focus of Che Guevara's poetic reading during his early travels when he arrived in Chile in 1951 and knew about the travails of the poet at the hands of the anti-communist president Gabriel González Videla.[32] Neruda had fled to Guevara's native Argentina, and Kuteischikova and Ospovat suggest that Che may have sought in him some poetic anticipation of his own fate, perhaps confirmed by the "Farewell" story.[33] Taibo writes that, even at the height of the guerrilla campaign in Bolivia, Che was recalling the words of Neruda's "Un canto para Bolívar" with reference to the death of Eliseo Reyes, a veteran of the Cuban campaign and an important pillar of the Bolivian guerrilla unit: "... of his obscure death we can only say, for a hypothetical future that may become real: 'Your little brave captain's body/has spread its metallic shape out into the immense void.'"[34]

Even in the last weeks of Che's life and in his death, poetry figures in his story. Anderson quotes a poem he wrote in those final weeks of the Bolivian campaign that took the form of a last will and testament to his wife Aleida and suggested he knew his time was running out: "This poem (against wind and tide) will carry my signature./I give to you six sonorous syllables,/a look which always bears (like a wounded bird) tenderness...".[35] Taibo adds that in a green notebook found among items in the knapsack, he had copied down poems by Neruda and Guillén, although there are conflicting accounts of exactly which works the notebook contained and Castañeda suggests it included the work of Felipe.[36] Either way, all three of these celebrated poets — Neruda, Guillén and Felipe — would write poetic tributes to Guevara.

Given his interest in literature, it is not surprising that Guevara himself also wrote poetry as a youth and into adulthood.[37] Anderson argues, for example, that as an adolescent Guevara confronted his crowded feelings through poetry, and quotes a dark and troubled verse he wrote in 1947 while working away from home in his first full-time job after leaving college: "I know it! I know it!/If I get out of here the river swallows me.../It is my destiny: Today I must die!/... The bullets, what can the bullets do to me if/my destiny is to die by drowning.../Die, yes, but riddled with/bullets...".[38] His correspondence with his sweetheart María del Carmen ("Chichina") Ferreyra displays tangible passion.[39] A letter he wrote to Chichina a few days after their romance had blossomed on a night in October 1950 begins with a verse that Castañeda describes as "both hesitant and obvious in its intent": "For those green eyes, whose paradoxical/light announces to me the danger of/losing myself in them".[40] However, it was in Mexico that Guevara became more active as a writer, and he penned a number of poems in this period (September 1954-November 1956). Such was his interest in poetry during his time in Mexico, that Taibo refers to him as a "physician-poet" moved, for example, to write a poem, "Vieja María", about the death from asthma of an old lady on the wards of the General Hospital of Mexico City where he was working in December 1954.[41] Taibo writes: "If poetry is an intimate space, and the poet, good or bad, uses poems to say what he would not put down in a journal, his memoir, or his correspondence; if the poem or a snatch of lyric gives us a glimpse of the inner life — then young Dr Guevara's Mexico poems will say more about him than his essays."[42] The ruins of ancient Mexico also inspired Che to follow in the footsteps of Neruda and express his feelings about the physical grandeur of pre-Columbian civilisation. At the end of his honeymoon trip with Gadea in south-eastern Mexico, he wrote a poem entitled "Palenque" which combined obligatory anti-American snipes — especially about "gringo tourists" — with an invocation of the mourned Incas and observations about the eternal youth of King Pacal's city.[43]

It was also in Mexico that Guevara wrote what is probably his most oft-cited poem in which he praised Fidel Castro and reaffirmed his willingness to support the Cuban leader in his efforts to free his homeland. "Canto a Fidel" ("Song to Fidel", sometimes called "Come Blazing Prophet of the Dawn", from the poem's second line), was written either while Che languished in the Miguel Schultz jail in Mexico City just after Castro's release or while Guevara was training for the Cuban expedition on the Santa Rosa ranch in Chalco, Mexico: "... Let's go, blazing prophet of the dawn/Along the unfenced winding pathways/To free the green alligator you love so much/.../And if iron should cross our path,/we shall ask for a shroud of Cuban tears/To cover the guerrillas' bones/On the road to Latin American history./Nothing more./...".[44] Although there is disagreement about when this poem was written, it is generally agreed that it was not one of Che's best and that he never in fact gave it to Fidel and may have handed it over to Gadea.[45] In an analysis of this poem, Mañalich Suarez (2001) argues that it reveals an attraction to epic poetry and the use of metaphor. Taibo says that while this poem reflects the high esteem in which Che held the Cuban leader — and the seriousness with which, by that stage, he was taking the revolutionary cause — it also reflects the irony that a man later the subject of so much heroic poetry found it so difficult to pen a credible eulogy of his own and, indeed, regarded poetry as a private affair.[46] Che did not consider himself to be a writer — a title, he told Ernesto Sábato, that was the "most sacred" in the world.[47] Years later, "Canto a Fidel" was published by Leonel Soto, editor of the magazine *Verde Olivo*, to whom Che sent an angry note warning him not to publish anything else without permission, especially "those awful verses".[48]

Che Guevara's poetic preferences and his own writing can give us insights into his personality and also into how he understood the role of the writer. It is important to note that many poets in the developing world, particularly in Latin America, have been associated with progressive and revolutionary politics and that, in turn, Che was not the only revolutionary figure to have written poetry — so did Mao Tse-tung and Ho Chi Minh, for example. Lucío Cabañas Barrientos, the Mexican guerrilla influenced by Guevara who died in 1974, even wrote his own elegy to Che: "The world is singing an anthem with sorrow/while the machine-guns keep up their rat-tat-tat/because struggling for our freedom in the Sierra/Commander Che Guevara has died."[49]

Common threads emerge when one examines what the young Ernesto read, encountering at a young age both French symbolism and the poetry that emerged from the Spanish Civil War. Guevara's youthful preferences seem to have favoured, on the one hand, poets with a disregard for moral and social conventions, such as the symbolists; and on the other, Hispanic poets who gave voice to notions of solidarity and brotherhood as epitomised by the Republican sacrifices of the Spanish Civil War and Latin American struggles for independence. His reading matter reflected the ideas of determined non-conformists and the struggle between good and evil as expressed by radical writers.

Baudelaire is often considered the foremost precursor of symbolist poetry and had himself taken part in the revolutions of 1848. His convictions incorporated anarchism and republicanism, as well as a candour about sex and death that in his day was considered unwholesome. Verlaine — initially a French Communard — used the expression "accursed poet" to refer to a number of other like-minded poets such as Mallarmé who fought against poetic conventions and suffered social rebuke.

Poets linked to the Spanish Civil War were also a staple. Alberti — who knew Ernesto's family — was an exile from the war and his collection *13 Stripes and 48 Stars* (1936), published when Che Guevara was aged seven, brings together songs of protest against the role of "yankee imperialism" and intervention in the Americas. García Lorca was killed by Nationalist partisans at the beginning of the war and Antonio Machado y Ruiz — initially close to the French symbolists — died as he fled Franco's Nationalist forces. Vallejo was also greatly moved by the Spanish civil war, in which he was deeply engaged at an intellectual level.

The Guevara family also had its own poetic links with the Spanish Civil War. Ernesto's uncle, Córdova Itúrburu was a former editor of the 1920s avant-garde literary magazine *Martín Fierro* and an active, radical participant in the struggles of the Agrupación de Intelectuales, Artistas, Periodistas, Escritores (AIAPE, the Association of Intellectuals, Artists, Journalists and Writers) against the perceived onslaught of fascism on Argentine culture under José F. Uriburu.[50] As vice president of AIAPE, Córdova Itúrburu travelled to Spain in 1937 during the civil war and published accounts of his journey. The young Ernesto's Aunt Carmen and her two children went to live at his home in Alta Gracia in this period, and he was exposed to all the dispatches, notes and articles that Córdova Itúrburu sent back and that passed through the house.[51] It is interesting to note that Nicolás Guillén, described as "the poet laureate of revolutionary Cuba", was at the same anti-fascist congress of writers and intellectuals in Spain in 1937 attended by Córdova Itúrburu, whom there is a high probability he met.[52]

Latin American anti-imperialism and solidarity were also key themes within Che's reading matter. Kuteischikova and Ospovat suggest that José Martí — often called the apostle of Cuban independence and the father of the Spanish-American literary movement *modernismo* — represented for Guevara the most important fusion of artist and revolutionary, and also cherished a compelling vision of his people's moral rebirth.[53] Che often repeated the poet's maxim that "Doing is the best way of saying" and his invocations of solidarity within Latin America.[54] It was Neruda, however, who best combined all these various thematic strands among Che's poetic interests. While in Spain during the Civil War, the Chilean befriended many of the poets the young Guevara would read, and it had been Neruda's experiences of the war — and in particular the murder of García Lorca — that had transformed him into an ardent communist and a supporter of the republican cause. Che often quoted the role of such fraternal friendships in words taken from the epic Argentine poem *Martín Fierro* by José Hernández, "If brothers fight, strangers devour them" ("Si los hermanos se pelean, los extraños los devoran"), but he found the highest realisation of this idea of solidarity in Neruda's *Canto general*, whose verses he knew by heart and quoted during his visit to the Incan city of Machu Picchu.[55] It is notable that Neruda's own journey to Machu Picchu in 1943 had been a decisive influence in the crystallisation of this epic poem, portraying the majesty of the indigenous inheritance as a source of unity in Latin America. The *Canto general* became one of the most important books in Che's life, as it did for millions of Latin Americans, with accounts by those who met him suggesting that not only did he read it in the Sierra Maestra but spoke recurrently to peasants he met there about it.

These preferences and his own poetry give us an insight into aspects of Che Guevara's character. First, his writing reveals a romantic strain and he either wrote poetry to, or shared an interest in poetry with, all of his closest female companions. Carlos María Gutiérrez (1969), for example, suggests that it was something akin to romanticism, brought out by the charisma of Castro, that prompted Guevara to join the revolutionary band within hours of having first met the Cuban leader in Mexico City.[56]

Second, despite the connotations of the term that Guevara himself would have decried, it must also be said that he was, undoubtedly, in some respects an idealist. He possessed a sensibility to ideas and a powerful imagination that enabled him at times in his life to transcend his own difficult reality — a characteristic, one could speculate, that he put to good use during those years as a sickly child spent reading in bed. Kuteischikova and Ospovat cite the Mexican writer Emmanuel Carballo, who suggested that Che's character combined polar qualities that were, at first sight, incompatible — realism and fantasy — and it was this that helped to explain his ability both to rise above his condition and convert his dreams into reality.[57] At times, Guevara even described himself as an *artist of the will*: someone with weak lungs who had turned willpower into an art form, and Kuteischikova and Ospovat also argue that a belief that willpower can transform ideas into reality are also evident in his interest in Cervantes' Don Quixote.[58] Quixote, enthused by dreams, constructs his own revolutionary life — he writes his poems with his lance and thus from fantasy comes concrete acts. Kuteischikova and Ospovat suggest that Che Guevara fully apprehended this image, and they noted, as do several poets, how he identified with the character in his last letter to his parents before leaving for Bolivia: "Once again I feel beneath my heels the ribs of Rocinante..." ("Otra vez siento bajo mis talones el costillar de Rocinante...") — a line quoted at the start of Ernesto Con's ode to Guevara in this collection. In León Felipe's own elegy to Che, "The Great Neigh", written in 1968 shortly before the poet's death, he transforms himself into Rocinante to mock the US:

> People often say, the Americans,
> the North Americans often say:
> León Felipe is a "Don Quixote".
> Not so much, gentlemen, not so much.
> I carry the hero nothing else...
> and yes, I can say...
> and I like saying:
> that I am Rocinante.
> I am not the hero
> but I carry him on the lean bones of my back...[59]

It is worthy of note that Castro has often said that his favourite literary hero is also Quixote and has himself been compared with Cervantes' character.[60] Other revolutionaries who have given themselves over to a fate determined almost entirely by their ideals, such as the poet Roque Dalton, have been compared with Quixote as well.

Che Guevara's idealism was also reflected in a sense of destiny, and Castañeda suggests Che had a strong fatalistic notion of his own historical mission that would lead him to an inevitable, preordained death.[61] Kuteischikova and Ospovat argue that references to death in Che's writing suggested a strong inclination towards a metaphorical interpretation of life.[62] Guevara's childhood reading also helps to contextualise his wanderlust based on a lifelong fascination with the rest of the world. An ambivalence towards being attached to one place was a characteristic feature of his personality, and he would become angry with journalists who referred to his "former homeland" of Argentina, insisting that his homeland was "Latin America".[63] Taibo notes that during the two years he stayed in Mexico there were 161 mentions of possible or hypothetical journeys in his correspondence with his family and two friends alone, and Che's poems from this time reflect this.[64] As an itinerant ambassador for the young Cuban revolutionary regime, Guevara travelled widely and formed attachments with many international figures.

Lastly, Che Guevara's own poetic preferences and references to poetry and literature in some of his writings offer an insight into the role he attributed to artists and creative pursuits in the new socialist society. His interest in the ethical dimensions of the revolution grew in his last years and in perhaps his most famous essay he envisaged the creation of a socialist "new man".[65] This idea was already in formation by 1964 as well a vision of artistic creation that he would weave into it that coincided with the ideas of Neruda and the Russian poet Vladimir Mayakovsky, both of whom believed that poetry could find a place in man's struggles and so could work for the majority. Che's formulation of these ideas crystallised around the verse of Felipe whose *El Ciervo* (The Stag, 1954) was one of the few books he said he kept on his bedside table.[66] The central image of *El Ciervo* is symbolic, suggesting a man persecuted throughout history. In a speech to workers on 15 August 1964, Che Guevara cited Felipe when talking about the relationship man will have with his work in the new society.[67] In a letter to Felipe a week later, he recounted how "the failed poet within" had drawn upon Felipe's words when addressing those workers. The Italian cineaste Gianni Toti, found in *El Ciervo* the key to Che's personality: "He would have wanted to realise what had already been realised by the eternally hunted stag... but to confront all his own persecutors with everyone on the planet...".[68] Guevara's "Man and Socialism in Cuba" ("El socialismo y el hombre en Cuba" 1965) advocates the creation of a new consciousness in man, "a complete spiritual rebirth in his attitude", and in this essay he devotes considerable attention to the role of the artist and of creativity. Guevara argues that Cuban art suffers not from the exaggerated dogmatism of "socialist realism" but from the opposite

— the fault of Cuba's artists and intellectuals lay in their original sin: they were not truly revolutionary. As Che writes: "We can try to graft the elm tree so that it will bear pears, but at the same time we must plant pear trees. New generations will come who will be free of the original sin."[69]

THE SELECTION

The poets whose work is included in this book come to the theme of Che Guevara from a broad range of experiences and political traditions, but we can identify some common experiences that contribute to an understanding of their motives. First, as with Guevara himself, the Spanish Civil War was a profound influence on the lives of many of the older Hispanic poets who either experienced it at first hand or started writing poetry under the influence of exiled Spanish teachers who had fled Franco's regime. Second, a number of the poets whose work is reproduced in this collection had met Guevara or were in contact with him. Alberti's poem derives from his friendship with the Guevara family; Otto-Raúl González met Che in Guatemala before the Cuban Revolution; the Haitian poet René Depestre was invited to Cuba in 1959 by Guevara; Changmarín met him in Havana at a meeting of Latin American communist parties; the Mexican José Tiquet knew both Che and his first wife Hilda Gadea; according to Taibo, the Argentine poet Juan Gelman passed on a message to Che that he had received in Buenos Aires from the journalist Jorge Ricardo Masetti who, together with Guevara and others, had conceived of an operation to set up a guerrilla flashpoint in Argentina.[70] The Russian poet Yevgeny Yevtushenko visited Cuba where he met Guevara, and the Canadian Al Purdy recalled shaking Che's hand while in Havana.

Third, there are also discernible links between some of our contributors themselves, especially those who were active in social struggles in the era of Che Guevara's death. The Uruguayan protest singer Aníbal Sampayo, for example, would have met Carlos Puebla, Ewan MacColl, Peggy Seeger and the Italian editor of a subsequent collection on Che, Meri Franco Lao, as well as key figures later responsible for the *Casa de las Américas* magazine's issues dedicated to Che at the Encuentro de la Canción Protesta held in Havana in the summer of 1967, just months before Che's death.[71]

Fourth, a number of the poets in this book — especially those from the developing world — experienced at first hand the violence of warfare or anti-colonial resistance. Fifth, much of the poetry and song included here was written by men and woman active in revolutionary, leftwing or progressive politics then and now. A number of the poets included in this book were either active in revolutionary organisations and warfare or in communist parties and politics. These poets often combined, as Margaret Randall wrote of the rebellious Salvadorean Roque Dalton, "a visionary poetic with a visionary politics", whether writing about Che Guevara or radical themes in general.[72] Dalton, for example, found it simply impossible to separate his poetry from his militancy, writing:

> "If the revolution, or rather, the struggle of my
> people, my party, my revolutionary theory, are
> the fundamental pillars upon which I want to
> base my life and if I consider life in all its intensi-
> ty as the great source and great content of poetry,
> what sense is there while I am creating of aban-
> doning my duties as a man and as a militant?
> Undoubtedly there is no sense."[73]

Many of those in this book remain engaged in progressive struggles and Third World issues today. Some of the translators in this collection were or are also social activists in their own right or have worked in conflict situations. Sixth, a significant number of the poets in this collection wrote about Che Guevara at a time of great risk during the Cold War in countries under authoritarian regimes. Some of our contributors also suffered *artistic* persecution for their work or have been involved in struggles to defend artistic integrity.

Another experience that many of the poets whose work is included in this book have shared is that of exile, from the period of the Spanish Civil War to the present. A large number of the Latin American and Caribbean poets included in this collection were exiled, or went into self-exile because of the threat to their safety, at least once during their lives and some several times. Other poets were marginalised in a more metaphorical sense by angst, trauma, the colour of their skin or a sexual identity or ideas that challenged the established norms of the societies in which they lived.

Lastly, several poets also suffered persecution for writing the poems that are included in this volume or were unable to publish them when they were written because of political repression. For example, K.G. Sankara Pillai's poem "Dear Che" — one of a series named "Red Diary" to mark an upsurge of popular activism in the state of Kerala and other parts of India — was written in 1972 for a journal edited by the poet, *Prasakthi*, but police confiscated the issue and the poem was never published.

A great deal of verse has been written about Che Guevara and, as a result, the selection reproduced in this collection can only be suggestive, rather than comprehensive. We have followed the approach adopted by other collections that draw together diverse strands around a single common theme and *Che in Verse* is not intended to be an authoritative record of poetry and songs about Guevara.[74] Many different styles of poetry and songs deriving from different traditions are included and our principal objective has been to be as expansive in our reach as possible. Although Cuba and Latin America are, inevitably, the main sources of poetry about Che, we have consciously limited the number of Latin American and Caribbean poems included in order to highlight and explore verse from other regions of the world.

This collection contains mainly poetry, but also includes protest songs in an effort to draw attention to the close relationship between poetry and ballads that take as their theme a heroic or martyred figure. Although many songs are poems put to music, other songs in fact highlight the limitations of verse as it becomes more popular, often reducing to a small and repetitive repertoire the images and ideas about a theme in comparison with their poetic cousins. Nonetheless, the Guevara story lent itself well to song, and a significant number of recordings by individual artists or collections about Guevara have been released since the 1970s, many initially produced through the Cuban record company Empresa de Grabaciones y Ediciones Musicales (EGREM). Today a number of websites provide lists of songs or offer downloads of them.[75]

In Latin America Che Guevara's story inspired many songs that fit within the broad tradition of the *canto popular* — an important vehicle calling for social change. In a survey of Che Guevara in Latin American songs, Mariana Martins Villaça (2004) concludes that these reveal how Che has been elevated into a species of "martyr of all struggles" and/or a "generalised hero of resistance".[76] Yet Guevara clearly appealed to musicians beyond Latin America, and songs from a number of other countries — France, Egypt and England — are also included in this book. Che has also been — and continues to be — adapted to contemporary rock, a Latin American example of which is the "Red Cockerel" ("Gallo rojo") sung by Los Fabulosos Cadillacs, the Argentine band that assumes a fraternal, intimate position towards him. Rock or rap songs by popular non-Latin American artists making reference to Che have included those of David Bowie ("Panic in Detroit"), Against Me! ("Cliché Guevara"), the Manic Street Preachers ("Revol") and Nas ("My Country").[77]

The aim of this book is to explore the global impact of Che Guevara in verse, and our priority has been to give readers a balanced meal and not to gorge them with the richest dishes and finest wines on the poetic menu. Che is the subject of this book, not poetry itself, and this collection aims only to be a literary footnote that makes a small, but genuine, contribution to knowledge about the impact of an important historical figure within one cultural medium. For this reason, this collection also includes some works that — by poetic standards — may seem naïve, over-optimistic or ill-judged, or that contain references to events or people related to the Guevara story that have subsequently proven inaccurate.[78] A small number of the poems in this book have not been published before either in their original language or in English, and we have also selected several poems in which Che makes an appearance only as an incidental figure in an effort to portray a different and equally important dimension of the inclusion of this character in verse. The translations are mainly literal, but at the same time we have aspired to achieve literary merit. They have been kept as faithful as possible to the originals to the extent, for example, that we have left the diacritical mark in the name Ché where that is what the poet has done (and in the case of Allen Ginsberg, mischievously, also in the name Guévara). In most cases the works in this collection are dated according to the known year in which they were written, first published or first compiled within a collection but in some cases caution is required. In the case of Sebastião Alba (Mozambique), for example, the work was unpublished before his death in 2000 then published posthumously in 2003, and so it is not known with precision exactly when he wrote it.

The poems and songs are compiled by country but the collection does not offer anything like a representative sample of material from each — merely a selection of what we have found, or what we have been able to gain permission to reproduce. As a result, it is not possible to make judgments that are empirically watertight about the approach taken to the theme of Che Guevara by poets from different countries or regions. However, although the sample is too small to go beyond useful generalisations, we can make observations about the traditions in which some of these poems have been written and draw attention to similar features within poems from these. We can also identify key themes across all of these poems and songs that can tell us something about depictions of Che Guevara in this branch of literary culture.

Such an endeavour should start with Cuba itself, where poems about Che Guevara before and after his death reflect a broader period of creative writing following a somewhat barren period in literature during the Batista era and fuelled by the new national historiography that was developing from within the Revolution.[79] Many members of an older generation of poets who had begun publishing in the 1930s and 1940s and who were later identified with the Revolution had not been in Cuba during the late Batista period.[80] This had meant that a characteristic of older poets who came to dominate the country's literary infrastructure was their knowledge of other literatures, and their work was often coloured by an individualism that only turns into a slow integration with the revolutionary project.[81] To one of Cuba's greatest poets, Nicolás Guillén, for example, Che is inserted into a progression that had only by the 1960s moved to an open assault on imperialism and a celebration of the Revolution.[82] The work of poets who began publishing or became prominent after the Revolution, such as Miguel Barnet and Pedro Pérez Sarduy, was in some ways less expressive yet turned with more force to the themes of daily life, speaking *from* the Revolution and not *about* the Revolution.[83] Just as the documentary novel was one of the most popular forms of narrative to emerge in Cuba after the Revolution, we might also consider many of the Cuban verses about Che as a species of documentary poem.[84] They did not address a coterie audience and adopted an open stylism while taking their lead from established poets who had embraced the Revolution such as Guillén.[85] They turned away from some of the preoccupations of the past, such as national identity, and began to aspire in their audience, unspokenly, to the notional "new man" of the kind envisaged by Che — emancipated of territorial constraints and past ideas.

A large number of Cuban poems and songs about Che Guevara written both before and after his death have been published, and the main and very obvious reason for this is that poets had a natural patron willing to print their work in the revolutionary state: Cuban poets could publish about Che without apparent fear or favour. Although we have included only seven Cuban works in this collection — a small fraction of what is available — it is very clear that in most of these there is a sense of ownership of and an intimacy with the Guevara story. In this respect, Cuban poems and songs about Che Guevara do not differ markedly from those of the rest of Latin America. Nonetheless, discernibly different perspectives and stylistic methods that derive from diverse social conditions can be identified in the approach taken by other Latin Americans whose work is incorporated in this study. Many works hail Che's prowess as a warrior; by contrast, Víctor Jara's song, "Apparition" ("El aparecido") praises his heroism but does not endorse his guerrilla tactics — reflecting the powerful tradition of the Chilean workers' movement of mass struggle and the existence of strong, established socialist and communist parties.

This sense of ownership of the Guevara story was not confined to Cuba or Latin America and the first collection of poetry about Che to appear in book form after his death, *Poemas al Che* (1969), brought together poems from both the Americas and Spain.[86] The Catalan poet and critic José Batlló had collected the work of Spanish poets with something to say about the fallen hero with the initial intention of publishing these in his home country.[87]

Outside the Hispanic world, there is one other country whose poets demonstrate a sense of ownership in this story: Ireland. Ethnic connection and its many contradictions is a powerful theme in the Irish understanding of the world, and Guevara has been of interest to some writers because of Irish antecedents on his father's side, the Lynch family. It was an Irish artist, Jim Fitzpatrick, who created the iconic two-tone black on red portrait of Che Guevara in 1968 based on Alberto Korda's celebrated photograph that influenced so many of the poets in this book. Che Guevara himself made reference to this connection with Ireland when he wrote to his father in late 1964 while stopping over in Dublin, referring to the "emerald isle of your ancestors" and how fascinated Irish journalists had been with the Lynch family history.[88] In 1969, two years after Che's execution, his father reportedly said: "The first thing to note is that in my son's veins flowed the blood of the Irish rebels. Che inherited some of the features of our restless ancestors."[89] Two of the Irish poets included in this collection, Liam Ó Comain and Val Nolan, make this connection.

By contrast with this intimacy, works from other traditions purposefully ensure a distance is kept from Che Guevara. In much of east Asia, for example, there is little tradition of poets writing about foreign figures, even though they may be world famous revolutionaries. This means that, despite much evidence of popular interest in Che Guevara in countries such as Thailand, Korea, Taiwan, China and Japan through healthy sales of his works and biographies of him, there is little poetry. A Thai journal dedicated to the ideas of Che Guevara in 1976, when students fled to the jungles following the bloody crackdown by the military at Thammasat University, contains poems about Sri Burapha, a Thai writer persecuted for his views, yet none that makes mention of Che.[90] Even the Korean poet Lee Sanha, who translated Che's works into Korean, has not written about Guevara himself. The Korean poems included in this collection address Che through proxies. Min Yeong's mournful poem "Before the Grave of the Poet Kim Namju" compares his dead protagonist's revolutionary commitment with that of Che Guevara in an effort to question his own, personal failings. Kim was a socialist poet and leader of South Korea's National Liberation Front in 1970s and was often likened to Che. Ko Un's poem is possibly autobiographical, addressing Che through the thoughts and concerns of an old man. The Japanese poet Renji Ono — who was debilitated by tuberculosis and its consequences all his life — examines Che through an asthma clinic, and the Chinese poems included in this volume are all very contemporary, suggesting the same iconic fascination among younger writers as can be found in any consumer society. The poem by Zhang Guangtian, taken from the play "Che Guevara", represents a very contemporary critique of liberalism and globalisation that attributes China's social problems to the abandonment of Maoism, the embracing of market reforms, and integration into the world capitalist economy, and opened deep divisions among Chinese intellectuals when it was first performed in 2000.[91]

Surprisingly little Russian and former Eastern Bloc poetry could be found for this collection, and the only works of note that have been included are by the Russian Yevgeny Yevtushenko, who travelled extensively outside the Soviet Union, and Dmitro Pavlichko, a Ukrainian diplomat. The Soviet establishment was clearly troubled by Che Guevara's inconvenient commitment to spreading revolution, and in Eastern Europe the individualistic strains of his idealism were anathema to corrupt bureaucratic regimes. This ambivalence or even hostility has persisted, and in the new post-communist dispensation Czechs and Hungarians contacted for this collection were dismissive of the very notion of compiling such a book. There is some irony in this position, for Che's image was much in evidence during the Prague Spring, and Hungarian dissident poets such as Miklos Haraszti and Tamas Szentjoby are believed to have published samizdat poetry about Guevara praising him as the only "genuine" Marxist.[92]

The popular character of poetry about Che is much in evidence when we consider that most of the poems written about him are not, in the main, epic in the traditional sense of *scale*. However, the poems by the Haitians René Depestre, Jean Métellus and Anthony Phelps — all originally written in French — are long, quasi-epic works weaving together incidental and global imagery into which Che is inserted as one of many themes and characters. This is very evident in Phelp's vivid poem which engages with the character of Guevara from the marital bed and the protagonist's relationship with the woman in his life. In the epic tradition, the Haitians also draw upon themes from antiquity, with Depestre beginning his poem by quoting Euripides and Phelps alluding to the USA as Cain "nourished on Abel's blood".

Writing poetry is an instrospective process in which the poet reflects constantly on the significance of his or her theme, and a number of the contributors to this collection depict Che as a natural subject for poetry or themselves explore the relationship between poetry and the Guevara phenomenon. The Argentine Juan Gelman, for example, struggles throughout his work to understand the role of the poet in a process of deep self-reflection. Many of the writers in the collection are also aware of Che's own interest in poetry.

Given the qualifications above about the general nature of the observations that can be made from the limited sample of works included in this collection, the poems incorporated can loosely be categorised according to three periods: those written before Che Guevara's death; those written from the time of his death into the late 1970s; and those written since the 1990s. Notably absent from this periodisation is, of course, the 1980s — a period in which few of the works in this collection were written or published. The 1980s was a time of rightwing ascendance across both the industrial world and also Latin America that would eventually bring to an end the Cold War. Although a few poets writing years later, such as Jorge Enrique Adoum, have reflected thoughtfully on this era and the "ideological vacation" of the Left, it would seem that at the time even fewer were writing poetry about it.

Several poems and songs in this collection were written while Guevara was still alive. These are revealing for predating his transformation into a global icon of rebellion, and hint at what it was about him that was then of interest to poets and songwriters. Pedro Pérez Sarduy's poem, written in 1965 after Castro's October speech informing the Cuban people of Guevara's resignation and departure to fight in foreign fields, captures presciently the later sense of loss that permeates much of the poetry in this book, a departure made all the more poignant by the growing mythology around him. Carlos Puebla's influential "Till forever, Comandante", written at the same time, is revealing for its premonitory tone, a hint of comprehension that the guerrilla is no longer with the Cuban people although his presence is still felt. Similarly, Miguel Barnet's "Ché" speaks of the hero's omnipresence and benign influence in Cuban life, beginning with a phrase commonly used to show respect that may have as its origins the comments of Simon Peter to Jesus: "Ché, you know everything…". Víctor Jara's "Apparition", written in 1967 months before Che's death but portending it, advances themes that would later shape the Che story in poetry and draws upon biblical comparisons.

Many of the poems included in this book belong to the period 1967-79 and were written in mourning and anger as poetic responses to Guevara's death. The most active period was 1967-71, although the 1970s remained a fertile decade and the tenth anniversary of Guevara's death in 1977 generated renewed interest in the theme. Outside Cuba, however, fewer Latin American poets in countries under the grip of harsh military regimes wrote about Che Guevara after the early 1970s, reflecting — like Turkey — the risks involved in such an endeavour. Poems from the late 1960s often also employ Guevara as a form of rallying cry in an era of protest, cultural turmoil and Third World struggles. The Vietnam war is invoked, and not only did poets writing in this period often identify Che with the struggle of the Vietnamese people, some even experienced the latter's suffering: Roque Dalton lived in Vietnam and worked there in a bicycle factory, and he spoke in correspondence of how the suffering of the Vietnamese would be the lot of the Latin Americans in their quest for freedom.[93]

The poems from this period tend to be highly narrative: these poets are lyrical reporters, inserting Che's death into a news environment amply filled by social protest and Third World struggle. Allen Ginsberg positions Che alongside such characters as De Gaulle, Kosygin, Kennedy, McNamara, Dulles, Acheson, Truman and Rusk. The Australian Richard Tipping's "Soft Riots" is perhaps the best example of how poets tried to capture the rebellious spirit of the late Sixties across the world, but he is also already aware by

1969 of the Christ-like qualities of his subject, whose execution he re-enacts within the panorama of demonstrations disrupting an angry society. La Loca's reflections, published with the benefit of years of hindsight but fully *of* this era, put Che on the walls of those US student dorms in which the drama of the sexual revolution was played out. Her observations were also telling, for the use of Che as a rallying cry reflected both how the reformist left was able to embrace Guevara from a distance as an exotic symbol of justice and hence as a *substitute* for violent Marxist revolution at home; but also how Che was to become a brand in the consumer society that grew out of the Sixties that many poems written later were so critical of.

The 1990s inaugurated a new phase in poetry about Che Guevara — particularly after 1997, when his remains were located in Bolivia and transferred to Cuba — as writers already established by the 1960s began to reminisce and a new generation of poets untouched by that radical era, and with a different set of priorities when it came to interpreting and recounting this story, came of age. Poems written by poets who were children when Che Guevara was alive often express a sense of longing to have met him.

Many of these poets have only known Guevara through popular culture, and this is a prominent current in their work. The New Zealander Mark Pirie associates Che's image with that of James Dean, and his poem summarises his view of Guevara's misguided pop icon status. Michael O'Leary, also from New Zealand, inserts Guevara firmly into the popular culture of the era: "'Looks a lot like Ché Guevara,' I heard David Bowie say/…". It is notable how poetry from this period — from the English-speaking world to China — often reflects upon and even at times mocks the transformation of Guevara's image into a brand in the post-Cold War era of global consumerism. The American Patrick Hyland, the Canadian Martha Chaves and the French poet Francis Combes all reflect on this and, similarly, the work of the Chinese poets Yi Sha and Jun'er attest to the very realistic assessment of Che's contemporary relevance in a rapidly changing society. Perhaps more significantly, however, many of the poems about Che since the early 1990s seek to understand his contribution or even insist upon his continuing relevance as a source of ideological integrity.

Themes in verse about Che Guevara

A number of key themes emerge when the ideas and images contained within poems and songs about Che Guevara are examined:

Iconography

Che Guevara's story is known globally in part because of the iconography that has developed around his portrait — in particular the photographs by Alberto Korda and Freddy Alborta — through which the vast majority of people have, inevitably, encountered this historical figure. Poets who make reference to images of Che both confirm this well-known feature of the Guevara phenomenon and, at the same time, reveal the importance of simple images to poetic inspiration. It is through the image of Che, and the unlikely places where this turns up, that many poets have been introduced to this theme or become aware of its significance. The Zimbabwean poet Cosmas Mairosi, for example, wrote his poem after visiting the offices of the Progressive Teachers Association of Zimbabwe (PTUZ), where he saw T-shirts emblazoned with Che's image on display. S.K. Kelen (Australia) finds the image of Che in Koki market, Papua New Guinea, on the shirt of a youth with Afro hair who "screams revolution at the seagulls". Jun'er (China) refers to the visit of poet Yi Sha to the city of Tianjin with "a handsome foreigner on his T-shirt" and Francis Combes's poem is inspired by Che staring out of a photograph in his home.

While the Korda image that formed the basis of the famous silhouetted poster of Che is clearly the most well known and has itself been the subject of study, it is arguably the image of Che Guevara's body on display in the laundry house of the Nuestro Señor de Malta hospital in Vallegrande, Bolivia — that of a waxen fallen hero staring into eternity — that has had the most influence on poets.[94] This latter photograph by Freddy Alborta has been compared to the painting of "The Lamentation over the Dead Christ" by Andrea Mantegna (c. 1490) and has itself been the subject of much scrutiny.[95] Jorge Enrique Adoum (Ecuador) writes of how Latin Americans pored over the famous photograph: "… (and we were… trying to find in them the sign that he was alive/all of a sudden turning into experts in logic as if gorillas had our powers of rea-son/experts in photographic illusion analysing his beard fearing it was him but talking about the christ of mantegna and of baroque sculptures...)/...".

Several poets make reference to the light of this photograph, and the texture of Che's skin. In an evocative poem coloured with a sense of changing light, Nuno Guimarães (Portugal) recreates the death of Guevara on a photographic sheet, the very recomposition of this image in the darkroom offering an escape from death: "... Now the light is expanding. guiding/the body, between the foliage, with arms/of light, sobrieties of fire, air, crackle/in the rig-orous space – rigor mortis –/.../in the rigidity of skin, another picture. /...". Derek Walcott (Saint Lucia) compares the image of the dead Che to that of an old master: "In this dark-grained news photograph, whose glare/is rigidly composed as Caravaggio's,/the corpse glows candle-white on its cold altar/...".

Representations of Che and his recurrence in popular culture as a form of branded lifestyle accessory provide a way into this theme for a number of, mainly non-Latin American, poets. Contemporary poetry reflects extensively on Che's appearance as a brand on con-sumer products, often starting with Fitzpatrick's famous poster. These and our own interactions with consumer paraphernalia pro-vide a shared context in which poets from Canada to China can interpret this figure, because today the same winds of globalisation – and the very same products – touch us all equally.

Several poets adopt a light-hearted tone when considering the commercialisation of Che Guevara's image, revealing a sense of frustration and setting their work up to make the inevitable con-trast between the large variety of products he adorns and the ideas he stood for. This observation even extends to China, the newest entrant to the consumer club. Jun'er (China) depicts Che with the biting humour that would appear to be a characteristic of many contemporary Chinese poets: "... Yi Sha and Che Guevara went shopping at the foreign goods market/ ...".

The strange sense of disconnection with the reality of Latin America that is felt in a consumer society is captured well by poets from the industrialised world such as Kevin Cadwallender (UK) and Michael McClure (USA) as they stare at their television screens.

Poems and verse in which Che is an incidental figure portrayed on a T-shirt or poster say much about how his image intervenes as a form of romantic punctuation mark in otherwise mundane lives. This is explicit in the poem of Cliff Wedgbury (UK) and Alexander Scott's beautiful and pithy verse in Scots — the only poem in the collection in dialect. The story of the young Guevara's almost beatnik wanderlust clearly lends itself well, as Castañeda suggested with some prescience, to "a kind of road book or road movie", as well as to what is now often referred to as "youth culture" more generally.[96] The poem of John Greeves (Wales) talks about how Walter Salles' film *The Motorcycle Diaries* offers a youth on a date the opportunity to impress his girlfirend.

The sensitivity to the icon's conversion into a consumer brand is at times a prelude to a bitter assessment of his legacy. Here consumerism implies betrayal, an inversion of what the poets believe Che Guevara stood for. As early as 1971, Yevgeny Yevtushenko was bemoaning the commercialisation of the Guevara myth, and Patrick Hyland (USA) brings this right up to date when he writes: "… Ideals of Revolution/are a joke/when your picture/may as well be/on a fucking cereal box/…". Yet at the same time some of the same poets seek a more positive assessment of the icon's presence in consumer products, attesting to how this may in fact confirm his universal significance.

Global appeal

It is notable how little emphasis poets place upon Che Guevara's identification with an individual country — be it Cuba or Argentina — and poets across the world often used his temporary presence in their own countries to drape their poems upon. Guevara is portrayed as a man freed of petty territorial limitations traversing the world. Jofre Rocha takes his reader from the Andes to the rice paddies of Vietnam and the swamps of Guinea, depicting Guevara as a "monument to brotherhood" whose country is "the whole World". Djamel Amrani inserts Che into a broad, sweeping poem that takes the reader from Cuba to Madrid, Beirut and El-Ayoun, and Jean Métellus's poem is remarkable for its expansive focus. John Haines (USA) depicts Guevara's universal territorial reach beautifully: "Somewhere inside me,/perhaps under my left shoulder,/there is a country named/Guevara./…". The idea of revolution, especially Marxist revolution, is by its very nature universal. Cu Huy Can (Vietnam) captures this well: "Che Guevara,/many people asked you:/Where is your real home?/And you replied:/My home is where I can fight the/revolution./Your home is where people suffer,/and you can join in their struggle./…". For many poets detached completely from the Latin American experience, Guevara provides a more straightforward opportunity to reflect on the circumstances of their own countries. Poems written after Che's death outside Latin America often saw him as a harbinger of revolution, especially in societies in which struggles against colonialism were unfolding or had shaped lived experience.

Outside Haiti, only the works about Che in this collection by the Guatemalan Otto-Raúl González and Klaus Høeck from Denmark can be described as epic. This might be considered surprising, given that Guevara's dramatic life and death lend themselves naturally to epic poetry. However, many of the poems in this collection have an epic *aspiration* that depicts Guevara as an itinerant hero of global appeal. This aspiration is reflected in the Bolivarian quality attributed to his travels in Latin America, and the way many poets set Guevara's exploits within an epic landscape characterised by the physical grandeur of mountains and rivers, the elements of wind and sun, the majesty of eagles and jaguars, and under a bright, overarching sky or star-studded universe. This positioning of Che within an epic landscape is not confined to Latin America and it is notable how Arif Damar and Metin Demirtaş both associate Che with the mountains or fighters in the hills of their native Turkey.

The epic aspiration is also revealed through Guevara's insertion into a lineage of the key figures from Latin American nationalist historiography. A recurrent theme among Latin American poets is the identification of Guevara with indigenous heroes or civilisations. The Chilean Floridor Pérez, for example, identifies Che with Galvarino, the celebrated Mapuche warrior. He writes: " … He was the Antilles-Mapuche/'CHE of the Mapu: the man of the earth' /...".[97] It is more difficult for poets from outside the region to exploit the possibilities offered by a pantheon solely composed of Latin American figures, and so non-Latin Americans broaden their heroic references. These epic lineages can sometimes appear eclectic and chosen only to provide as extensive a reach across the developing world as possible. The allusion to a heroism of legendary stature sometimes takes the form of references to local legend, ancient chivalry or Greek mythology. Floridor Pérez, for example, draws upon the first epic poem written in the Americas, Alonso de Ercilla's *La Araucana* (1569).

Che's last days

A significant number of poets recount the story of Che's last days in Bolivia, often recreating these events in theatrical terms. Klaus Høeck's "Topia" is the most remarkable example of this approach, putting Che and his comrades in Bolivia on to a stage and playing out the drama of their last days in scenes and acts. This device allows the Danish poet to draw attention to the universal appeal of the story and, in particular, to the hypocrisy that he identifies in the audience. There is a fascination for the exotic scenery — the rich flora and fauna — upon this dramatic stage. The Canadian poet Al Purdy notes the movie-like qualities of the story and writes: "... 'Where is Che Guevara?' is answered: / deep in Bolivian jungles leading his guerrillas/from cave to cave with scarlet cockatoos screaming/.../his men crawling under hundred-foot trees/where giant snakes mate in masses of roots / ...".

Che's last day and the circumstances and even minutiae of his execution in the schoolhouse at La Higuera are a particular focus. Efraín Huerta's powerful work is a good example of how poets conjure up the moment in colour and shade: "The yellow death of blind eyes was unleashed,/of blind eyes the yellow death was unleashed./Bitter blue steps amid the foliage and the mire./Bitter and dense searching death, mortal whore./...". The severing of Che's hands is a potent recurrent theme providing a valuable set of metaphors about power and powerlessnes. The hands have a symbolic resonance with the crucifixion story allowing for further comparisons with Christ (see below). Anne Delana Reeves (USA) is among those poets who combine these themes in her haunting work depicting a nun visiting the body of the dead Che before the hands are symbolically severed: "... Kneeling, she kissed his fingers. Warm bands/of gunpowder lashed cupped palms. The taste/metallic stained her lips and throat like love./From his hands water flowed. She couldn't drink enough.". Among the metaphorical possibilities offered by Che's hands is that of their potential replacement heralding a revival of the warrior. Floridor Pérez's poem is built upon the coincidences with the mutilation of Galvarino, the indigenous Chilean Mapuche warrior whose own hands were cut off by the Spanish *conquistadores*, and he delivers unto Che the hands of this legendary hero. Similarly, the Ukrainian Dmitro Pavlichko writes: "... But, like some fabulous blood-stained bird,/Those hands then came to life, and trembling stirred,/And flew out of the prison cell afar,/...".

Several poets go even deeper into the circumstances surrounding Che's death to undertake a much more intimate exploration of what he may have been thinking in his last moments and after death. Lawrence Ferlinghetti (USA) enters Che's mind and explores his thoughts — a day after his death — in his own interpreted Spanish (left as such in the original for this collection). Many of the words he employs will be recogniseable to the English reader, allowing the poet to create a curious and confused atmosphere that forces us to follow the language carefully as it pales into an inevitable oblivion. The dead Che speaks graphically of his family, the Cuban campaign, his comrades in Bolivia, pubic lice and lesions, his boots, hunger, thirst.

Like the death of any celebrity, Guevara's execution is recorded by many poets as a specific moment in time recalled in terms of the news agenda of the day, allowing them to contrast such a life-changing moment with the monotony of daily life elsewhere. In a similar way a number of poets record the circumstances in which they themselves heard the news of Che's death as if taking snapshots of their surroundings in a poetic aide memoire to a traumatic event. The best example of this approach can be found in the work of the Finnish poet Anselm Hollo in which he recounts how he strolled with his daughter on the Isle of Wight, off the south coast of England, with the news fresh in his mind. Hollo's poem reflects how the immediate images of one's surroundings become part of the ontology of poetry at a dramatic moment.

These references confirm that Che Guevara's death was a moment of transcendent importance, and how in some cases the possibilities and dreams offered by this character make it possible to step out of otherwise humdrum lives. The Australian Duncan Richardson, for example, writes: "Sorry Mum, can't come for dinner/you see Che Guevara's last bodyguard is in town/and I really can't miss him/Sorry darling, can't do the washing up/I know it's my turn but Che Guevara's last bodyguard is in town...".

Anger and grief are common reactions among poets to the news of Che's death.[98] The poem of Mario Benedetti (Uruguay) for example, overflows with rage and Jorge Enrique Adoum (Ecuador) refers to the killing of Che "... filling us with more hate than any human can bear/...". It was one of those rare moments when it was okay for men to cry: Thiago de Mello writes: "... I sobbed/in that masculine weeping of men./...". Masa Mbatha-Opasha (South Africa) says: "... It was for you, brother Che,/that many of us cried at great length/for your early death./...".

The United States cannot escape widespread perception of its negative role in Latin America, and invariably it is Washington that is blamed for Che's death, with the Bolivian regime held in contempt as a junior partner. The Latin American poets are those that find the most critical metaphors with which to depict the US. Alfonso Gumucio Dagron (Bolivia) writes: "...sons of bitches/clumsy soldiers with northern star and eagle/on their chest/...". Nelson Osorio Marín (Colombia) portrays the US sarcastically as a happy giant, "... who shares out among the kids/pats on the back and lollipops./ ..." but nonetheless "...devours children and men./ ...". Poets across the world can share the possibilities offered by the idea of one man confronting the might of an imperium with near universal reach. Che's killers are frequently described as carnivorous or scavenging beasts such as "wolves". The attribution to the US of a principal role in Che's death — and recognition of the epic struggle that he was waging against imperialism — was much in evidence in the poetry of American writers themselves.

Betrayal

Many poets, particularly those in Latin America, believed that Che Guevara had been betrayed by the Left and by his own continent. Jorge Enrique Adoum (Ecuador) is still writing about this sense of betrayal in Latin America in 1997: "... he was doing what we knew had to be done but were not doing/what we wanted to do but we did not do/what inevitably we have to do but we are not doing/...". Bolivia's Communist Party and Mario Monje, its leader at the time of Che's campaign, comes in for particular criticism and there is a strong sense among Latin American poets that Guevara's sacrifice had been insufficiently acknowledged. There is also a confessional tone to many of these poems in which the poet speaks of his or her own impotence or contrasts the seemingly insignificant challenges of daily life with the momentous importance of Che's sacrifice. Pentti Saarikoski (Finland) confesses, on a hot sunny day while reading Che's memoirs, of trying to hide behind "... all manner of posters/and platitudes/and quotations/so that no one will question my duplicity./...". Ted Willis (UK) builds his entire poem upon a sense of shame.

In these poems hypocrisy and betrayal act as universal themes when set against the practical course chosen and pursued by Guevara himself. Attention is commonly drawn to Che's activism in comparison with that of more complacent comrades in the industrialised world. Min Yeong (Korea) evokes betrayal through the character sitting at the grave of a fellow poet, Kim Namju, who is likened to Che, yet is Korean: "... This cowardly workmate of yours who used to loiter hiding/behind your back, busy just keeping up with you/as you put your life on the line and fought ...". Poets often acknowledge that their poems were written to exculpate themselves or out of personal grief.

When discussing Che Guevara, poets draw attention to several personal characteristics: his good looks, and in particular his bearded smile and penetrating eyes that transmitted a potent charisma;

his asthma; and his common touch and integrity. Sennur Sezer (Turkey) speaks of Che the doctor looking at children, and asks: "... Did you see the joy in his eyes/The passion/How he looks, the cure in his eyes.../...".

Che was clearly as attractive to some men as he was to many women, and his status as a gay icon was epitomised in the offset print Che Gay (1974) which takes the Korda image and adds make-up to Che's face.[99] Allen Ginsberg (USA), for example, a pioneer of gay rights, described Che as "... One radiant face driven mad with a rifle/..." and speaks delicately of the dead guerrilla's physical appearance. That Che has become something of an erotic icon is also found in contemporary poetry, such as that of Greg Hewett (USA), which is as radical and challenging in its way to the con-stricted mores of the orthodox old left as the revolutionary himself may have been in his day.

A number of poets make reference to Che's asthma, a physical weakness that can both be understood universally and a means of highlighting the hero's very human qualities.[100] The point that asth-ma is a universal condition highlighting the similarities between people is made by Renji Ono (Japan), whose entire poem centres on an asthma clinic: "... But in the end, I cannot deny the thought that we are linked originally by asthma./.../We are joined by having asthma,/Each person is completely alone./...". Che's asthma also serves as a device that allows the writer to draw attention to the revolutionary's unflappable determination.

References to Che Guevara's physical characteristics are comple-mented by those that draw attention to his emotional qualities. Poets and songwriters often depict him as a selfless man of integri-ty with the common touch, wielding authority with an ease and camaraderie. Nicolás Guillén (Cuba) writes: "...Your voice is firm,/without the edge of command in it,/as you command com-pañera, friend,/affectionate and responsible,/leader, comrade./We remember you, each day, at the Ministry,/each day, in the Army,/each day, as an easy companion,/each day, as an uncompro-mising man,/pure, as a child and as a man,/...". The common touch is very evident in Val Nolan's lucid poem about Guevara's visit to a pub in Limerick: "Elbow-touch by elbow-touch he meets/The old men in old cloth caps, farmers/In their good tweeds or labourers with/Their hands lime-sallow from the sites./...". Guevara evokes a strong sense of fraternity, and he is often referred to as a brother to whom the people will remain loyal. His integrity is often characterised as a set of practical virtues, living fairly and the desire to practice what he preached. To Maggie Jaffe (USA) the Guevara moral universe is encapsulated by a simple fairness: "... And he divided men into two groups:/those who can sleep/on a mattress while others suffer,/and those who cannot."

Quasi-religious symbolism and narrative

Poems about Che Guevara included in this collection make a significant number of references to Christ, and even when these are not overt, many use language inspired by biblical themes. Roque Dalton's remarkable poem is the best example of how revolutionary poets appropriated the Passion of Christ as the most potent tale of love, betrayal and sacrifice available at a universal level. Dalton (El Salvador) refers to Guevara as "Ché Jesus Christ", then leads his protagonist through a Christ-like ordeal, the main characters of which are all key figures in the story — Caiaphas Monje, Pontius Barrientos — until Christ Guevara is crucified with bursts from an M-2.

The case that the use of Christian imagery is a purposeful and at times mischievous device is strengthened by the fact that other poets like Dalton who were or are avowed communists or socialists also use Christian metaphors. We have noted above how Miguel Barnet speaks of the hero's omnipresence with a phrase that may evoke the comments of Simon Peter to Jesus (John 21:17) — "Lord, you know everything". Peter Weiss (Germany) observes that: "... He was like a Christ taken down from the Cross...". Otto-Raúl González writes: "... Peter Weiss has said Peter Weiss has written comandante Guevara/that you looked like a Christ taken off the cross I agree we agree/.../Christ of the twentieth century dialectic theoretical and practical Christ /...".

A number of themes through which the life and death of Che Guevara is compared with that of Christ are discernible. First, Che is sometimes depicted in messianic terms, as someone whose arrival will bring salvation or liberation. Anthony Phelps (Haiti) writes, for example: "... oh land of America in search of a Messiah/the friend the comrade Che is dead/...". Poets reflect upon Che's childhood and personal development, as if searching for clues to his subsequent impact, and several portray his mother as the biblical figure Mary. There are clear resonances with the mother of Christ in Roberto Vecchioni's poem about Celia de la Serna, which imagines her in a dialogue with her son.

The horizon, sunrise, fire and light are often employed as metaphors to depict the messianic Che's coming. Pablo Neruda (Chile) talks of "the illustrious fire of Guevara" dying in the mountains; Nicolás Guillén (Cuba) writes: "... In spite of your fall,/your light is undiminished./A horse of fire/celebrates your glory as a guerrilla,/...". and Zhang Guangtian (China) writes: "Who lit the dawn's reddish glow on the horizon?/A millennium of dark nights shall today be no more./Perhaps the light will arrive early; We can hear you calling out to us — Che Guevara./...". Vicentico of Los Fabulosos Cadillacs likens Che to the "Sun of May", the Sol de Mayo national emblem of his native Argentina that is featured on the country's flag. As with Christ, the notion of a star bringing Che or as a harbinger of his arrival also recurs. The star is sometimes the five-pointed star of communism, but at other times a hybrid that allows a poet to combine a reference to revolution with a more universal constant.

Another theme that recurs in this poetry that is also redolent of the story of Christ is that of love, and many poets make reference either to Che's love for the meek or the love felt for Guevara. Efraín Huerta's beautiful poem evokes at once the common depiction of Christ as a dove and the message of love that is attributed to Che Guevara. These notions of love and affection are important universal characterstics. Alan C. Brown (UK) builds his entire poem around a love that appears accidental: "No one is fated to love; but accidents happen./.../One man can make a difference; many with equal/Love as yours — a new horizon./...".

As with the story of Christ, poets also portray Che's martyrdom as bringing him sanctification or sainthood. Kieran Furey (Ireland) writes: "... Like Christ you lived/(Though you ceased to turn the other cheek): /Bearded, wandering, badly dressed, misunderstood;/Fighting hypocrisy left and right;/Ejecting money-changers from your temples./Like Christ you died/(Though you fought to the last):/Hunted, betrayed, captured, tortured and killed/By ill-paid servants of a mundane power./...". As with Christ, Guevara is often said to have died for mankind in general. Masa Mbatha-Opasha (South Africa) writes: "...It was for many of us, Guevara,/that you died that violent, merciless death./.../You have been crowned a hero, a legend and a myth./You have been elevated to the holy seat of saints, prophets and gods./..." and Mario Benedetti (Uruguay) refers to Che bringing the "good news". Hans Magnus Enzensberger (Germany) takes a more critical position, conscious of the constructed nature of this imagery and writes of Che's memory after his death: "... *A mystical adventure*, and/*a passion irresistibly reminiscent of the image of Christ:*/that's what his followers wrote....". These references to Christ and sainthood are not limited to the poets of countries with a predominantly Christian tradition. The Indian poet K.G. Sankara Pillai describes Che as "... the Jesus of the modern age/crucified by America./..." and Bagdaad Maata, a poet originally from Algeria who has been actively engaged in the struggle for the rights of Muslim immigrants in France, refers to Che as "... this modern Christ...".

Other potent Christian themes recreated in this poetry are immortality, by which Che Guevara is said to remain present in a ghostly, spectral form, and the notion of a second coming by which he will return, bringing revolution and vengeance. Allusions to his continuing presence can be likened to those Cuban poems written before his death but when he was no longer in the country that convey a strong sense of what Carlos Puebla called his "cherished transparency". In many of the poems written in the immediate aftermath of his death — and in particular Latin American and Caribbean poems — Guevara was still seen as a latent and potent force. Thiago de Mello (Brazil) writes: "... I know that they keep you, powerful,/in the warm earth of your heart./As powerful as ever,/powerful as a brother." Juan Cristóbal (Peru) says: "... you will never die, 'contemporary bloodhound' of history/...". The theme of immortality is not confined to Latin American poets. To Alasdair Clayre (UK) the dead Che continues to embody the vengeful poor: "... And yet the dead man still/is with his wounds alive/will with his wounds survive/the dictator's will/and the rich man's mind/who when he will not give/to let the poor man live/turns and sees behind/a man with a broken knife/a man not pure or good/a slaughtered man...". The sense that Che could not be dead, or that he lives on through the memories of him, is well captured in the period immediately after his death by the defiant haiku of Christopher Logue (UK), and to Adrian Mitchell (UK) he was only "Technically dead". Immortality or spiritual continuity is often expressed through the ghostly, organic presence of Che in the landscape, flora and fauna. Pablo Neruda's wild stag returns to the greenery, and Eugénio de Andrade (Portugal) writes: "... Pale voices seek you in the mist;/.../Eyes wide with fear/awaiting the midday sun at night,/the vibrant face of the sun where you arise,/where you mingle with the branches/of summer's blood or the rumour/of rain's white feet in the soil./...".

Poets for whom Che Guevara is immortal or who long for his return also often allude to a second coming, like that of Christ. Roque Dalton writes: "... In view of which Ché has been left no other path than resurrection/and to remain standing on the left-hand side of men/commanding them to quicken their pace/for ever and ever/Amen." The Chilean Leopoldo Marechal talks of waiting to see how a "phoenix can arise from its ashen place of rest", and Kieran Furey (Ireland) writes: ".../Some say you'll come again./There are those who wait for you./And if you do return,/What will happen on Judgement Day?/...". A new dawn is sometimes the preferred metaphor for this return. The Galician poet Xosé Luis Méndez Ferrín writes: "... And so the most eagerly awaited dawn is arriving,/...".

The culmination of the second coming is, ultimately, uprising: Che's death is often seen as the spark of a future conflagration, and fire again is often a preferred metaphor — also evincing comparisons with the biblical day of judgement. Vicente Feliú (Cuba) writes: "... The tear, the poem and the memory/are carving on the fire the song of death/with golden machine-guns from wherever you are./...". Dmitro Pavlichko (Ukraine) writes: "... So take good care, you butchers, all the same./Because he'll rise from the grave to punish your souls,/And your foulness wipe away with flame./...". Ingemar Leckius (Sweden) also recounted the guerrilla campaign of a man "... carrying the passport of brotherhood/ .../until the rifle muzzles thicken/And an invisible flame erupts.".

Nonetheless, allusions to immortality and a second coming are problematic for the materialist left, and some declared socialist poets or those writing from the perspective of then socialist systems are more measured in their evocations. This is captured well in the lines of Yevgeny Yevtushenko to whom the sense of immortality is both rotten yet overwhelming: "... I detect with every nerve/the putrid smell of immortality./Remembering you, Comandante/overwinds the soul,/and the quiet inside/pulsates like an earthquake./...". The ideological tension on the left between the desire for Che to live on, yet the prohibition against this in theory, is very evident in Mario Benedetti's poem.

Other poets debate the dangers of a cult of personality growing up around Che and some seek through their words to neutralise this possibility and to justify their eulogies. Vicente Feliú's "A necessary song" is an appeal not to raise Che upon a shrine and Anselm Hollo (Finland) adds to this a call not to turn Che into a cult. For this reason, some poets use other devices to evade, yet acknowledge, the notion of immortality. André Benedetto's highly original poem "The Stranger Left on the Terraces of Baalbeck" depicts Guevara as otherwordly, someone who has fallen to earth as if from outer space, yet combines this with religious metaphors: "... I see that there would be:/'the God with 5 heads/the Star with 5 heads/of the Rebellion'/in front of whom will/the flying saucers kneel/...".

Ideological themes

An examination of the political, economic and social ideas addressed in these poems allows us to highlight those the poets most commonly associate with Che, while also permitting us to consider the role of ideological themes in poetry more generally. Most of the poems in this selection avoid engaging with complex ideological questions and tend to deal with only one or two themes. Che Guevara is portrayed mainly as a practical archetype and, save for a few notable exceptions, poetic portrayals of Che tend not to dwell upon his ideas other than drawing attention to a broader humanism. Those exceptions include Peter Schütt's poem, which is suffused with an ideological fury yet still puts in generalised terms and on a par with the class struggle Guevara's role as a fighter against injustice and oppression. It is the poem of Jean Métellus (Haiti) that discusses Che's ideas in most detail, its last stanza associating him with a number of themes generally passed over in other poems: revolutionary contagion, internationalism, agrarian reform, the nationalisation of oil and banks, social conditions in Latin America, nationalism, the political education of the masses, and even the corrupted bureacracy in revolutionary Cuba.

Where ideas are engaged with explicitly, two themes in particular recur: Cuba and its Revolution, and the idea of the "new man". Verses by Cuban poets and songwriters often associate Che with the fighting in Santa Clara during the Revolution. Given the influence of the Cuban Revolution on neighbouring countries it is no surprise that poets such as Jan Carew (Guyana) also position Che firmly within an appraisal of the Revolution. Jorge Enrique Adoum (Ecuador) refers to Che's role in Cuba only as a metaphor for Latin America and depicts the Revolution as a success by contrast with the mainland's failure to respond to Guevara's call. Outside Latin America and the Caribbean, Cuba is clearly also a monument and aspiration for the Left, and some poets approach Che through the Cuban revolutionary story. The ballad of Ewan MacColl (UK) is a straightforward account of Che's story from the moment he sets sail from Mexico with his Cuban *compañeros*. "How to kill Cuba" by Adrian Mitchell (UK) suggests that everything — people, buildings, photographs — must be burned and the ashes guarded in order to erase the Revolution's impact, and it is perhaps no surprise that Sebastião Alba from Mozambique, where Cuban forces served in a non-combat advisory role, makes reference to Che's importance in the revolutionary story.

Yet Cuba and Castro are also sometimes associated with disillusionment. Michael O'Leary (New Zealand) writes: "... His conception/Became disenchantment as the Realpolitik in Cuba too/Began to make Castro's ideals seem to ring untrue/...". Hans Magnus Enzensberger (Germany) examines Cuba in order to present a more candid assessment of the man: "... But economy didn't listen to his speeches. There was no spaghetti./Nor any toothpaste, and what is toothpaste made from?/The banknotes he signed were worthless./The sugar stuck to shirts. Machines, paid for with hard currency,/decayed on quais. La Rampa rumbled with rumors./Bowing and scraping in Moscow, new credits. The people lined up,/were unreliable, cracked hungry jokes./...".

The theme of the "new man" developed by Guevara and referred to earlier was of particular appeal outside Latin America. Anthony Phelps hints at this creation of a new man in the memory of Che as he muses from the marital bed. Volker Braun, whose poem "After the Massacre of Illusions" is reproduced in this collection, incorporated Che Guevara's conception of the New Man into his documentary play *Che Guevara und der Sonnenstaat*, which also makes reference to the German Expressionist idea of the New Man ("Der neue Mensch"). A variant on this theme is provded by the Galician poet Xosé Luis Méndez Ferrín who compiles a proclamation on behalf of the "new peasant" that will emerge in his homeland. Yet although Méndez Ferrín's poem is one of the few that makes reference to peasants and, indeed, issues of class itself, even the message he articulates is reducible to a more simple freedom from oppression: "... Our class raises over the valleys of terror and the greenery/a new tool/known by the name of liberation./...".

More often than not, political ideas in these poems are boiled down to slogans or digestible humanistic themes about how the guerrilla hero brings hope for justice and the fight against oppression, turning Che into what Efraín Huerta describes as the "... father and son of independence,/grandson of all the freedoms of all the world,/...". This is well summarised in Auguste Macouba's "Hope is Speaking": "... The last of man's songs/today, hope is speaking./All of you oppressed breathless/kneeling and humiliated world/brothers in hunger offended without strength/...". Otto-Raúl González, a veteran communist, writes: "... the children ask me ask us what for why he fought/.../he fought I say we say for human dignity/he fought breaking his arms so that in the world there would not be/exploiters nor exploited nor poverty nor ignorance/he fought against the caste of those gorillas that crush/all citizens' liberties/he fought always for man and his best causes/...". Bagdaad Maata (Algeria) sums up well the simple virtues that many poets read into the Guevara story: "... His spirit still moves, his strength still penetrates,/Because Lies, Deceit, Hatred and Arrogance/Cannot win over Truth and the Love for the wretched/They cannot triumph, but only engender Suffering." This sense that Che was less an ideological beacon and more an archetype, a practical inspiration, is well captured by Ted Willis (UK) and Daniel Schechter (USA), and the inspirational dimension of Guevara's role is alluded to in several references to Don Quixote and his steed Rocinante in these poems, suggesting a belief that his story also belongs to the stuff of legend. Cervantes' characters are used as metaphors for a determined struggle against the odds for justice, regardless of ideological questions.[101]

The legacy

Che's ideas fuel reflections about his legacy among poets and it is notable that, behind many of the sympathetic allusions to Guevara, there is often a more candid and pessimistic assessment of his life. Latin American poets are less inclined to debate the legacy of Che and it is the poets from outside the region who engage in a more realistic effort to do so, often conveying a sense of ambivalence about it. Al Purdy writes: "... Well it is over/Guevara is dead now and whether the world/is any closer to freedom because of/of Che's enormous dream is not to be known/...". The poem of the American Lyman Andrews cuts off without a conclusion as the dying figure tries to speak. He captures a sense of futility, depicting a barefoot character waiting to kill a tank with an old gun with which his father killed rabbits. Similarly, Daniel Schechter's poem is built upon this question: "Was his death in vain?", and he suggests death was inevitable for a "romantic adventurer" wedded to the guerrilla life. Some of the contemporary Chinese poems are sarcastic in their assessment of Che, exploiting him above all for the opportunity he offers to play with words. Volker Braun's poem is a tirade against the mundane repetition of "fine phrases" and Francis Combes leaves open his assessment with a kind of poetic riddle: "… Comandante Che/tonight/in front of my typewriter/a cigar in my mouth/surrounded by house plants/I wonder who once said:/'Revolution is a bicycle;/if you stop/pedalling/you fall.'" Some poets even dare to voice criticism of the path chosen by Guevara. Masa Mbatha-Opasha (South Africa) attacks the choice of violence as a path: " … /You taught revolution not evolution/you chose liberation but not revelation/which won us freedom without any wisdom./You were for rebellion and never changed that opinion,/but maybe I'm too young to say you were wrong./…". Kerry Upjohn also concludes with the bleak assessment that Che's sacrifice was ultimately a gesture: "… Did you ever realize that/Potatoes fill peasant bellies with a sustenance/That raw revolution will never equal?"

CONCLUSION

A number of themes emerge as prominent in an examination of the poems contained in this collection. First, many of the poets and songwriters shared or share common experiences and political outlooks. Second, the Guevara story has found its way into the imaginations of many poets across the world through the iconography — in particular, images of Che — and works of popular culture that have spread globally since the Sixties to the extent that the Che phenomenon is inseparable from this. The aesthetic sensibilities of many poets and songwriters were often galvanised by the image of the living and the dead Che, and these poetic reflections on images in photographs only strengthen the thesis that has often made that Guevara has become, above all, a *cultural* icon — the emblem of a generation.[102] They confirm the inevitability that many of the poets and songwriters come to this theme from a position of detachment, through popular culture more generally. The English poet John McGrath was candid about this: "I don't know what you were like./I've looked at the photos,/read what Fidel had to say,/gone through your books, speeches./I've got a feeling that if I'd met you,/I might have found you arrogant or mad./...". Third, it is notable how few poets identify Guevara with an individual country and he is seen as an heroic everyman of truly global appeal in poems that mostly have an epic aspiration. Fourth, Che Guevara's last days are often depicted in an almost theatrical narrative in which the poets and songwriters aim, above all else, to inject drama into this story. Poems and songs written in response to Che Guevara's death often convey emotions of anger and grief, and it is the USA as an enemy or force with a global reach that is blamed with the Bolivian regime held in contempt only as a junior partner. Fifth, there is a discernible sense in the work of many poets, particularly those in Latin America, that Che Guevara had been let down or betrayed by his own continent and by the Left globally and there is a confessional tone to many poems. Sixth, poets tend to draw attention to similar personal characteristics when discussing Che Guevara: his smile and penetrating eyes; his asthma; and his common touch and integrity. Seventh, there are a significant number of direct and indirect references in these poems and songs that liken Che Guevara to Jesus Christ or to themes that have resonance with the New Testament, even by poets from countries that do not have a predominantly Christian tradition. Finally, most poets whose work is included in this collection avoid engaging with complex ideological questions, and he is portrayed largely as a practical archetype bringing hope for justice, freedom and the fight against oppression.

Che Guevara has the qualities of martyrs throughout the ages: a charismatic figure in prophetic conflict with the norms of society who lived fast, stayed faithful to his principles, and died young. These qualities were embedded in the imagination of writers and musicians everywhere at a key period in the expansion of popular culture globally in the 1960s and 1970s. Castañeda argues that the international and cultural context in which Che's death took place was key to explaining why this event became the leitmotif of an era.[103] As the militant Salvadorean poet Roque Dalton said, the moral and political lessons of Guevara's life and death formed an invaluable part of the revolutionary patrimony of *all* peoples of the world.[104]

As the themes above suggest, many of the poets in this collection have sought out universal notions upon which to base their work and interpret this character. This aspiration to forge a universal archetype is very evident in the employment of Christian metaphors, although we must account for the likelihood that in many cases poets who used such metaphors did not stumble upon these themselves and were responding to notions already in circulation. The use of Christian imagery represents an important theme in the study of Guevara as cultural icon, and has been examined in some detail in terms of images of Che.[105] The many parallels that have been drawn between images of Christ and images of Che are well known aspects of the Guevara phenomenon. A recent exhibition (2006) at the Victoria and Albert museum in London, for example, explored among other things, the quasi-religious connotations of some of the images derived from Korda's celebrated photograph. Kunzle (1997) has argued that the fusion of Korda's Che with Christ involves the accretion of some highly symbolic characteristics in art, and in particular the identification of what is often understood to be "Latin American" with Christ's Passion. Such images incorporate the bitterness and tragedy of crucifixion — be it the crucifixion of countries on the cross of the International Monetary Fund or of individual martyrs fighting for justice — with the iconography of resurrection, peace with justice and saintly divinity.

The theme of love in this poetry provides a good example of how Che Guevara's own positions have allowed poets to make parallels both with the physical sacrifice of Christ, but also with the ideas associated with him. In "Socialism and Man in Cuba", for example, Che Guevara wrote: "At the risk of seeming ridiculous, let me say that the true revolutionary is guided by great feelings of love. It is impossible to think of a genuine revolutionary lacking this quality. Perhaps it is one of the great dramas of the leader that he or she must combine a passionate spirit with a cold intelligence and make painful decisions without flinching. Our vanguard revolutionaries must idealize this love of the people, of the most sacred causes, and make it one and indivisible. They cannot descend, with small doses of daily affection, to the level where ordinary people put their love into practice."[106]

Another theme that has also developed as one strand of the

analysis of Guevara as a cultural icon but different in terms of scale from comparisons with Christ himself, is that of saintly divinity. In an examination of the "secular sainthood" of Guevara, Passareiello (2005) defines a saint, as compared with a hero or an icon, as "an officially recognised, often institutionalised person who is entitled to public veneration beyond simple respect and admiration and who also may be someone who is capable of interceding with the cosmos — someone with not only special status but perhaps even special power".[107] In Latin America and beyond there are many examples of "popular saints" — those not recognised in the Catholic canon yet, nonetheless, enjoying a local, institutional recognition. The haunting "Zamba del che", for example, a song written by the Mexican Rubén Ortiz and popularised by Víctor Jara, makes reference to "San Ernesto de La Higuera", the popular sainthood of Che that has developed in parts of Bolivia.[108] It must be noted that popular sainthood does not just belong to a Christian tradition. Saints are an important component of popular Islam, to take just one example, and the traditions and sayings of scholars of Islam allow for a definition of the qualities of sainthood that is not inconsistent with those above, and in particular the acknowledgement by the consensus of the orthodox that the person is a saint.

Much of the verse in this book belongs to that category depicting Che as Christ-like and not as a mere saint lower down the cosmological food chain. Che is more likely to be the "solar prophet" than the "saint layman" both referred to by the Guatemalan poet Otto-Raúl González. Guevara has sometimes, for example, been referred to locally as "El Cristo de Vallegrande", particularly with reference to Alborta's photograph. It is likely that this is because it is Christ — as Messiah or prophet — that allows for universal comparisons, whereas saints are often associated with locality or country. The notion of Christ is also particularly valuable for addressing themes of messianism, self-sacrifice and immortality. In this way, many of these poems recreate the cult of martyrdom and adoration for the spiritually superior individual on a certain path to death that is at the heart of the Christian tradition everywhere. Whether poets subscibe to that Christian tradition or not, in many countries they remain profoundly influenced by it. Even Dalton, for example, was influenced by his own upbringing, and his poetry reveals both the angry militancy of many Jesuit positions in their quest to forge a popular church and a very Jesuit precision.[109]

The absence of ideological themes in these poems and songs about Che Guevara complements this search for universal metaphors. Most of the poets in this collection have avoided engaging with complex ideological questions and decanted from this story just one or two broad messages about justice and freedom. Roberto Fernández Retamar warned just after Che Guevara's death about the danger of his ideas being lost to emotion and generalisation when he wrote:

> "As in the case of Martí, his undoubted brother, we run the risk that the transparent and uncontainable grandeur of his sacrifice makes one forget that in this being boiled dazzling ideas, that sought to be structured coherently in a vision of the world."[110]

Yet poets themselves often have explicit and considered reasons for adopting such a strategy based on their understanding of the limitations of poetry as a medium for conveying political and economic ideas. Dalton wrote:

> "It's beautiful to consider the poet as a prophet. This in itself is a poetic act in which the creator of the poems appears to us to be looking down from the heights upon the future of humanity and showing us the best way forward. However, I prefer to consider the poet more as someone who investigates his own time than the future because, like it or not, if we are too insistent about what is coming we lose at a certain level a more immediate perspective and we run the risk of not being understood by all men that find themselves submerged in their daily reality."[111]

The veteran British poet Alan C. Brown, who crafted his trade in the pubs of the north of England, suggests: "... a poem is not the same thing as an accurate political statement, it should be something different but not opposite to the truth; it uses a different approach to that of plain statement — such as irony, metaphor and subtle hinted statements, to make one think at a deeper level. One German poet said his poems were like a bomb on a slow fuse — I hope the best of mine are that."[112]

The limited ability of poetry to convey explicitly political statements is a recurrent frustration among poets given to assuming dramatic postures. In place of blunt polemic, throughout the ages they have opted for metaphor, allusion and emotion that address political themes through ostensibly innocent images. Anthony Phelps, for example, appears to allude to revolution in his Haitian homeland in this way: "... but how can I talk about the star in this lady's ear/when the birds peck at our words/...". The danger for poets inherent in assuming overtly political postures is captured by Croft and Mitchell (2003) in their description of much British socialist poetry as "worthy, naïve, earnest, hectoring and, well, boring".[113] One irony, then, of much of this poetry about Che Guevara is that, while perhaps no other ideology inspired so many twentieth-century poets more than socialism, much of the work in this collection cannot be described as socialist. Although he concludes with a rallying cry: "... So let's unite and build/A loving socialist planet", Liam Ó Comain makes the point in the foreword of his poem that Che's appeal was indeed emotional, and that changing human hearts was as important as changing economic and social structures.

The absence of complex political statements in much of this poetry alongside a focus on the more emotive aspects of the story reinforces a sense that, like Che Guevara himself, many of these poets have embarked on an odyssey. They have set out to find, understand and capture on the page those universal qualities they associate with true heroism and sacrifice. As we have seen, Guevara's life and death and his personal attributes have provided them with a rare, and perhaps unique, set of creative possibilities for constructing a universal archetype in a period when the ambition to fashion such a poetic holy grail has been at its most insistent and the prospects of a welcoming audience drinking from this have been more auspicious than ever before. As a result, their work either nurtures or responds to a vision of a martyr of epic stature over and above the constraints of the very specific historical and regional context in which the individual himself was acting. The sense of brotherhood and solidarity evoked by Che Guevara is clearly of more fertile potential for these rebels with pens than his ideas themselves, and the response of poets and songwriters to this underlying theme of fraternity may help to explain why this favoured son of Latin America has had such an enduring cultural impact at a global level.

NOTES

1. Eradam, Yusuf. 2007a. "No Poem for Che Guevara No More!" Correspondence with the editors, 12 February 2007; adapted by the editors.
2. Eradam, Yusuf. 2007b. "Arif Damar's Defense". Correspondence with the editors, 12 February 2007; adapted by the editors.
3. Kuteischikova, Vera and Lev Ospovat. 1977. "La literatura en la vida de un revolucionario. (Para un retrato de Ernesto Che Guevara)", *Casa de las Américas*, Año XVIII (Sept.-Oct. 1977), pp. 24-34.
4. See Brunk, Samuel and Ben Fallaw (eds.), *Heroes and Hero Cults in Latin America*. (Austin, 2006).
5. Castañeda, Jorge G., *Compañero. The Life and Death of Che Guevara*. (London, 1997), p. 8.
6. *Ibid.*, p. 4.
7. Taibo, Paco Ignacio II. *Guevara, Also Known as Che*. (New York, 1999), p. 2.
8. See, for example, Guevara Lynch, Ernesto, *Mi hijo el Che*. (Barcelona, 1981).
9. Kuteischikova and Ospovat, *op. cit.*, p. 26.
10. Castañeda, *op. cit.*, p. 12.
11. See Taibo, *op. cit.*, p. 9; Castañeda, *op. cit.*, p. 19.
12. Taibo, *op. cit.*, p. 9.
13. Anderson, Jon Lee, *Che Guevara. A Revolutionary Life*. (London, 1998), p. 35.
14. *Ibid.*
15. See Granado, Alberto,*Travelling With Che Guevara*. (London, 2003).
16. Kuteischikova and Ospovat, *op. cit.*, p. 26.
17. Taibo, *op. cit.*, p. 36. Granado suggests that Che discovered Vallejo through Dr Hugo Pesce at the Guía hospital and leprosarium in Lima, *op. cit.*, p. 124.
18. Taibo, *op. cit.*, p. 59.
19. *Ibid.*, p. 36.
20. *Ibid.*
21. *Ibid.*, p. 37.
22. Castañeda, *op. cit.*, p. 92.
23. Kuteischikova and Ospovat, *op. cit.*, p. 26.
24. *Ibid.*, p. 27; Castañeda, *op. cit.*, p. 113.
25. Kuteischikova and Ospovat, *op. cit.*, p. 26.
26. *Ibid.*
27. Taibo, *op. cit.*, p. 272.
28. Guevara de la Serna, Ernesto, "El Patojo" (1963) in *Reminiscences of the Cuban Revolutionary War*. (Melbourne, 2005), p. 131.
29. Castañeda, *op. cit.*, p. 265.
30. Guillén wrote a number of poems in honour of Che Guevara, his first — and possibly the very first eulogy to Guevara — within days of the revolutionary victory in Cuba in January 1959. See Anderson, *op. cit.*, p. 380.

31. Fernández Retamar, Roberto. 1968. "Aquel poema", *Casa de las Américas*, Año VIII, No. 46 (Jan.-Feb. 1968), pp. 47-48.
32. Kuteischikova and Ospovat, *op. cit.*, p. 28.
33. *Ibid.*
34. Taibo, *op. cit.*, p. 515; see also Guevara de la Serna, Ernesto, *The Bolivian Diary.* (Melbourne, 2005).
35. Anderson, *op. cit.*, p. 730, author's translation.
36. Taibo, *op. cit.*, p. 574; Castañeda, *op. cit.*, p. 100.
37. See, for example, the rhyme reproduced by Taibo, *op. cit.*, p. 14, translated by Roberts.
38. Anderson, *op. cit.*, pp. 43-44.
39. See Castañeda, *op. cit.*, p. 37.
40. Ernesto Guevara de la Serna, 1951, cited in Castañeda, *op. cit.*, p. 38.
41. Taibo, *op. cit.*, p. 57; see also Anderson, *op. cit.*, pp. 182-183.
42. *Ibid.*, p. 44.
43. Ernesto Che Guevara, 1972, in Hilda Gadea, *Años decisivos.* (Mexico City, 1972) pp. 235-236; see Castañeda, *op. cit.*, p. 87.
44. Taibo, *op. cit.*, p. 67; see Gutiérrez, Carlos María. 1969. "Los motivos del Che", *Casa de las Américas*, Año IX, No. 54 (May-June 1969), pp. 23-24; and Castañeda, *op. cit.*, p. 89.
45. See Anderson, *op. cit.*, p. 201. The green alligator or caiman is a metaphor for Cuba coined by Nicolás Guillén.
46. Mañalich Suarez, Rosario. 2001. "La competencia literaria en Ernesto Che Guevara", on *Puntos de Vista*, No 4 (October 2001). Ocean Books: http://www.oceanbooks.com.au/espanol/puntos/pun40.html.
47. Guevara de la Serna, Ernesto. 1960. Letter to Ernesto Sábato in Argentina. 12 April 1960, cited in Kuteischikova and Ospovat, *op. cit.*, p. 30; see also: San Cristóbal de la Habana, Sitio del Che, Che Guia y Ejemplo: Epistolario. http://www.sancristobal.cult.cu/sitios/Che/Index.HTM.
48. Taibo, *op. cit.*, p. 595.
49. Lucio Cabañas quoted in Alberto Ulloa Bornemann, *Surviving Mexico's Dirty War.* (Philadelphia, 2007), pp. 74-75.
50. See Cane, James. 1997. "'Unity for the Defense of Culture': The AIAPE and the Cultural Politics of Argentine Antifascism, 1935-1943", *Hispanic American Historical Review*, Vol. 77, No. 3 (Aug. 1997), pp. 443-482.
51. Castañeda, *op. cit.*, p. 14.
52. Márquez, Robert, *¡Patria o Muerte! The Great Zoo and Other Poems by Nicolás Guillén.* (Havana, 1973), p. 13.
53. Kuteischikova and Ospovat, *op. cit.*, p. 27.
54. *Ibid.*
55. *Ibid.*, p. 28.
56. Gutiérrez, *op. cit.*, p. 23.
57. Kuteischikova and Ospovat, *op. cit.*, p. 25.
58. *Ibid.*, p. 29.
59. León Felipe, "El gran relincho" in José Batlló and A. Fornet, *Poemas al Che.* (Havana, 1969), pp 5-7, editors' translation.
60. See Skierka, Volker, *Fidel Castro: A Biography.* (Cambridge, 2004), p. 378.
61. Castañeda, *op. cit.*, p. 100.
62. Kuteischikova and Ospovat, *op. cit.*, p. 31.
63. Taibo, *op. cit.*, p. 336.
64. *Ibid.*, pp. 51 and 57.
65. Guevara de la Serna, Ernesto. 1965. "El socialismo y el hombre en Cuba", *Marcha* (Montevideo), Uruguay, 12 March, 1965.
66. Guevara de la Serna, Ernesto. 1964b. Letter to León Felipe in Mexico. 21 August 1964, cited in Kuteischikova and Ospovat, *op. cit.*, p. 29. See also: San Cristóbal de la Habana, Sitio del Che, Che Guia y Ejemplo: Epistolario
67. Guevara de la Serna, Ernesto. 1964a. "On creating a new attitude", *Obra Revolucionaria* (Havana), speech of August 15, 1964.

68. Kuteischikova and Ospovat, *op. cit.*, p. 29, editors' translation.
69. Guevara de la Serna, Ernesto, 1965, *op. cit.*
70. Taibo, *op. cit.*, p. 394.
71. See: Canción Protesta, *Casa de la Américas*, Año VIII, No. 45 (Nov.-Dec. 1967).
72. Randall, Margaret, "Introduction" in *Roque Dalton: Poemas clandestinos/Clandestine Poems.* (Willimantic, 1990), p. XII.
73. Dalton, Roque.1963. "Poesía y militancia en Améria Latina", *Casa de la Américas*, Año III, Nos. 20-21 (Sept.-Dec. 1963), p. 18, editors' translation.
74. See, for example, Croft, Andy and Adrian Mitchell (eds.), *Red Sky at Night. Socialist Poetry.* (Nottingham, 2003).
75. See, for example, www.marxists.org/subject/art/music/index.htm; www.sancristobal.cult.cu/sitios/Che/canciones.htm; www.echeguevara.com.ar/htm/canciones.htm.
76. Martins Villaça, Mariana. 2004. "'El nombre del hombre es pueblo': as representações de Che Guevara na canção latinoamericana". Anais do V Congresso Latinoamericano da Associação Internacional para o Estudo da Música Popular. Available at: www.hist.puc.cl/historia/iaspm/rio/Anais2004%20(PDF)/MarianaMartinsVillaca.pdf.
77. A useful summary of popular non-Latin American artists whose songs have made reference to Che has been compiled on Wikipedia: http://en.wikipedia.org/wiki/Che_Guevara_in_popular_culture.
78. Castañeda, *op. cit.*, points out that the body was not cremated by the military, but merely buried beneath the airstrip at Vallegrande.
79. See, for example, Hassan, Salah Dean Assaf. 2002. Introduction: "Origins" of Postmodern Cuba, *The New Centennial Review*, Vol. 2, No. 2 (Summer 2002), pp. 1-17.
80. See Goytisolo, José Agustín, *Nueva Poesía Cubana. Antología poética.* (Barcelona, 1969), p. 14.
81. *Ibid.*, p. 19.
82. Márquez, *op. cit.*, p. 28.
83. Goytisolo, *op. cit.*, p. 19.
84. See Gónzalez Echeverría, Roberto. 1980. "'Biografía de un cimarrón' and the Novel of the Cuban Revolution", *NOVEL: A Forum on Fiction*, Vol. 13, No. 3 (Spring, 1980), pp. 249-263.
85. Márquez, *op. cit.*, p. 13.
86. See Batlló and Fornet, *op. cit.*
87. *Ibid.*, p. xi.
88. Taibo, *op. cit.*, p. 401.
89. McDermott, Peter. 2005. *Irish Echo Online*, March 16-22, 2005. Available at: http://www.irishecho.com/archives/archivestory.cfm?newspaperid=16187&issueid=406.
90. See Phaithun, Sun-Thon, *Lom Laichai yang mai sin.* (Bangkok, 1976).
91. See Cheng, Yinghong 2003. "*Che Guevara*: Dramatizing China's Divided Intelligentsia at the Turn of the Century". *Modern Chinese Literature and Culture*, Vol. 15, No. 2, (Fall 2003), pp. 1-43.
92. See Robinson, William F. 1974. "A new blow against Hungarian non-conformists". Radio Free Europe Research, Hungary/14, 6 November 1974. Open Society Archives (OSA) 1956 Digital Archive, Box-folder report: 35-5-287. Central European University, Budapest.
93. See Randall, *op. cit.*, p. VIII.
94. See Ziff, Trisha (ed.), *Che Guevara: Revolutionary and Icon.* (London, 2006).
95. See, for example, Katz, Leandro, *El Dia Que Me Quieras*, VHS film. (Argentina, 1997).
96. Castañeda, *op. cit.*, p. 46.
97. It is interesting to note that the word "che" can be found in both the Mapuche language, Mapudungun, spoken in southern Chile and Argentine Patagonia, and in the Guaraní language, spoken in Paraguay, parts of northern Argentina, eastern Bolivia and south-western Brazil.
98. See Lao, Meri, *Al Che. Poesie e canzoni dal mondo.* (Rome, 1995), p. 15.
99. See Ziff, , *op. cit.*, p. 83.
100. *Ibid.*, p. 9.
101. See Lao, *op. cit.*, p. 11.
102. See, for example, Castañeda, *op. cit.*, p. 410.
103. *Ibid.*, p. 409.

104. Dalton, Roque. 1968. "Combatiendo por la libertad de américa latina ha muerto nuestro comandante Ernesto Guevara", *Casa de la Américas*, Año VIII, No. 46 (Jan.-Feb. 1968), p. 20.
105. See, for example, Kunzle, David. *Che Guevara: Icon, Myth, and Message*. (Los Angeles, 1997).
106. Guevara de la Serna, Ernesto, 1965, *op. cit.*
107. Passareiello, Phyllis. "Desperately Seeking Something: Che Guevara as Secular Saint", in James F. Hopgood (ed.), *The Making of Saints. Contesting Sacred Ground*. (Tuscaloosa, 2005), p. 75.
108. "La Zamba del Che" was written in November 1967 by Rubén Ortiz Fernández. It premiered at Mexico's national university UNAM and was played during demonstrations held during the 1968 student movement in Mexico, later being recorded by Víctor Jara in Chile in 1970.
109. Randall, *op. cit.*, p. II.
110. Fernández Retamar, *op. cit.*, p. 46.
111. Dalton, 1963, *op. cit.*, p. 19, editors' translation.
112. Alan C. Brown, correspondence with the editors, December 10, 2006.
113. Croft and Mitchell, *op. cit.*, p. 4.

References

Anderson, Jon Lee. 1998. *Che Guevara. A Revolutionary Life*. London: Bantam Press
Batlló, José and A. Fornet. 1969. *Poemas al Che*. Havana: Instituto del Libro
Brunk, Samuel and Ben Fallaw (eds.). 2006. *Heroes and Hero Cults in Latin America*. Austin: University of Texas Press
Canción Protesta, sección, *Casa de la Américas*, Año VIII, No. 45 (Nov.-Dec. 1967)
Cane, James. 1997. "'Unity for the Defense of Culture': The AIAPE and the Cultural Politics of Argentine Antifascism, 1935-1943", *Hispanic American Historical Review*, Vol. 77, No. 3 (Aug. 1997), pp. 443-482
Castañeda, Jorge G. 1997. *Compañero. The Life and Death of Che Guevara*, Translated from the Spanish by Marina Castañeda. London: Bloomsbury
Croft, Andy and Adrian Mitchell (eds.). 2003. *Red Sky at Night. Socialist Poetry*. Nottingham: Five Leaves Publications
Dalton, Roque. 1963. "Poesía y militancia en Améria Latina", *Casa de la Américas*, Año III, Nos. 20-21 (Sept.-Dec. 1963), pp. 12-20
Dalton, Roque. 1968. "Combatiendo por la libertad de américa latina ha muerto nuestro comandante Ernesto Guevara", *Casa de la Américas*, Año VIII, No. 46 (Jan.-Feb. 1968), p. 20
Eradam, Yusuf. 2007a. "No Poem for Che Guevara No More!" Summary translation of the defence by counsel for Metin Demirtaş in his trial in Turkey that began on 25 March 1968. Correspondence with the editors, 12 February 2007
Eradam, Yusuf. 2007b. "Arif Damar's Defense". Summary translation of Arif Damar's own defence in his trial in Turkey that started on 12 July 1968. Correspondence with the editors, 12 February 2007
Fernández Retamar, Roberto. 1968. "Aquel poema", *Casa de las Américas*, Año VIII, No. 46 (Jan.-Feb. 1968), p. 46
Gadea, Hilda. 1972. *Años decisivos*. Mexico City: Aguilar
Gónzalez Echeverría, Roberto. 1980. "'Biografía de un cimarrón' and the Novel of the Cuban Revolution". *NOVEL: A Forum on Fiction*, Vol. 13, No. 3 (Spring, 1980), pp. 249-263
Goytisolo, José Agustín. 1969. *Nueva Poesía Cubana. Antología poética*. Barcelona: Ediciones Península, Nueva Colección Ibérica
Granado, Alberto. 2003. *Travelling With Che Guevara. The Making of a Revolutionary*. Translated by Lucía Álvarez de Toledo. London: Pimlico

Guevara de la Serna, Ernesto. 1951. Letter to Chichina Ferreyra, February 1, 1951. Unpublished. Cited in Castañeda, 1997, p. 38

Guevara de la Serna, Ernesto. 1960. Letter to Ernesto Sábato in Argentina. 12 April 1960, cited in Kuteischikova and Ospovat, 1977, p. 30

Guevara de la Serna, Ernesto. 1964a. "On creating a new attitude", *Obra Revolucionaria* (Havana), speech of August 15, 1964 ("Discurso en la entrega de certificados de trabajo comunista en el Ministerio de Industrias")

Guevara de la Serna, Ernesto. 1964b. Letter to León Felipe in Mexico. 21 August 1964, cited in Kuteischikova and Ospovat, 1977, p. 29. See also: San Cristóbal de la Habana, Sitio del Che, Che Guia y Ejemplo: Epistolario: http://www.sancristobal.cult.cu/sitios/Che/Index.HTM [Accessed March 2007]

Guevara de la Serna, Ernesto. 1965. "El socialismo y el hombre en Cuba" ("Man and Socialism in Cuba"), *Marcha* (Montevideo), Uruguay, 12 March, 1965. [Originally titled "From Algiers, for *Marcha*", Letter to Carlos Quijano, *Marcha*, Montevideo, 12 March 1965]

Guevara de la Serna, Ernesto.1972. "Palenque", quoted in Hilda Gadea, *Años decisivos*. Mexico City: Aguilar

Guevara de la Serna, Ernesto. 2005a. "El Patojo" (1963) in *Reminiscences of the Cuban Revolutionary War*. Melbourne: Ocean Press

Guevara de la Serna, Ernesto. 2005b. *The Bolivian Diary: The authorized edition.* Melbourne: Ocean Press

Guevara Lynch, Ernesto. 1981. *Mi hijo el Che.* Barcelona: Planeta

Gutiérrez, Carlos María. 1969. "Los motivos del Che", *Casa de las Américas*, Año IX, No. 54 (May-June 1969), pp. 23-24

Hassan, Salah Dean Assaf. 2002. Introduction: "Origins" of Postmodern Cuba, *The New Centennial Review*, Vol. 2, No. 2 (Summer 2002), pp. 1-17

Katz, Leandro. 1997. *El Dia Que Me Quieras*, VHS film. Argentina: Caterina Borelli

Kunzle, David. 1997. *Che Guevara: Icon, Myth, and Message.* Los Angeles: University of California

Kuteischikova, Vera and Lev Ospovat. 1977. "La literature en la vida de un revolucionario. (Para un retrato de Ernesto Che Guevara)", *Casa de las Américas*, Año XVIII (Sept.-Oct. 1977), pp. 24-34

Lao, Meri. 1995. *Al Che. Poesie e canzoni dal mondo.* Rome: Erre emme edizioni

McDermott, Peter. 2005. *Irish Echo Online*, March 16-22, 2005. Available at: http://www.irishecho.com/archives/archivestory.cfm?newspaperid=16187&issueid=406 [Accessed: April 2007]

Mañalich Suarez, Rosario. 2001. "La competencia literaria en Ernesto Che Guevara", *Puntos de Vista*, No 4 (October 2001). Ocean Books: http://www.oceanbooks.com.au/espanol/puntos/pun40.html [Accessed: March 2007]

Márquez, Robert. 1973. *¡Patria o Muerte! The Great Zoo and Other Poems by Nicolás Guillén.* Edited and translated by Robert Márquez. Havana: Editorial de Arte y Literatura

Martins Villaça, Mariana. 2004. "'El nombre del hombre es pueblo': as representações de Che Guevara na canção latinoamericana". Anais do V Congresso Latinoamericano da Associação Internacional para o Estudo da Música Popular. Available at: http://www.hist.puc.cl/historia/iaspm/rio/Anais2004%20(PDF)/MarianaMartins

Villaca.pdf [Accessed: April 2007]

Passareiello, Phyllis. 2005. "Desperately Seeking Something: Che Guevara as Secular Saint", in James F. Hopgood (ed.). 2005. *The Making of Saints. Contesting Sacred Ground*. Tuscaloosa: The University of Alabama Press

Phaithun, Sun-Thon. 1976. *Lom Laichai yang mai sin* [Collected articles on Che Guevara and Progressive Thai Writers]. Bangkok: Banna Kit

Randall, Margaret. 1990 "Introduction" in *Roque Dalton: Poemas clandestinos/Clandestine Poems*. Willimantic: Curbstone Press

Robinson, William F. 1974. "A new blow against Hungarian non-conformists". Radio Free Europe Research, Hungary/14, 6 November 1974. Open Society Archives (OSA) 1956 Digital Archive, Box-folder report: 35-5-287. Central European University, Budapest. Available at: http://files.osa.ceu.hu/holdings/300/8/3/text_da/35-5-287.shtml [Accessed: March 2007]

Salkey, Andrew (ed.). 1977. *Writing in Cuba Since the Revolution. An Anthology of Poems, Short Stories and Essays*. London: Bogle-L'Ouverture Publications Ltd

San Cristóbal de la Habana, Sitio del Che, Che Guia y Ejemplo: Epistolario: http://www.sancristobal.cult.cu/sitios/Che/Index.HTM [Accessed: March 2007]

Skierka, Volker. 2004. *Fidel Castro: A Biography*. Cambridge: Polity

Taibo, Paco Ignacio II. 1999. *Guevara, Also Known as Che*. Translated by Martin Roberts. New York: St. Martin's Griffin

Ulloa Bornemann, Alberto. 2007. *Surviving Mexico's Dirty War. A Political Prisoner's Memoir*. Edited and translated by Arthur Schmidt and Aurora Camacho de Schmidt. Philadelphia: Temple University Press

Ziff, Trisha (ed.). 2006. *Che Guevara: Revolutionary and Icon*. London: V&A Publications

ALGERIA

D<small>JAMEL</small> A<small>MRANI</small>   1976

Shadows which dream of me

Shadows which dream of me
which accompany me untangling my wanderings
a scrawny tune of embers! a volcano's delirium
Oh! how long has it taken for our hands
to join up...
Shadows which gather
on the scar of a river bank
in the musical joy of life
in the lyrical peace of memories.
And we shall impose our will
to the sun's flesh
to the waterlilies' anger
— revengeful crocus with a clenched fist
moist faces on the cutting edge
of the skies
Reflections multiplied on the mire
of gaols
watchful chests under the
beating sun.
How bitter is the spiteful elegy
the lagoon marked out with beacons
the incarceration under the soul's skin
while laughters scald the tip
of flames with spring showers
with naked bodies burnt at the stake
with bunches of palm tree dates.
Luxurious tree of El-Ayoun,
draped with the southern lyre, with turbulent wood,
I salute you.
O fiendish blindness of tyrants
those who hurled stones at Federico and Neruda

at the time of flashes of a hard tooth
at the time of the outcasts of golden distinction —
O Beirut, chained, surrounded and paralysed city
where fear is taught to children
where one catches oneself killing and setting fires in the innocent
and broad daylight just to defend oneself.
O my brothers with nails and chains
with volcanic chests
with salty tears that hit everyone's eyes
O my first fear at the very root
of my tree
Pablo dreamt of Madrid in spring
Blas de Otero of lemon trees in Paris
and both were howling in the moonlight
the invertebrate freedom
the maddening and bloodthirsty usurpation.
Che was sweating with the coffee farmers
in the vibrating land of the *zafra*
In the boiling rocks of all oceans
on the way to all weapons
in the generating
elevating
life-giving flame
of man's revolution.
And what a surprise to be hidden still
behind the frizzy landscapes of exiled hearts.
— bodies which shiver in the straightjacket
of misery and hemmed ordeal.

Translated by Alexandra Stanton

Editors' note: El-Ayoun is the largest city in the Western Sahara, disputed since Spain abandoned its former colony in 1975; the reference to Federico is to Federico García Lorca, the Spanish poet killed at the start of the Spanish Civil War; Blas de Otero is the Spanish poet Blas de Otero Muñoz; a *zafra* is a field of sugar cane.

BAGDAD MAATA   2005

Che.. Che.. Here's to you!

Do you know, Madam, seated in the first row
This ageing man all dressed in white?
He is the father of sorrow, of suffering and tears
Of all the pains, and of the secret of weapons.

The valiant fighter that was this doctor
A penniless Argentine, Cuban or Bolivian,
With an angelic face and child's beard,
With such a powerful gaze, so pure, so moving,

This hero without glory devoted to the world
The champion of his cause, ignored, rarely praised,
Paid with ingratitude, and more bad luck
With suffering and pain without knowing good fortune,

One could not rob his soul nor his reason
So he was tracked down, in the mountains and in small valleys,
He was hunted down, parched, and finally handed over
So as to finish off the Great Che Guevara!

It is true that the body of this modern Christ
Was manhandled, and thrown to
Thirsty dogs, and to stinking hyenas,
His principles nonetheless survive, his deeds are still alive.

His spirit still moves, his strength still penetrates,
Because Lies, Deceit, Hatred and Arrogance
Cannot win over Truth and the Love for the wretched
They cannot triumph, but only engender Suffering.

Translated by Alexandra Stanton

ANGOLA

Jofre Rocha   1969

Song for Guevara

Over the mountains of the Andes
your thunderous voice still reverberates today.
And from Alaska to Patagonia
on certain nights of uprising and uproar
your unforgettable face descends among the villages
to give breath to the desperate
and a lesson of perseverance to the people.
Everywhere they seek your embrace
to lay the foundations of future homelands
and although you died in a Bolivian forest
your heart beats forever
in every field of struggle
from the rice paddies of Vietnam to the swamps of Guinea
always living at the side of every combatant
capable of fighting and dying for freedom.
Escambray and Sierra Maestra
sing loudly with your blood
and so the assassins' bullets
only disseminated to the four winds
your order for combat

because you are a monument to brotherhood
and your country, the whole World.

Translated by Richard Bartlett

ARGENTINA

Julio Cortázar   1967

I had a brother

I had a brother
we never saw each other
but it didn't matter
I had a brother
who passed through the mountains
whilst I slept.

I loved him in my own way
I listened to his voice
free like the water,
I walked sometimes
near his shadow.

We never saw each other
but it didn't matter;
my brother wide awake
whilst I slept.

My brother showing me
behind the night
his chosen star.

Translated by Gavin O'Toole

GABRIEL FERNÁNDEZ CAPELLO (VICENTICO)
LOS FABULOSOS CADILLACS   1991

Red cockerel

There was a time you were strong
and battled like a fighting cock,
red cockerel, such a brave
commander of this barrio,
no matter if there were ten,
twenty or a thousand,
you were immense, Sun of May.
Nowadays people sleepwalk
none can wake them up.

So this is why I beg you
to bring us back to life
to wake up all the blood
that is asleep.
Some day this block
is going to be as you wanted
and tomorrow it'll be the whole barrio
that's behind you.

When the tide is rising up
I'll stay in this barrio
because I follow your footsteps
and your coursing blood.
And tomorrow there'll be ten,
twenty or a thousand
beside you, Sun of May.
There was a time you fought
and that time is coming.

So this is why I beg you
to bring us back to life,
to wake up all the blood
that is asleep.

Some day this block
is going to be as you wanted
and tomorrow it'll be the whole barrio
that's behind you.

Translated by Georgina Jiménez

Translator's note: The Sun of May, or Sol de Mayo, is the national emblem of Argentina and is featured on the country's flag.

JUAN GELMAN   1968

Conversations

I am from a country where a short while ago Carlos Molina
Uruguayan anarchist and minstrel
was arrested
in Bahía Blanca in the south of the south
facing the immense sea as they say
he was arrested by the police
Carlos Molina was
singing, spinning ballads
about the vast ocean voyages
the monsters of the vast ocean
or ballads for example
about the horse that lies down on the pampas
or about the sky one supposes Carlos
Molina was singing as ever beauties and sorrows
when
suddenly Che began to live and die in his guitar
and so
the police arrested him

I am from a country where they cry for Che or in any case
they sing for Che and
some are happy with his death
"see" they say "he was wrong the thing
isn't like that" they say but they do not say what the hell the thing
                                                        is like or

they prefer to recite old biblical verses or
suggest point advise whilst
the rest stay quiet
look into the air with lost eyes

Comandante Guevara entered death
and wanders thereabouts they say

I am from a country where it was hard to believe he was dying and many
your humble servant among others
was consoling themself thus:
"but if he says you don't have
to fight to the death but that you have
to fight unto victory then he isn't dead"
others were weeping too much like someone
who had lost his father and I believe
that he is not our father and
with all due respect I think that
it is wrong to weep for him thus

I am from a country where the enemies could
not make stick a single insult a single
obscenity a single little indecency
about him such that some even
mourned his death not
through kindness or
humanity or pie
ty
but because those old hounds
or deads on leave sensed at last an enemy who
was worthy
that a flash of danger
entered the scene and then
they would be able to die seriously
by real hands or bullets "and not
in the embrace of that type of dissolution

in which we merely dissolve" as
someone with an important surname said

I'm from a country where they happened or happen
all these things and yet others
like betrayals and wickedness on an excessive scale
and the people suffer and are blind and none
defends it and only
Che stood up against this

but
now
Comandante Guevara entered death
and wanders thereabouts they say

I am from a very complicated country
Latineurocosmopoliturban
creolejudaipolispanitalianish
so say the texts and the texts that say
well they say and
as they say
thus is thus but I
assure them that it's not true
that from this fantasy land
Guevara left one morning and
another morning he returned and always
he will return to this country although not for
more than
looking at us a little a big little and
who will endure it?
who will endure his glances?

but
just now
Comandante Guevara entered death
and wanders thereabouts they say

I ask
who will endure his glances?
you the mummies of the Argentine communist party?
you let him fall
you so-so lefties?
you let him fall
you the owners of the revealed truth?
you let him fall
you who looked at China without understanding that
looking at China really
was looking at our country?
you let him fall
you petty
theoreticians of fire by mail partisans
of violence by telephone or
of the metaphysical mass movement?
you let him fall
you priests of *foquismo* and nothing more?
you let him fall
you members of the club
of big arses seated upon "reality"?
you let him fall
you who spit
on life not
realising that in fact you are
spitting against the great wind of history?
you let him fall
you who don't believe in magic?
you let him fall

I am from a country where Comandante Guevara
was left to fall by:
the soldiers the priests the homeopaths
the auctioneers
the refugees Spaniards masochists Jews
the bosses and
the workers as well for now

"What a man what a great man" however
a worker said to me pedro
he was called is called has
a wife who cannot bear
living babies and pedro
told me "what a man what a great man how
I love him" said the mason thinking
of his mother a whore
famous throughout Córdoba and the mother
of seven children whom she raised with love
Pedro now with a capital letter
how I salute your bitterness
how I kiss the foot of your failures!
"what balls" Pedro said to me one day speaking of Che
of certain appendages that boil
beneath the conjectural peace
of this cosmopolitan country

Comandante Guevara entered death
and wanders thereabouts they say

I am writing this
because the Casa de las Américas of Cuba
a very respectable institution
has resolved to publish a special issue
of its magazine dedicated
to testimonials about Che
now that they have killed him
so they say and Roberto
Fernández Retamar a very close friend
but more
a part of my life who travels there
through the formidable and
phosphorescent and cherished and conspicuous Caribbean
Roberto as I said
has thought it necessary that I

write something about this or perhaps someone else
thought this should be so and requested
articles poems etcetera from
contributors who
will feel even more miserable
if this were possible if this
were really possible

I am from a country where I give you your due
Roberto but
say or tell me please
what do you ask for or are you asking?
that I actually write?
I can give you news from my heart nothing more
does anyone really know
what is the news from my heart?
does or will anyone believe that
I have refused to weep except
with my wife or with
you Roberto now
that I narrate these questions
and I know that sadness like a dog
always follows men bothering them?

I am from a country where it is necessary
not to love but to kill
the melancholy
and where
one must not confuse
Che with sadness

or as Fierro said
swelling with fatness

I am from a country where I myself
let him fall
and who will pay for this
who

but
what matters is that truly
Comandante Guevara entered death
and wanders thereabouts they say
beautiful
with stones under his arm

I am from a country where now
Guevara has to endure other deaths
each one will solve his death now:
he who laughed is now worthless dust
may he who wept reflect
may he who forgot forget or remember
and he who remembered merely have the right to remember
Comandante Guevara entered death of his own
accord but
you
what are you going to do with that death?

my little ones
what?

(as no one is spared
between parentheses I want
not because of stupid comments possibly
aimed at me
nor for piety or
mere precaution
those decaying chunks of flesh that cannot
pray at midday
I want as I repeat
to repeat a story that not everyone knows and
in which there are some who
distrust:
the poet who writes his poem
leaving in it the marvel of

the life and death of Comandante Guevara
that Cordoban *porteño* with the piercing gaze
of a god or gods
surprised in the middle of his miracle his
boot rotted by the jungle of the world
I mean that this poem or thing
of which one has to distrust
in which one has to believe
does not end on these pages
kind reader I beseech you
to follow the news in the dailies
of the sip and sap — Section for Ageing Pain for
              example or
Seraphims Are Powerful
or
Such an Abundance of Police — I beseech you great reader
to read carefully
lines in blood written each day in Vietnam
and also in Bolivia for fuck's sake
and also in Argentina
dearest reader I beseech you to read)

Comandante Guevara went to his death
and wanders thereabouts they say
I know few things for example I know
that I must not weep Ernesto
I know
that
you depend on me now
I can bury you with great tears but
really I cannot

the poet really
abstains from crying abstains
from writing a poem be it
for the Casa de las Américas be it
for whatever it may be the poet

barely cried in reality
continues looking at the world
knows
some day beauty will come
but not today that you are absent
the poet
just knows how to watch over
che
guevara

now I want a great silence
to descend upon my heart and enwrap it
father Guevara, what will become of your children?

why did you leave beautiful one
on the horses of song?
who will put you together again?

Translated by Gavin O'Toole

Translator's note: A *porteño* in Argentina is someone from Buenos Aires; *foquismo* is the theory of guerrilla warfare attributed to Che; sip refers to the Sociedad Interamericana de Prensa.

LEOPOLDO MARECHAL   1967

Words to Che

When this great dishonour gravitating over Latin America has
                                    been redeemed;
When this great shame has been washed with the good soap that
                                    the blood of heroes makes;
When freedom is not a cheque in dollars and a deceitful illusion,
Then, comrades, we will see how a phoenix can arise from
                                    its ashen place of rest.
And it does not matter if the very sun itself illuminates
                        both the tomb of a guerrilla just fallen
And the barren back of the most miserable generals.

What are you angry about, man? Why are you crying, woman?
Did you not know that a hero must die and dies, as if taken
                                        by his own beautiful wind?
The hero was an advocate who knew not how to sleep
And a sleeplessness with its mouth full of clamour:
A danger, in sum, and an uncomfortable irritant.
That is why, when the hero succumbs, the cursed ones caught in
                                        the act face you with a grin
And the cautious blessed ones grieve with their heads to one side.
Oh, Che, it's not I that has to weep over your defeated flesh!
Because again I contemplate a scale already balanced by your
                                        last battle.
And facing this balance, I will tell your enemies and ours:
"You have made of a warrior in motion a motionless engine".
And this motionless engine fuelled in Santa Cruz
Now organises the pace of future battles.

Translated by Gavin O'Toole

AUSTRALIA

S.K. KELEN   1972

Koki Market

Koki market on the beach
next to the village on stilts
over the water. Where you can
buy fruit and vegetables at native prices.
Red stains of betel nut spat
everywhere on the ground. Pedlars sit
behind their goods all laid out
on small grass mats. Gossiping
and arguing in Pidjin and Motu.
Fifty Papuan soldiers march by to the joy
and pride of a gang of native transvestites.
Naked children play while a red-brown man
with no legs, held up by crutches, looks sadly over
a universe of waves to heaven. A youth
with Afro hair and a shirt with a picture of Che
screams revolution at the seagulls
but the sounds of living drown him.

I buy a coconut from a woman
whose tattooed head's a thousand years old.
Smells of cooking and tobacco and
rotting fruit pervade the air.
Pure sky touches the horizon of the jade desert.

Old women wade into the sea,
naked, cast their fishing lines.
Out on the reef the wing of a Japanese
transport plane stands like a broken soldier.

Port Moresby, 1972

JOSEF LESSER   2006

What did you make of it?

(for Che Guevara)

Hey buddy
when you witnessed the speed of light
in that flicker of your life arrested
        in the eye of a humming bird
what did you make of it
the light - - - - - - your life?
mesmerised by the speeding train
you boarded at the station of social change
you graduated to conductor,
Fidel the driver had memorised the route
steered you from the scalpel to the gun.

Hey buddy
what did you make of it
the light - - - - - - your life?
inside a wheel within a wheel
rotating seed of fellowship sown together
by the thread of history eased through
the eye of a revolutionary needle.

Who was the needle who the thread
who stitched the quilt of Cuba
soul body and head?

Hey buddy
what do you make of it now?
the spinning yarn the patchwork streets
where sewing circles save a dime to buy
a one way ticket on the leaving train,
and from the window streamers
the colour of heritage seek refuge in the sky.

DUNCAN RICHARDSON   2002

Che Guevara's Last Bodyguard

Sorry Mum, can't come for dinner
you see Che Guevara's last bodyguard is in town
and I really can't miss him.

Sorry darling, can't do the washing up
I know it's my turn but Che Guevara's last bodyguard's in town
It's getting late and I've got to go.

No son, I can't pick you up from the Mall
you see, Che Guevara's last bodyguard is speaking
and there's a chance he'll set me free.

The pile of worthy magazines grows too tall beside my bed
and the Havana head bangers wear
their baseball caps backwards
so when Che Guevara's last bodyguard is in town
one more betrayal would be
too much.

RICHARD TIPPING   ·   1969

Soft Riots / TV News

6pm july 4

    theyre marching on the American consulate

               be/cause

      theres nowhere else to go

its cold in the city   wind off the water
             trains on time

marching
marching for
marching for reasons

in adelaide a man takes off his coat
in melbourne a man sits down and sighs
in sydney a woman changes channels
in brisbane its windy southwest change max 25

THE CAMERAMEN ARE READY   action
action
the spotlit streets   action
spit back cats cars   action

a spearhead of radicals bearing red flags urged
on and led by other radicals a drawing of the prime
minister was also burned a petition police wielding
batons kicked and punched 1000 independence day
ball with 99 arrested and constable green hit by
a stone & allowed to leave

i tell ya jude
you cant beat the sheriff

che che che che
che guevara
che che guevara
che che che guevara
che che guevara
che

angelic hip christ holding
bulletholes to his poems :
crucified dead & buried
after three days he didn't
rise / no rock rolled back

who live out your lives
   who live out your lives
      in darkness
         in darkness

                  a match
                  three butts
                  ashes all
                  on a box
                  of pins

the police were unable to find a motive for the killing.
they suggested three alternatives :

READY

         up against the wall
         they pin the target
         to your chest & share
         your last cigarette

         up against the wall
         clawing at

AIM

            spotlights arclight gutteral swing bark
            blinding the wire ripping through your outstretched
         fingers tearing at your machinegun gut gut to
         shredding clothes a shirt flagged above bones the
            wire flashing with the sun wire barbs gaa sssh ing

         when i shut my eyes its dark in my brain

zzzoooooooooooooomm shot
reversed to full screen
panoramic wall

strung by the hungry prisons of

FIRE

click

goodnight melbourne
lights out adelaide
brisbane shut your eyes
sydney
see you in the morning

Note: In the section referring to Che, the first part is a chant beating out a rhythm with the emphasis on the word "Che": 1 2 3 4 / 1 2-3-4 / 1 1 2-3-4 / 1 1 1 2-3-4 / 1 1 2-3-4 / 1

KERRY UPJOHN   1974

Che Guevara

Displayed, your corpse still guards the mystery —
Silent Indians file past — enveloped in
Hazy hallucinations of forgotten pasts and heroes.
The chiselled profile, a bearded face,
While dark eyes dimly stare —

For years chasing the socialists' shadows,
Throughout most of South America, you sought Revolution.
In romantic visions submissive Indians became
Tall Inca warriors. The sturdy peasant
Would symbolise your future triumph.

And always, the sun hung like
A red backdrop against the sky
Burning with energy. In bare ungrassed patches
The naked bones of dry Bolivia
Were seen in summer; like your cheekbones.

Life's epic moments fortunately are rare.
You spent months in Government
As the resident saviour of the people
(Where prophets are never welcomed ...)
Living off the fat white pages of official documents.

Scorning the UN speeches you fled
Again life was a series of exalted disasters.
Your bands of followers, jovial, but alert.
Relentlessly through jungle the soldiers followed
Determined to encircle your independence.

Dead, but now enshrined as saint —
Your Quixotic quest was ageless.
Did you ever realize that
Potatoes fill peasant bellies with a sustenance
That raw revolution will never equal?

BELGIUM

FRIEDA GROFFY   1996

To Che

I'm not going to write an ode to you
Others have done that before me
I'm not going to turn you into a hero
Others have done that before me
I'm not going to build you a statue
Others have done that before me
I'm not writing down history
That, you did by yourself
I'm not making the Revolution
That, you did by yourself
I'm not creating the legend
That, also you did by yourself
But I do want to sell my soul to you
To become one of those 'new people'
You were dreaming about
To pass on your message
Carried by the stormy winds
Of our tormented times
Finally you returned home to that
Small, bold, tiny island
Where the love of the common people
Smiles at you from every street corner
And from every square the palm trees
Whisper over and over again the same song
'Comandante Che Guevara'

BOLIVIA

ALFONSO GUMUCIO DAGRON   1971

Che

there will forever be a shadow
over there, a shadow a nearby light
here forever a forehead in the thickets
not seen but felt in the dampness
of every tree
                    fluttering down
the living heartbeat of the living jungle
since the blood
found there its true carapace

in spite of sons of bitches
clumsy soldiers with northern star and eagle
                    on their chest
this land will be torn
ties and stripes will have to die
and even speaking in Spanish will be shameful

the murmur is already running as rivers
the leaves echo
                    even
the snow the heights the sea
tremble with hope but the song is
still sad the shadow
moves slowly
                    multiplied
cries laughs rants does not forget loves rises up
and there is none who can stop it
because it loves

Translated by Georgina Jiménez

BRAZIL

José Carlos Capinam and Gilberto Gil   1968

I'm crazy for you, America

I'm crazy for you, America!
I shall bring with me a lady from the beachside
whose name must be Martí
I am madly in love with you!
Having as her colours
the white froth of Latin America
and the sky as flag

I'm crazy for you, America
I'm madly in love with you!

A smile that is almost pure cloud
the rivers sing, the fear,
body filled with stars.
How do you name such love
of these nameless countries?
This tango, this rancho,
this fire of sowing,
the fire of knowing.

I'm crazy…

The name of the man who is dead
now cannot be spoken, who knows,
before the dawning day.
the name of the dead man
before the definitive night
spreads across Latin America,
the name of the man is People.

I'm crazy…

You are the morning which sings
the name of the dead man
there are no sad words
I'm madly in love with you!
A poem still exists
with palm trees, with trenches
songs of war, who knows,
songs of the sea,
hey, awaiting the uprising.

I'm crazy...

I am passing through here,
I know that one day I'm going to die
from fright, from a bullet or from neglect
with no precipice of light,
among sobs of longing,
I am going to die
face down in the arms, in the eyes
in the arms of a woman.

More passionately still
in the arms of a peasant
warrior mannequin, oh woe is me!
in the arms of someone who wants me.

I'm crazy...

Translated by Richard Bartlett

Translator's note: This song combined both Spanish and Portuguese.

THIAGO DE MELLO 1977

Blood and dew

When I heard the news
I was almost ten years old,
first was that deafening thud
in the depths of the chest and the arteries
biting the salt of blood,
tearing the sun of cartilage.

Afterwards I sought refuge with anger in tears
which, more than the face, burnt my life.
A red-hot love, castle
of my heart, you taught me:
I'm not going to cry. But I sobbed
in that masculine weeping of men.
I stayed staring for a long time
at your portrait, at your face
in the foreign newspaper:
that was when, suddenly, I discovered
that we, the people,
we are descended from birds.

(Certainty which, some time later, I confirmed
staring, in the fortress of exile,
the flame which burnt in the eyes
of the poet Ho Chi Minh,
emblazoned on the cover of *Time*,
on the day of inevitable triumph
of the people of Vietnam.)

I have never written you a poem.
But I have chatted often and at length,
it has been many, many dawns,
relating your life,
your lucid dream, your struggle,
for the peasants of my land
and of other lands as well.

Today I am far from them. But I know
that they do not have your portrait on their wall.
But I know that they keep you, powerful,
in the warm earth of your heart.
As powerful as ever,
powerful as a brother.

Because you, comandante of hope,
brother of the men of this world,
brother of those who want to share,
brother of those who fell with you,
before and after you,
in the building of a worthy life.
Brother of the child newly born
in the painful land of my childhood.
Above all brother of the man
who is being born, now,
within man.

It is only for this, comandante Che Guevara
that I wish to write you today,
while navigating the Amazon river,
beneath the clarity of midday.
I am, at this moment of the world and of men,
steering beside the San Pablo Leprosy hospital,
from where your long
and illustrious journey began.

Just to let you know that it's growing,
that every day it's growing more
the hand of man,
the hand of the good and upright man,
who is your brother, for whom you lived
and in whose heart you remain alive,
that miserable hand, but so beautiful,
that picks from the American earth
that corner you planted, love and generosity,

the road you opened, star and earth,
which for all of us is like a sun
— a sun humid from blood and dew.

Translated by Richard Bartlett

FERREIRA GULLAR   1975

Extract from **In the swift night**

In the Yuro ravine
it was 13:30 hours
          (in São Paulo
it was later; in Paris night was falling;
in Asia sleep was silken)
          In the ravine
of the Yuro river
the clarity of the hour
displayed its dark depths:
the clear waters washed
without past and without future.
A cracking in the forest, call
of a bird, breeze
in the leaves
          was the noisy silence
the landscape
(which moved)
that immovable, moved
within itself
          (much like a washing machine
washing
          beneath the Bolivian sky, the landscape
with its sheaves and currents
          of air)
          In the Yuro ravine
          it was no particular hour
          just rocks plants and waters

It was no particular hour
        until a shot
exploded into birds
and animals
        until steps
voices in water face in leaves
chest heaving
        the chlorophyll
        penetrates human blood
                and history
it moves
    the landscape
    like a tram
                beginning to travel
In the Yuro ravine it was 13:30 hours

Ernesto Che Guevara
your end is near
it is not enough to be certain
to win the battle

Ernesto Che Guevara
throwing you in prison
it is not enough to be sure
to not kill you with a bullet

Ernesto Che Guevara
don't be deluded
the bullet enters your body
as in any other bandit
Ernesto Che Guevara
why do you still struggle?
the battle will be over
before the day is done

Ernesto Che Guevara
your time has come
and the people ignore
that you fought for them

The waters of the Yuro flow, the firefight now
is more intense, the enemy advances
and closes the circle.
     The guerrillas
divided into small groups
     keep up
the fight, protecting the rear
for wounded comrades.
     On high,
great masses of clouds shift slowly
traversing countries
in the direction of the Pacific, its blue head of hair.
A strike in Santiago. Rain,
in Jamaica. In Buenos Aires there is sun
on the tree-lined streets, a general plans a coup.
A family celebrates a silver wedding anniversary in a train
                       which approaches
Montevideo. Alongside the road
a cow from Swift moos. The Stock Exchange
in Rio closes higher
     or lower.
Inti Peredo, Benigno, Urbano, Eustáquio, Ñato
bemoan the advance
of the rangers.
     Urbano falls,
     Eustáquio,
     Che Guevara sustains
fire, a burst hits, hits again, disintegrates
     a knee, in the melee
     his comrades return
     to fetch him. It's too late. They flee.
The swift night closes over the remains of the dead.

The night is much swifter in the tropics
(with its on the edge of the leaves in rubbish
explosions) of dirty waters
 dulled
 in the swamps
 it is much faster under the skin of darkness, in the
  conspiracy of blues
  and reds pulsating
  like vaginas fruits mouths
  vegetables
  (confused in dreams)
 or
 a blossoming branch in lightning
 halted over a pool of water
  in the dark
It is much deeper
the night of dreams
of a man in the flesh
of coca
of hunger
and within the jug an old
tin mug of peas
of the Armour Company

Suddenly we come to the world
and we call Ernesto
Suddenly we come to the world
and we are
in Latin America

But where is life
we ask
 In the pubs?
in the eternal
tardy afternoons?

in the shantytowns
where history stinks of shit?
in the cinema?
in the female cavern of dreams
and of urine?
or in the ungrateful
tedium of a poem?
(the life
that seeped away
in the Prata estuary)

Will I be a singer
will I be a poet?
The copper answers (of Anaconda Copper):
You will be an assailant
and police
spy assassin snitch

Will I be a paedophile and murderer?
will I be an addict?
The steel answers (of Bethlehem Steel):
You will be a minister of state
and commit suicide
Will I be a dentist?
perhaps who knows ophthalmologist?
otorhinolaryngologist?
The bauxite answers (of Kaiser Aluminium):
you will be an abortion doctor
to earn more money

Will I be a shit
I want to be a shit
I want in fact to live.
But where is this filthy
life — really filthy?
In the hospice?
in a holy

office?
        in the orifice
of an arse?
Ought I to change the world,
the Republic? Does life
have to be displayed like a banner
in a public square?

Life changes like the colour of fruit
        slowly
        and forever
Life changes like a blossoming flower
        swiftly
Life changes like water in sheets
        dream in electric light
        rose unfolds in ashes
        the bird, of the mouth
        but
        when it is time
And it is time all the time
        but
a century is not enough to create a petal
        that only takes a minute
        or not
        but
        life changes
        life changes death into multitude.

Translated by Richard Bartlett

CANADA

Martha Chaves   2006

Ernesto Guevara Chez Everywhere

You run into Ché's face everywhere
this summer
Ché's face repeating

like a photocopy of a broken record

with a fixation of déja vu

On t-shirts

tank-tops

panties

coffee mugs

key-chains

can openers

bongs

even

wallets

Items of every colour

size

and shape

sometimes phosphorescent

and divided by four

Like Andy Wharhol's portrait
of Marylin Monroe

El Ché assaults you everywhere

At exclusive boutiques and
even at Goodwill

You can't escape Ché's face

ticket priced and whored

At a très chic pet store
in Westmount, Quebec

I saw a woolen sweater

      for a dog
a mere $100.00
        no more

bearing the bearded mug

of Ernesto Guevara A.K.A. El Ché

Comandante Guerrillero Revolucionario Extraordinaire

If he could see

how much

A poodle's sweater costs

spinning

in the dirt

he has probably got
to the land
of   Mao

For maybe only two

out of ten people know

the man behind the face

and his legacy
for the human race
              some say
"I wear it because he is handsome"

Had Ché been homely looking
Like Sandino

Or butt ugly
like   Levesque
he would not be bought
and sold

by people who don't know 'bout him

I asked some young guy
"but, tell me, can you identify
this portrait, this man known as el
Ché?"

He said:

"The lead singer of 'Rage
against the
machine'?

Elvis when he was thin?"

You run into Ché's face everyway
this summer

Editors' note: Levesque is probably a reference to René Lévesque, the founder of the Parti Québécois.

AL PURDY   '   1968

Hombre

— Met briefly in Havana
among the million Cubans waiting
Fidel's speech on May Day 1964
under a million merciless suns
He came around and shook hands
with the foreign visitors
a guy who looked like a service station attendant
in his olive drab fatigues and beret
but with the beard and black cigar
the resemblance ended
— the Argentine doctor and freedom fighter
Che Guevara
And I remember thinking the North Vietnamese ladies
looked especially flower-like beside him
I remember his grip particularly
firm but perfunctory
half politician and half revolutionary
for he had many hands to shake that day

Later he disappeared from Cuba
and there were rumours of quarrels
between himself and Castro
and US newspapers asked nervously
"Where is Che Guevara?"
Then Havana Radio reported Guevara
had joined guerrillas in "a South American country"
but the US expressed some small doubt
about the reliability of Havana Radio
while I thought of him — shaking hands

Back home in Canada I remembered Guevara
along with structural details of Cuban girls
the Grand Hotel at Camaguey with roosters
yammering into my early morning sleep

an all-night walk in Havana streets with a friend
a mad jeep-ride over the Sierra Maestras
where sea-raiders attacked a coastal sugar mill
and Playa Giron which is the "Bay of Pigs"
where the dead men have stopped caring
and alligators hiss in the late afternoon
Again May Day in Havana 1964
with a red blaze of flowers and banners
and Castro talking solemnly to his nation
a million people holding hands and singing
strange to think of this in Canada
And I remember Che Guevara
a man who made dreams something
he could hold in his hands both hands
saying "Hiya" or whatever they say in Spanish
to the flower-like Vietnamese ladies
cigar tilted into his own trademark
of the day when rebels swarmed out
of Oriente Province down from the mountains

"Where is Che Guevara?" is answered:
deep in Bolivian jungles leading his guerrillas
from cave to cave with scarlet cockatoos screaming
the Internationale around his shoulders
smoking a black cigar and wearing a beret
(like a student in Paris on a Guggenheim)
his men crawling under hundred-foot trees
where giant snakes mate in masses of roots
and men with infected wounds moan for water
while Guevara leads his men into an ambush
and out again just like in the movies
but the good guy loses and the bad guys always win
and the band plays the Star-Spangled Banner
Well it is over
Guevara is dead now and whether the world
is any closer to freedom because
of Che's enormous dream is not to be known

the bearded Argentine doctor who translated
that dream to a handshake among Bolivian peasants
and gave himself away free to those who wanted him
his total self and didn't keep any
I remember the news reports from Bolivia
how he was wounded   captured   executed   cremated
but first they cut off his fingers
for fingerprint identification later
in case questions should be asked
and I remember his quick hard handshake
in Havana among the tiny Vietnamese ladies
and seem to hold ghostlike in my own hand
five bloody fingers
of Che Guevara

JOE ROSENBLATT   1968

The Bee Hive

I don't believe in ghosts
yet surgeons transplant a living heart
into the chest cavity of a dead man
a fisty pulping orange
... a new ticker!

But for a bullet hole in the heart
there is no second valentine for a Marxist.
The worms have murdered the tiger. Che is dead.
And in time, we too shall face the bee keeper
for they who move with tender feet
through the saw-mills of the hive
they shall hear a hymn of Carpenter bees
whose furnace song is dum-dum's liturgy.

In secret ground they've buried Che's dust
trembling like monks who hide religious radium
from the lead eyes of the poor.

CHILE

Víctor Jara   1967

Apparition

He finds paths among the mountains
leaves his footprint on the wind,
the eagle gives him flight
and the silence shelters him.

He never complains of cold,
never complains of fatigue,
the poor hear his passing
and blindly follow him.

Fly, fly, hide,
here, there, everywhere,
fly , because they will kill you,
fly, fly, hide.

The vultures with golden claws
have put their price upon his head.
The fury of the powerful
has crucified him.

Son of the revolution
followed by twenty and twenty,
because his life is dedicated
they want to murder him.

Translated by Joan Jara

PABLO NERUDA   1969

Sadness at the Death of a Hero

Those of us who lived this history,
this death and resurrection
of our grief-stricken hope,
those of us who chose combat
and watched the flags growing,
knew that those who said the least
were our only heroes
and that after the victories
came the vociferous
their mouths stuffed with boasting
and salivating exploits.

The people shook their heads:
and the hero returned to his silence.
But silence mourned
until it choked us with grief
when dying in the mountains
was the illustrious fire of Guevara.

The comandante ended up
murdered in a gully.

No-one breathed a word.
No-one cried in the Indian villages.
No-one climbed the belfries.
No-one raised their rifle,
and those whom the murdered comandante
came to save
cashed the reward.

On these events, the contrite reflect,
what happened here?

And the truth is not told

but this misfortune of metal
is covered up with paper.
The route was just being opened up
and when the defeat arrived
it was like an axe that fell
into the cistern of silence.

Bolivia went back to its rancour,
to its rusted gorillas,
to its intransigent misery,
and like terrified sorcerers
the sergeants of this shame,
the petty generals of this crime,
hid with efficiency
the warrior's corpse
as if the body would burn them.

The bitter jungle swallowed
the movements, the paths,
and wherever trod the feet
of the exterminated militia
today the lianas whispered
a green voice of roots
and the wild stag returned
to the greenery with no explosions.

Translated by Georgina Jiménez

FLORIDOR PÉREZ   1968

The hands

And now with what can I greet you, friends.
With which hands caress the children
and toast with my glass of wine.
With what the hell shall I write my poem
now that they've mutilated the warrior.

He was the Antilles-Mapuche
 "CHE of the Mapu: the man of the earth"
But it's not for me to tell you who he was,
and this is not a poem.
                         This is nothing
more than a cry of pain or rage
— it's not that I'll grieve for him — nor does
it mean that an immortal
will miss this life
But how could it be possible?! The scoundrels
gave the order to cut off both his hands *
and so what I bring him is no poem:

— Here are the hands of Galvarino,
Comandante.

* Alonso de Ercilla, in *La Araucana* (1569), referring to the ordeal of
the *toqui* Galvarino.

Translated by Gavin O'Toole

Translator's note: Galvarino is celebrated as one of the most valiant Mapuche warriors
for his defiance towards the conquering Spanish in 1557 when, as an exemplary punish-
ment, they cut off his hands. *La Araucana* was the first epic poem about America. *Toqui*
was the title conferred by the Mapuche on those chosen as leader during times of war. In
the Mapuche language, Mapudungun, the word "che" means "people".

JAIME VALDIVIESO   1977

Spectre of the Warrior

I plead for breathing most pure
most faltering and deep
to talk of a warrior;
I beg to speak of water of air
of his everyday presence
like the air and like the water.

I would not like to invoke the hero
pasted on the walls
nor the warrior
halted at a distance
dead, the warrior.

I would like to talk about the child
like every other child,
about the youth with brown hair
flopping over his forehead
sitting two benches to
the left companion of
all youths.

Of the man who left the city
forgot his diploma
and went out on foot and on a motorcycle
(and then on a raft)
by the paths
of maize and malanga
looking for the man
in the lesions of leprosy.

You were born Ernesto Guevara de la Serna
last link with the wolf
first with the true man
that you yourself embodied
tearing your skin

116

against thorns and mud and with
just daily bread and water.

Child of an urban cradle
you were secretly preparing yourself, without knowing,
in Alta Gracia and Buenos Aires,
before the chess board
in the attics and on the roof tiles
or holding your breath
on football pitches
and in lonely barrios.

But somewhere,
there was a red star
pointing towards the jungle
towards the heights
of Cuzco and Machu Picchu
where air suffocates,
or to the depths of the earth
where pounds still
the heart of the Maya.

And in that way you left arriving
little by little
at the exact crossroads:
first in Guayaquil
and then in Guatemala
(where you lost your pawns
to the banana kings),
until you were led to the gunpowder and steel,
the same way we could arrive
you and me, without Marx or Lenin,
just by following the incline
of the lashings and hunger,
or observing how gold rises
out from blood
to its most merciless shine.

You sniffed history
before history,
before you were born, Che Guevara,
field doctor
hybrid of herb and cane.

Then you became the anecdote
the frustrated adventure, the "poor fool"
and finally the myth
crossing the island and carrying on forward.

Later you would be the terror
or the hope of every hour
in a thousand faces sitting on a bus
next to a wall at the exit of a cinema,
and in the shadows of the water
of all the jungles.

The little soldier didn't know
that with the first *coup de grâce*
he would awaken
from their final dream
all the beasts
of the city and the jungle:
from that very moment
a new ghost
of flesh and bones
would pitch its tent
right inside the mind
of all men.

You are now obliged to live
without closing your eyes
life will be your destiny.
Master of all
times and places
you won't need to dye your hair
to lose yourself:

you'll be born every day
and every hundred years
with any name
with any kind of hair.

Friar Bartholomew you were called
when you were pacing the lands
with your sandals,
Then Tupac Amaru among the flames
and Martí and Sandino behind bars
and now and tomorrow brother and comrade,
you said so yourself, of every youth
"who shudders at an injustice".

Every time the blood freezes
and someone takes a deeper breath
you will be amongst us;
every time someone
clenches a fist and looks to a star
you will be amongst us;
every time someone
sits before his own death
and stares at it face to face
until it vanishes,
and then sits before his own life
face to face
and leaves in search of other lives
you will be amongst us.

Translated by Georgina Jiménez

Translator's note: Malanga or yautia, also know as tannia, tannier and cocoyam, is a root vegetable resembling a yam similar to the related taro or dasheen, and is among the oldest root crops in the world. The title of this poem, Spectre of the Warrior (*El fantasma del guerrillero*), recalls the phrase of Marx in the Communist Manifesto: "a spectre is haunting Europe".

CHINA

Jiang Fei   2006

Che Guevara

in 1960, this cane-cutting peasant from the Americas
made a three-day visit to China
bringing his asthma and his wheezing
with his full beard and an empty satchel slung over one shoulder,
this bloke spoke threateningly in the middle of drought:
We must always stand with the People
when there was nothing left to eat, he ate the bullets
they shot at him

Translated by Simon Patton

Translator's note: In the 1960, China was undergoing terrible famine as a direct result of Mao Zedong's "Great Leap Forward" (1958-1962). In Chinese, the verb "to eat" [chi] can also mean "to suffer, incur". For this reason, it is quite normal to talk about "eating bullets" with the meaning of "being shot". Jiang Fei plays on the two meanings of the word in this poem.

Jun'er   2007

Yi Sha and Che Guevara

that year, in August
Yi Sha visited the city of Tianjin
there was a handsome foreigner on his T-shirt
and a red star on his cap
I asked Yi Sha who it was
he told me it was
Che Guevara

Che Guevara
Che Guevara

Yi Sha and Che Guevara went shopping at the foreign
goods market

Yi Sha and Che Guevara gave a talk on TV
Yi Sha and Che Guevara attended book signings
Yi Sha and Che Guevara went back to the ancient

> capital of Changi'an

via Beijing

Translated by Simon Patton

YI SHA   2004

Urban Landscape

with a cigar in his mouth
and the look of a cheerful talker
Che Guevara turns up in the city centre
on an enormous billboard
our business leaders have learnt a thing or two
they've started to leave behind piddly gimmicks
like "I love being a woman"
they know that using the images of idealism
to pick the pockets of idealists
is a more sophisticated more fashionable more high-class trick
I happened to pass beneath the billboard with my son
he asked me: Is that the Big Boss?
I thought for a moment
then said:
Yes, that's the Big Boss,
but he's got no money

Translated by Simon Patton

ZHANG GUANGTIAN   2000

Che Guevara

Who lit the dawn's reddish glow on the horizon?
A millennium of dark nights shall today be no more.
Perhaps the light will arrive early;
We can hear you calling out to us — Che Guevara.

Who pointed out to me the sky's shining star?
Heart and soul conquered the excess of vanity.
When at the crossroads searching for our home,
We spot the outline of your figure — Che Guevara.

Who led me to set forth once again?
Belief in justice shall once again be emboldened.
The road ahead needs new footsteps,
Rank and file we follow you — Che Guevara.

Who stands up never to be overthrown?
Blossoms fill the land behind you.
Devotion to revolution turns to steel,
We are as determined as you — Che Guevara

Chorus:

Red flags wave forth from my firm devotion;
Receiving your gun, I rush toward the battlefield.
Singing my song summons strength;
By walking along your path we find a new direction.

Translated by Jonathan Noble

Translator's note: "Footsteps" may be a reference to the famous last line of Lu Xun's short story, "My Hometown" (1921): "The road did not exist at first, but as more people used it, it became the road." Zhang Guangtian, director of Che Guevara, attaches important significance to this line in the play *Mr Lu Xun*, which he wrote and directed the following year in 2001.

COLOMBIA

Nelson Osorio Marín   c.1969

The giant

They told us that in the north
lives a happy giant
who shares out among the kids
pats on the back and lollipops.

But one day a man came
with a star on his forehead
and with chunks of mountain
coursing through his blood.

The man looks at us and says:
Somewhere in Bolivia
I left my body and my pipe
but I didn't forget life.

Nor did I forget that you
were told of a giant
without being told that at night
it devours children and men.

The giant invents bombs
and makes us spit blood,
so a way has to be found,
to kill it with one blow.

The man went slowly
growing in his immense shadow
and pointing towards a tree
where there was a pair of boots.

Translated by Gavin O'Toole

COSTA RICA

Ernesto Con   1996

Ode to Ernesto "Che" Guevara

> *"Once again I feel beneath my heels the ribs of Rocinante..."*
> — *Farewell letter from Ché to his parents*

Noble was his spirit,
to Bolivia he went to die;
Ernesto was his name,
the world called him "*Che*".

Valiant and rash
with Rocinante he set out;
for his appointment with the death
he did forever flout.

He hurried up his moves
towards his inevitable fate,
to the rhythm of the hooves
of his faithful Rocinante.

Shield in one hand,
in the other a flower;
of Neruda, the verses
sang the troubadour.

There death awaited
wielding its infamous scythe;
he was laughing at his fate,
silent fell his noble cry.

And under sombre nightfall,
on a cliff beneath the sun:
an eternal champion fell
with his shield and flower.

Translated by Georgina Jiménez

CUBA

Gerardo Alfonso   1996

Still it is the dreams

You emerged from the Southern cone
but were coming from long before then,
with love for the world deep within you.
It was a star that brought you here
and made you a part of this people.
In gratitude, many men were born
who were just like you,
who did not want you to leave
and have been different since that day.

After so long and so many storms
we continue following forever
the long, long route
that you walk.
The century's end presages an old truth,
good and bad times
both form part of reality.

I knew well you were going to return
you were going to return from some place,
because the pain has not killed the utopia,
because the love is eternal
and those who love you don't forget you.
You knew well since that time
that you were going to grow you were going to stay
because clear faith cleans the wounds,
because your spirit is humble
and you are reincarnated in the poor and in their lives.

After so long and so many storms...

Still it is the dreams
that pull people through
like a magnet that joins them day by day.
It is not about windmills,
it is not about Quixote,
but something tempered in the soul of men,
a virtue that is raised above
names and honorary titles.

After so long and so many storms...

Translated by Georgina Jiménez

MIGUEL BARNET   1965

Ché

Ché, you know everything,
Each nook and cranny of the Sierra,
Asthma over the cold grass,
The speaker's rostrum,
Night tides
And even how
Fruit grows, how oxen are yoked.

I would not give you
Pen in place of pistol
But it is you who are the poet.

Translated by R. Frank Hardy

VICENTE FELIÚ   1968

A necessary song

(To Ché, not in memoriam)

Your skin linked to the bone was lost in the earth.
The tear, the poem and the memory
are carving on the fire the song of death
with golden machine-guns from wherever you are.
And here, each night your books are searched
for the just motive of all action
and your memory opens up to all who are born again
but there is always someone who raises you upon a shrine
and creates a legend of your formative image
and makes impossible the dream of reaching you
and learns some of your phrases by heart
to say "I shall be like him" without knowing you
and proclaims them without love, without the dream,
                              without love, without faith
and your words lose a sense of respect
to the man who is born covered by your splendour.
Some poet said, and this will be fairest:
From this day our duty is to defend you from being god.

> *Callejas, 1968* (the line in italics is Vicente
> Huidobro's, from the poem *Elegy to Lenin*)

Translated by Georgina Jiménez

ANTONIO GUERRERO RODRÍGUEZ 2002

Che's example

Guerrilla fighter of the cause
I champion, let me tell you:
all you taught
later served me well.

All you taught —
resolute will,
impenetrable candour,
a star well-chosen,
the value of trustworthiness,
a look of the greatest assurance
hope, valour
love and joy.

Guerrilla fighter of my dreams
cherished until fulfilled.
We continue along the path
of irreversible victory.

Based on an anonymous translation, adapted by the editors

NICOLÁS GUILLÉN   1967

Che Comandante

In spite of your fall,
your light is undiminished.
A horse of fire
celebrates your glory as a guerrilla,
between the wind and the clouds, in the Sierra.
Even though they've silenced you, you speak,
and even though they burned you
and let you rot in the earth,
and lost you in the cemetery,
in the forest,
in the swamp,
they can't stop us from finding you,
Che Comandante,
Amigo.

With her filed teeth,
North America chuckles,
squirming, at this very moment,

in her bed of dollars.
And yet, her chuckling becomes a mask,
as your noble body of steel rises
and swarms everywhere in other guerrillas, like flies,
and your universality, bruised by mere soldiers,
lights up the American night, like a sudden star,
dropped in the middle of an orgy.
You knew all about it, Guevara,
but you said nothing,
in order not to draw attention to yourself,
Che Comandante,
Amigo.

You're everywhere. In the Indian,
made of copper and dreams. In the black man,
covered in the spittle of the white backlash.
In the oil refineries, in saltpetre,
and in the terrible helplessness of the banana,
and in the magnificant animal *pampa*,
and in sugar, salt and coffee,
you, a moving frieze of your own blood,
as they cut you down, breathing,
because they couldn't love you,
Che Comandante,
Amigo.

Cuba knows you, in her heart.
Your bearded face instructs us.
Like a young Saint, your body is ivory and olive.
Your voice is firm,
without the edge of command in it,
as you command *compañera*, friend,
affectionate and responsible,
leader, comrade.
We remember you, each day, at the Ministry,
each day, in the Army,
each day, as an easy companion,
each day, as an uncompromising man,
pure, as a child and as a man,

Che Comandante,
Amigo.

And so, you pass our way in your fading battle fatigues,
lived-in and torn, you,
in the jungle, just as you were, before,
in the Sierra,
half-naked,
secure in weaponry and the word,
churning the wind
and prising the slow-opening rose.
There's no peace.
Salud, Guevara!

Or better still, from the very depths of America,
wait for us. We will leave with you.
We want to die and to live,
as you have died,
and to live,
as you live on,
Che Comandante,
Amigo.

Translated by Margaret Randall

PEDRO PÉREZ SARDUY   1965

Che

just as if you were walking in the American jungle
and swollen with powder
just as if an urgent longing for the fatherland had interrupted
six rebel tears in the open street one night
just as if your mother proud woman had touched your shoulder
your guerrilla olive fatigues and told you
again about your next unknown journey
there is in the exactness of continents a whirlwind
as with wars
just as if a deep tumour were sucking a dying blind buffer
there are detonations of heroic words which shoot

the curve of the foetus
which hits back and returns to strike again
our shoulder of battles of bulky wounds is joined
and you are gone
there is an incredible myth like a sea like a chunk
of the Sierra around you
an agitated multitude a millennium of lore
immense like the morning which is waiting for you
in some place a presentiment
and you are gone with the sober drunkenness and you are gone
to live under the roof of the world
there was never any fear in the air that you sweated
in any of the circumstances
in my narrow streets of Santa Clara or among the thick beards
in December
your presence was low-keyed as it caressed the rough edge
the warmth of smallshot
and your brown steely glance penetrated like a mischievous child
the thunderous barracks of dead heroes who were robbed
and so the crisp new days came and January crossed leaving
in a corner of the sky clots of blood
and nobody stayed behind in the morning
and least of all you who in your suicidal fever knew how to wound
the most prepared heart by your departure
nevertheless and like yesterday today we begin again
the new guerrillas
and rejoice like the flapping seabirds in the legend
of the soul
all this touches us in our most simple essence
and you are gone
just like that
just as if your mother proud woman had touched your shoulder
your guerrilla olive fatigues and told you
again about your next unknown journey
so we fix you firmly as our presage in the core of humanity

Translated by John La Rose

CARLOS PUEBLA   1965

Till forever, Comandante

We learned to love you
from the historical heights
from the sun of your bravery
that laid siege to death.

> Here remains the clear
> cherished transparency
> of your beloved presence
> Comandante Che Guevara.

Your glorious and tough hand
opens fire on history
when the whole of Santa Clara
wakes up to see you.

> Here remains the clear...

You arrive burning the breeze
with suns of springtime
to nurture the flag
with the light of your smile.

> Here remains the clear...

Your revolutionary love
draws you to a new venture
where they await the resolution
of your liberating hand.

> Here remains the clear...

We will carry on advancing
as we remain at your side
and with Fidel we say to you
Till forever, Comandante!

> Here remains the clear...

Translated by Gavin O'Toole

DENMARK

Klaus Høeck   1978

Extract from **Act III of Topia or Che Guevara**

The canvas set is meant to represent
Bolivia: green stretch of meadowland
in poster paint and glue, a river gent
ly winds across the stage's coloured band.

There is a sky as tall and splendid as
a sapphire or as ermine. Distant in
the backdrop a white farmstead. Arganaz
the farmer housed under its roof of tin.

Let's assume for now we're looking at well
any old theatre anywhere on
the earth that now and then puts on this show

for the benefit of the rights of hon
est bourgeois and the well-to-do, also
the pseudo-revolutionary cell.

The curtain by the way has meanwhile gone
up. A small group of men all dressed in kha
ki are now crossing the river there on
the blue pseudo waves of the stage which are

with the aid of projectors all agleam
like sapphires and orange blossoms that peep
in early spring. The members of the team
say nothing for they push a cardboard jeep

that's in the process of getting stuck in
the white sand (or glue that hasn't quite
dried yet). It's Che Guevara and his part

isans arriving in November in
Ñancahuazú where they then all start
pitching camp in scrub with a cave in sight.

In spite of edema and asthma the
ambush works. Coco and his men open
fire from the ravine's steep slopes. And seven
soldiers fall to the ground in their own nose

bleeds. What we are witnessing is of course
just blanks and lots of ketchup. Although this
small skirmish here in terms of theatre is
a huge success. A wave with all the force

of wild approval causes the mighty
chandelier to jingle. The Liberté's
reviewer jumps to his feet and applauds.

When two home-made grenades explode towards
the front of the orchestra pit, the blaze
of the ovations swells to a tutti.

A tiny dummy plane dives from the flies
on what looks like a reconnoitring sor
tie. Reminiscent of a swift that tries
to enter its own space. Down on the floor

the lighting man swears: 'Bloody hell, don't say
the bulb's gone in the red projector!' There
is hardly any action in the play,
with actors lying dead just everywhere.

Soldiers and mortar fire, but no neat plot
no line that can aspire to hit the spot —
a cardboard cut-out of reality.

The reviewer, dictator, or would-be,
of his banana republic of writ
ers, will be successful and be proved right.

I know it sounds banal, at least it could,
but some people are evil and some good
independently of any blood-red
meridians of social structures. Dead

ly cruelty divides them like the slash
from a machete. The one in a splash
of boiling piss drowns his foe, the other
spurs on his love's Rocinante ever

and again to fight for truth's perfection,
rides through the arch of high tragedy in
to the magic circle of this small stage.

My two assumptions: even in this age
such men exist and: that Che Gue was in
deed a man familiar with affection.

Only the slash from the machete can
be seen from time to time in sun or star
gleam as tiger-striped lightning. And what far
goal are these stage characters, every man,

in search of in their green labyrinth on
the far side of legality,
what distant and imagined enemy
beneath the mountain's dark arch. Oh, I shun

to give an answer. Let each man answer
for himself and those of like ilk. The in
tellectual priest with his Judas silver.

The Marxist lodge member with villa on
the Côte d'Azur and Jag. Let such folk dare
to fashion an answer into thin air.

Che, there are many ways of dying, and
the easiest was not the one for you
when you became a guerrilla you knew
full well that you would fall into the hands,

calloused and filthy, of some hangman but
your life under the orange-blossom snow
was so pure that much more than they could know
it upweighed their blood and dirt and profit.

Now your real life is about to begin,
one you live inside us for here, within,
our motives and dreams will be your new home,
your ideas will be our Jerusalem...

Let then that photograph of him where he
is lying on his lit de parade
a corpse with clips and surgical scissors
inserted in his skin round his collar

bone (the little hollow's psalter) let it
become imprinted on your retina's
most sensitive surface, let it serve as
an eternal recollection, let it

not get lost in the book's closely glossed
pages (which mainly deal with the prepar
ations in La Paz) in the great blue loss

of memory — forgetting Che Guevar
a and his death is like forgetting free
dom and suppression of all liberty.

Translated by John Irons

Editors' Note: Ñancahuazú was the river in Bolivia near to which Guevara set up his guerrilla camp.

ECUADOR

Jorge Enrique Adoum 1997

Che: the fleetingness of his death

thirty years already?
does this mean we continue to be useless after thirty years in a
world without him?
does this mean there is a generation able to have been born grow
and beget in a world for thirty years without him?
how does one conceive of the world without him for thirty years?
america without him?
(yes we were even telling the europeans that it must be a sad
thing not to be latin american
because he was the first example of that man of the future that
america was going to give birth to one day
he was this being made of flesh who was already a legend or vice
versa that epochal hero with whom until just recently we were
drinking coffee
he made our america feel noble feel dignified when in cuba it was
more america than ever
and we were going there proud of having been born in the same
continent in the same era as he
and of the admiration and the affection of humanity when one
spoke of any of his deeds or of his difficult virtues we had in a
certain way airs that we were a part of him ...)
or does this mean that it is us who are without che after we left
che without us
(he was being converted dangerously into an excuse for us
he was doing for us what we should have been doing ourselves
he was doing what we knew had to be done but were not doing
what we wanted to do but we did not do
what inevitably we have to do but we are not doing
and we were satisfied that he was doing it well he was doing
everything well
and we left him alone as a commander with no army
we his army were applauding his manliness from afar
admiring his fortitude being moved by his gentlemanly integrity)

perhaps for considering him so great we believed that under his
command we the insignificant were not needed
and because we believed him invulnerable we did nothing for
those impenetrable indians to crack the stone of their soul so as to
allow the future in once and for all and clear the mist away
nor did we do anything to enlighten that indian woman with a
sick daughter about who it was had long been murdering her and
who was going to save us
she took the fifty pesos from che and someone betrayed him
and we betrayed him because we were not with him in front of
him beside him behind him
when the soldiers and the wolves (wolves and wolves)
surrounded him

now it is difficult to believe that he would have died one day
but it was more difficult thirty years ago because the world could
not imagine that the small death of men would affect him
because death is such a minor thing and a lieutenant prado is an
insignificant thing and a general ovando is such an insignificant
thing
(and we were holding on to the lies of armed stupidity to the
contradictions of infamy trying to find in them the sign that he
was alive
all of a sudden turning into experts in logic as if gorillas had our
powers of reason
experts in photographic illusion analysing his beard fearing it was
him but talking about the christ of mantegna and of baroque
sculptures...)
when fidel said he had died
we lowered our heads brought together a little mountain of
memories as we do every time someone dies as if to reconstitute
him
so that he would be returned to us complete
his lungs and his belly without holes
complete bones that they said had been broken to fit into a jar
intact skin that they said had been burned so that his tomb would
not become a place of pilgrimage
but hell I said
if there is not a single bush in america in which he wasn't killed

there is not a single place that isn't his tomb as a fighter and
martyr
and we still feel miserable and a little guilty because he was alone
but again proud of that final slap in our honour that he gave to all
the colonels through the face of selniche
and filling us with more hate than any human can bear
against that barrientos a hybrid between a gorilla and a GI that
rubbed his hands
and against our own, what? cowardice dogma comfort mutilation?
and then only then did we want to have been in valle grande
to have died beside him
better still instead of him …
someone said that day that the great bearded one of the caribbean
island had been left alone
hell no I said
he is there with ten million comrades who love him and the
revolutionaries of the world who admire him
we are the ones now alone and without an excuse
the ones who always have been alone because we have wanted to
be alone viciously alone
busy with our domesticity blah-dee-blahing about the revolution
before going for a drink or sleeping
and the rest who do not even talk about revolution
and it was not about having died in his place but about gathering
together our solitudes and our trivias to replace him amidst us
now not to have been in his place but to go to his place
us, at least those of us who have not rotted…
and a long time afterwards even in the remote villages of asia and
africa we saw peasants discuss their agrarian problems around a
table on the soil beneath the flag of their country and a standard
with the image of the man with the star on his forehead
and painted on our city walls the image again of the man with the
star on his forehead
and the teenage girls who did not know him sport on their chests
over their breasts the image of the man with the star on his
forehead…

suddenly the bitch of history came
astonished we entered into something like an ideological vacation

and suddenly no-one knew anything or believed in anything any
more
and instead of loathing and hating ourselves as if crying for our
impotence
I went around asking what was done in which corner when in the
entrails of america
was lost to us the new man we had been waiting for and for
whose coming some gave their lives
what had been done since we abandoned him with his guerrilla
spectre in the jungle
what was done when neoliberalism became the "sole universal
form of government" with the unruly exception of cuba

when because they killed him they believed he had died and
announced the "end of history"
as if we all now think the same with the disobedient exception of
chiapas and cuba

but I know we know that history cannot end before the new man
that he announced returns bringing with him
something like the most beautiful utopia of america
and that is why I wait for him to be able to continue living
and to be able to continue awaiting what is coming

so che, forever unto victory?

Translated by Gavin O'Toole

Translator's note: Lieutenant Prado was Gary Prado Salmón, the Bolivian army captain
who captured Guevara. General Ovando was General Alfredo Ovando Candía, the com-
mander of the Bolivian armed forces when the campaign against Guevara was prosecut-
ed, who had wanted to decapitate the body of the guerrilla after his death, but was talked
out of doing so by the CIA. The Christ of Mantegna is a reference to "The Lamentation
over the Dead Christ" by Andrea Mantegna (c. 1490), a painting that has often been com-
pared with Freddy Alborta's photograph of the dead Che Guevara on display in the
laundry house of the Nuestro Señor de Malta hospital in Vallegrande, Bolivia, of 10
October 1967. Selniche is a reference to Lt. Col. Andrés Selich (sometimes referred to as
Selniche) who had angry exchanges with Guevara when trying to interrogate him in the
La Higuera schoolhouse where he was held after his capture. Barrientos is a reference to
René Barrientos, the anti-communist president of Bolivia who gave the order for Che to
be executed. The reference to Chiapas is to the guerrilla rebellion in Mexico by the main-
ly indigenous EZLN in 1994, after the end of the Cold War.

EGYPT

SALAMA EL TAWIL   1995

Che Guevara's Voice

The word, with my pulse,
Flows from my heart.
And my pulse draws on
The people's words.
The word, hand in hand,
Unites Love and Freedom,
Happiness and Independence,
For all.
In my heart
And the heart of the people,
I grow resolute …
Fixing my goals,
The goals of the people,
For the benefit of all.
For a new tomorrow,
The dawn of our dreams.

Translated by Sally Azzam

EL SALVADOR

Roque Dalton (as Jorge Cruz)   1974

The creed according to Ché

Ché Jesus Christ
was taken prisoner
after finishing his sermon on the mount
(to the din of machine guns)
by Bolivian and Jewish rangers
commanded by Roman-Yankee chiefs.

He was condemned by the revisionist scribes and Pharisees
Whose spokesman was Caiaphas Monje
while Pontius Barrientos was trying to wash his hands
speaking in military English
on the backs of the people chewing coca leaves
without even having the alternative of a Barabas
(Judas Iscariot was one of those who deserted the guerrilla
and showed the way to the rangers)

Later they placed on Christ Guevara
a crown of thorns and the robe of a madman
and hung from his neck a mocking sign
INRI: Instigator Naturalis of the Rebellion of the Ill-contented

Then they made him carry his cross upon his asthma
and they crucified him with bursts from an M-2
and they cut off his head and hands
and burned the rest so that the ashes
would disappear with the wind

In view of which Ché has been left no other path than
resurrection
and to remain standing on the left-hand side of men
commanding them to quicken their pace
for ever and ever
Amen.

Translated by Gavin O'Toole

FINLAND

Anselm Hollo   1967

**walking the beach with my daughter's eyes
& the news in my head**

smallest child fewest words
notices
            most
most impressive
stomping along the top of the sea wall

sun haze above the far out tide
acres of watery sand
small packs of dogs and humans
tons of kelp on the beach below
chunks of driftwood half a life saver
a plastic toy gun
block letter labeled STEPHEN
                        AGENT 009

the naked and headless
corpse of a swan

.

in a place named after Simon *Bolivar*
La Paz and CIA (*Washington*) money
paid for his death

so let us have
no epitaths beyond the true
american
lived fast died young made a beautiful corpse
no monuments no
cities or states
bearing
            his name
no speeches

muffled reports
like Policeman's Specials on Lake Erie shore
where the late Charlie Pfohl
rode with the Vultures
                            MC Club
the mortician gave him a head
it had to be paid for
                            of plaster
it was a necessity

'such flowers   all over the place'.

XII'67, Isle of Wight

PENTTI SAARIKOSKI   1969

On a hot sunny day

On a hot sunny day
I sit in the yard swing
reading Che Guevara's memoirs.
The wife knits
the child plays
the dog sleeps.
A man of such a pure heart!
The child walks down to the shore to look at fish.
I read the weather report
and check how much booze is left
in order to know how I'll think tomorrow
about things, and how I'll express that.
I try to hide behind all manner of posters
and platitudes
and quotations
so that no one will question my duplicity.
The wife picks up the coffee things
and all of us go inside,
in Indian marching file
wife and child and I and Che.

Translated by Anselm Hollo

FRANCE

ANDRÉ BENEDETTO   1968

The Stranger Left on the Terraces of Baalbeck

1. Serious question posed by a yankee professor
at the international symposium of Padua in 2028:

> "Did Guevara have the single x
> and the double y
> of criminals?"

2. Jesus! Mary! Joseph!, said the Bolivian lady making the sign
of the cross, how he resembles Christ! In that
small village slaughtered like a dog

3. I see that there would be:
> "the God with 5 heads
> the Star with 5 heads
> of the Rebellion"

in front of whom will
the flying saucers kneel
    and Us of Mount Ventoux
will return to another universe.

Translated by Isabel O'Toole

Translator's note: The city of Baalbeck in Lebanon is a world heritage site noteworthy for its colossal structures, boasting both the ruins of the largest Roman temples in the world but also the world's largest cut stone, which has fuelled speculation that alien civilisations were instrumental in its construction. Mount Ventoux in Provence is one of the most famous mountains in France and gained fame as the site of Petrarch's 1336 ascent. It is also said that it has been the scene of a number of UFO sightings.

FRANCIS COMBES   2003

Elegy for El Che

1

El Che has reappeared in my home
as he did in the heart of Mexico
in Chile and in Nicaragua.
His picture stands on my desk
between the globe
and the old typewriter
made in the USA.
El Che has settled in my place
with that gaze of a rebellious kid
sparkling fire
and his adolescent's beard
And he is smiling
despite the fever and the asthma
and history's contradictions.
El Che laughs heartily
happy and pure as the morning
When the water in the *mate* starts boiling
In the guerrillas' camp
encircled by mist
a fighting Christ of implacable softness
Southern Star
an utterly terrestrial Angel
with a merciless love
He smokes a cigar
and the ashes which fall on his tropical beard
despite the rain and the passing years
set fire to the hills.

2

Set against the faded blue sky of the map
                    South America
has the body of a tortured hanged man
and out of the open wounds left by the executioners

fall children of light.
Che is a child of light fallen on this earth.
And — after having walked
             the paths of human suffering
             on the back of this crippled continent —
the runaway child
picked up his doctor's case
and gathered his weapons.

3
In the Sierra Maestra
in times of revolutionary war
(This is an extract of the golden Legend of the Saints
sometimes bleeding from the Revolution)
harassed, the guerrillas cross the hills with a forced
        step
Che
            whose asthma prevents him going forth
                         says to Fidel:
"Leave me, I will hold you up"
but Fidel refuses to hear him.

4
"Beauty is not offended,"
you used to say,
"by Revolution."

5
Che,
comrade minister,
you are driving a tractor and you're playing
your hand is holding a machete
like the fighters of the *zafra*
the warriors of production
but even Cuba's soil
although light

sticks to your feet
and the sky is heavy.
"Socialist economy"
you say —
"without communist ethics
is of no interest to me."
Once the road is barely open
you have to set off again.

6
Che
you will not have known
the shame of growing old
of growing larger around the waist
of growing accustomed
to small honours
and great miseries.
You will not have known
the ashen and dusty taste
of resignation.

7
Betrayed by those
for whom you were fighting
you become lost
in the cold and the greenery
on the paths of an austere country
but the erring ways
military disaster
isolation and defeat
in the earthy night
and in the dark heart of peoples
as if by magic
have been transformed
into a source of light.

8
Che
you have reappeared in my home
and in supermarket aisles
on shop's shelves
on CD boxes
printed on T-Shirts
or on the chrome of zippos
a new icon to sell and to buy
fantastic product winner
in the great beauty contest
of martyrs and rebels.
Capitalism nourishes itself
from all rebellions
and feeds
itself
on what sets out to destroy it.
Che
you are the incurable dream
of a world without dreams
and without revolution
a dream that wakes one up in the middle of one's sleep.

9
Comandante Che
tonight
       in front of my typewriter
       a cigar in my mouth
       surrounded by house plants
I wonder who once said:
"Revolution is a bicycle;
if you stop
       pedalling
            you fall."

Translated by Alexandra Stanton

JEAN FERRAT 1967

The guerrillas

With their black beards,
their old-fashioned rifles,
their uniforms faded
as a cloth of hope,
they have made a decision
to live for tomorrow,
they have made a decision
weapons in hands.

The guerrillas, the guerrillas.

If there were only few
who followed their path,
they know that tomorrow,
they will be thousands.
There will be a time
that the world is a sierra,
that a whole continent
rhymes with Guevara.

The guerrillas, the guerrillas.

What they have in their hearts
is simply expressed:
their words full of sweetness
their words red with blood.
A hundred million mestizos
know that in that corner
is found justice
as well as dignity.

The guerrillas, the guerrillas.

The small smooth words

that give courage to an army
and all your police
will not change anything.
My brothers who know
that the most beautiful flowers
push through the dung,
see how the hour chimes.

The guerrillas, the guerrillas.

Translated by Georgina Jiménez

COLETTE MAGNY   1968

When the braziers are lit

We are seventeen under one very small moon.
The march has been dangerous.
Ernesto Che Guevara.
When the braziers are lit
one should but see the light.
Ernesto Che Guevara!

Thirty days passed between the wind
and the clouds of the Sierra.
Behind us the sea, the plains,
the paddy fields in front.
The thorns, the dust, the stings
and the wind.
Our skin is but a cloth of misery.
Put the field to the torch!

When the braziers are lit...

It has been eleven years already, from the port of Tuxpán
all fires extinguished
left the Granma,

the effigy to the eternal
or the perfume of the Cuban petal.

When the braziers are lit...

From other lands in the world
hail my modest forces.
I leave Cuba the purest part
of my hopes as builder
and this that they most loved
among the beings whom I love.
The honours they bestowed upon me.

When the braziers are lit...

Beat the yankees hard,
brother of Guatemala, of Colombia,
of Venezuela.
Beat the yankees hard,
brother of Bolivia and of Brazil.
Beat the yankees hard!

When the braziers are lit...

It matters little the place where death surprises us:
she'll be welcome that is
providing our call is understood,
that other hands are tendered to grasp our weapons.

¡Hasta la victoria, siempre!

Translated by Georgina Jiménez

MARTINIQUE

AUGUSTE MACOUBA   1970

Hope is Speaking

Today, hope is speaking.
The night's silence beats with both hands
its tambourines
Outside, in the blackness, not a single star is looking down
from the darkened celestial vault
and no nocturnal figure
looms on the footpath.
Not the slightest breeze on the
fainted flowers
of the tall palm trees.
Nor a flight from the firefly with its emerald glow
the frogs have stopped their daily
refrain
Tonight
silence is King, standing tall as a lion
In the city
in the valley
in the hills
as the only woken whisper… Guerrilla ay Guerrilla!
The boom of
the carved tom-tom
resounds a rebellious cry
on a tamed donkey's skin!
The last of man's songs
today, hope is speaking.
All of you oppressed breathless
kneeling and humiliated world
brothers in hunger offended without strength
I declare that never again shall we see incomplete niggers,
rawboned hindus
no yellow would ever be a peril

man shall never see napalm again
for Vietnam and for China.
There shall never be any more dogs in Alabama
or in Salisbury or Johannesburg
no Bay of Pigs
no marines in Santo Domingo or elsewhere.
I declare that there shall no longer be any dust
which will not fully exist.
Oppressed comrades
under the tyranny of the falcons in power
our hands together with other hands beyond the seas
will triumph in a brotherly crowning piece.
Today, Hope is speaking.

Translated by Alexandra Stanton

GERMANY

VOLKER BRAUN   1990

After the Massacre of Illusions

Guevara under the runway with his hands
Hacked off, he doesn't "work i' the earth" any more so now
The ideas are buried
Out come the bones
State funeral FOR FEAR OF RESURRECTION
O Sacred Head Sore Wounded Marketing
FOLLOW YOUR FINE PHRASES
TO THE POINT OF THEIR INCARNATION
Valery Chodemchuk, covered up
In the sarcophagus of the reactor, can wait
How long will the earth endure us
And what shall we call freedom

Volker Braun's note: 'FOLLOW YOUR FINE PHRASES' is said by Deputy Mercier to his fellow prisoners in Act III of Büchner's Dantons Tod. Danton replies: 'Nowadays they do everything in human flesh . . . They will use my body too.'

Translated by David Constantine

Hans Magnus Enzensberger   1975

E.G. de la S. (1928-1967)

For a while thousands wore his little beret on their heads,
and thousands and thousands more carried big pictures
of his picture and hollered his name out very loud.
Those processions downtown now seem
as unreal as the country and class he was born in.

Far from the slaughterhouses and barracks and brothels,
his father's villa crumbled on the river. The money evaporated,
but the swimming pool was maintained. A shy child,
allergic, often close to choking to death. Battled with his body,
smoked cigars, became (whatever that means) a man.

Jules Verne lay under his pillow. His first attack,
his first flight into reality: *Tristes Tropiques*.
But the lepers under the rotting veranda on the Amazon
didn't understand what he said, and kept dying. Only then
did he find the foe to whom he stayed loyal all his life,

and the foe of the foe. Just a few victories later,
the New Man appeared to him, an old idea, very new.
But economy didn't listen to his speeches. There was no spaghetti.
Nor any toothpaste, and what is toothpaste made from?
The banknotes he signed were worthless.

The sugar stuck to shirts. Machines, paid for with hard currency,
decayed on quais. La Rampa rumbled with rumors.
Bowing and scraping in Moscow, new credits. The people lined up,
were unreliable, cracked hungry jokes. Agents everywhere,
intrigues he never understood. A foreigner forever.

Tried to moralize to the Russians. The lover of humanity
yelled for the *hatred which shall transform humanity into
a violent, effective, cold killing-machine.* Actually
a mimosa: his favorite pastime, reading poems. (He knew

Baudelaire inside out.) A tender failure, food for secret services.

So he fled to the weapons, remaining there, where all was clear
and lucid: foe foe and treason treason, in the jungle.
But he himself seemed extinguished. *Round, beardless,*
                                        graying temples,
thick glasses, like a salesman, a duffle coat, in this
fancy dress in Ñancahuazú he went about his final work.

Spoke no Quechua, no Guaraní. *The silence of the Indians*
was absolute, as though we came from another world. Insects,
lianas, underbrush. *The peasants like rocks.* Colics,
coughing fits, edemas. Overdoses of cortisone. Adrenalin.
Gasping till the last injection: *Ave Maria purisima!*

The legend was spreading like foam. We're already
supermen, invincible. (Always that deadly irony,
unnoticed by his comrades.) *A human wreck,* an idol.
We would have hired him, the most progressive
of his enemies advertised. Instead they displayed his corpse

with hands cut off. *A mystical adventure,* and
a passion irresistibly reminiscent of the image of Christ:
that's what his followers wrote. He: *Les honneurs, ça m'emmerde.*
It's not that long ago, and forgotten. Only the historians
settle in like the moths in the cloth of his uniform.

Holes in the popular war. Otherwise, in Metropolis, only
a boutique that stole his name speaks of him.
On Kensington High Street, the incense sticks are glowing;
next to the cash register, the last hippies sit sullen,
unreal, like fossils, and unquestioning, and almost immortal.

The text breaks off, and calmly the answers keep ganging up.

Translated by Joachim Neugroschel

PETER SCHÜTT   1969

Saluting Che Guevara

Only giving arms to the revolution
to disarm the counter-revolution, long since violent;
only taking up class struggle
to put down class rule;
only starting civil war
to put an end to wars

will spare you the disgrace
of having left this disgraceful world unchanged.

His thoughts are hatred
for the oppressors; anger
at the exploiters; the rage of all the people
at what the despots do.
His acts: the oppressed revolting;
the exploited rising up;
prisoners fighting to be free.
What he means: the beginning of the end
of oppression, exploitation, slavery.

Translated by Mererid Puw Davies

PETER WEISS   1968

He died just when we needed him

He died just when we needed him
More than ever before.
Why did he die?
Was he sick? Had he lost faith?
Was it perhaps a sacrifice?
But if he was sick, why didn't we help him?
He was like a Christ taken down from the Cross …
I loathe the heroics of pain
I loathe the mystique of resurrection
We abandoned him
When we ought to have helped him with all our might.
The very earth which drank his blood was not his earth;
Only the land where you live is yours.
And now we're turning him into a martyr
To ease our own consciences.
Or am I making a mistake?
Was he perhaps strong and active and full of faith?
Was he perhaps the only one who *dared*?
Did his death teach us our cowardice?
Learn
Learn
Learn
The struggle continues.

Anonymous translation, from Alexandre (1968)

GREECE

Manos Loïzos   1972

Che

I came across a photograph of yours
A photograph of yours from another country
One of those that the students are holding
One of those that an informant would tear apart
One of those that the students are hanging against their hearts

Che Guevara, Che Guevara
Cheeeeee, Che Guevara

Shut the window
Seal the doors
I tremble over the man in the boots
What is he looking for as he is walking in the shadows?
What is he looking for as he is asking about you?
What is he looking for as he stares at our house every night?

Che Guevara, Che Guevara
Cheeeeee, Che Guevara

How many roses were burnt by the snow
Oh, this spring makes me bleed

Translated by Georgia Loukina

GUATEMALA

OTTO-RAÚL GONZÁLEZ   1968

Extracts from **Concert for Machine-gun:
Cantigas for Ché Guevara**

I

And how can I tell Haydée, my wife, that it is true?
with which words shall I start to tell her what she must know?
how can I tell her everything without making her or everyone
                                                    else suffer?
naturally she must know and I have to be the one to tell her
but...how can I make the news less bitter?
while I walk home I am we are thinking I go we go crying
I look we look with anger at the colour of the houses
I can't we can't hear the dogs that helplessly bark their longing
I dry we dry the tears the streets
and when I get home simply I say we say
it's true Haydée it's true *they killed him*
and Haydée my wife understands and that night we love each
                                                    other more than ever

IV

Did you know him dad asks everyone
and I answer we answer yes that we knew you
that I heard that we heard your voice
that I felt that we felt your gaze
that I shook that we shook your hand
and that voice gaze and hand were of this and other worlds
and then all turned into chimes clapping shrieks joy
and we listen to violent carols and sacred music
in which thunder lightning and shooting echo
I transfigure we transfigure I have we have
silk on our touch
light in the eye
bread in the mouth

honey in the ear
flowers in the air
and I feel we feel that I am we are before the gleam of your gaze

VIII
I write to my mother we write
dear mother here is your usual cheque
it is our wish that you are in the best of health
I want to tell you we want to tell that we are very happy
because I am we are between us all writing a great poem
a tiny poem for him that since october
(the most beautiful month of the year because it is the month
of revolutions)
he turned into immortal symbol tiger sword symbol crystal
and steel
p.s. he is mother comandante Ernesto (che) Guevara Okay

XI
The voracious bourgeoisie
the greedy bourgeoisie
the toesucking bourgeoisie
the plain bourgeoisie of gold chain and watch
the sweet clover bourgeoisie
the municipal and stupid bourgeoisie
the bourgeoisie of dazzling ring
of sweaty dazzling ring
the constipated and stubborn bourgeoisie
the bourgeoisie that still has pride in
defecating in a potty
the cretinous idle lying bourgeoisie
fool lacking judgement and mediocre
silly simple insensitive imbecilic
dumb sly uncouth dunce
greenback counter
pronounces your name comandante
and makes the sign of the cross

XII
I am we are washing my our hands
and suddenly a cockroach starts creeping on the wall
what shall I do? what shall we do? shall I kill it? shall we kill it?
I think we think about what you would do comandante
in this case before this situation so insignificant and delicate
before this grave but absurd and non-transcendental problem
must I must we kill the dirty insect
that keeps ascending the wall?
your answer reaches me reaches us like a hot gust from gunfire
and the cockroach the enemy the loyal symbol of filth and
                                                    backwardness
is dispatched from this world by a slap
and slowly it agonises at the bottom of the sewer
no more hesitation!

XVII
Sad endless uniform like the sticky rain
of the Andes
is this vast sorrow that besieges me and this clumsy sensation of
being useless
since it grows (grew) the tree the great solitary tree
of your death
like dry leaves that November twirls and gathers at the bottom
of parks
my sadness is gathering in the dark and blind outline
of these days
and I don't lack the will to go and search amongst the earthy roots
of the fog
or between the agile acid eagles that sharpen their claws on
tempests
a shaft of light to be able to ignite the great bonfire
of dry leaves
and to see rising your warrior figure enveloped by flames
comandante
and solar prophet saint layman with body of incinerated sun
and to follow
until the end the tracks left by your clean innermost generous
                                                    and universal
outbursts

XXV
the children ask me ask us what for why he fought
the warrior there in the turbulent mountains there in the bleak
and frozen highlands
he fought I say we say for human dignity
he fought breaking his arms so that in the world there would not be
exploiters nor exploited nor poverty nor ignorance
he fought against the caste of those gorillas that crush
all citizens' liberties
he fought always for man and his best causes
I put we put such shine such strength in the words
that the children even though they don't understand well
grasp something
and afterwards in their boisterous childish games and open
laughter
they all want to be comandantes Guevaras

XXXIX
Even though is true that the morning glory
closes its eyes before the rain falls
comandante
and that prince albert and laura victoria
are the beautiful names of certain stunning
flowers
in more than half the world I keep we keep listening to
the banging
of the old and broken and hard drums of millenarian
hunger
but now your name comandante is like the name
of a young volcano
or like that of a spear cast by a primitive avenging
god

LI
Now I go through we go through a tempest of realistic and drastic
words
now we are travellers in the air in all languages

in unison
and I know we know how to say pain vietnam guerrilla
                              combatant armed struggle
without tears

LVI
Peter Weiss has said Peter Weiss has written comandante Guevara
that you looked like a Christ taken off the cross I agree we agree
thus I look at you we look at you like that Christ on an exhausted
                              Andean mule
blind Christ violent Christ fighting alongside a few
to bring a new climate to the helpless
Christ angry at injustice
Christ taken prisoner and then despicably murdered not on
                              good friday
but bitter monday
Christ without cross bled mutilated incinerated
Christ of the twentieth century dialectic theoretical and practical
                              Christ

Translated by Gavin O'Toole

GUYANA

Jan Carew   1971

Ten Years: 1959-1969

I speak, today,
from the heartland, where the fires burn
under black lava skin,
threatening volcano,
when my peoples' wrath is full;
there are those three worlds
and mine's the Third,
the Human World.

Spartacus spoke for me,
with gladiators bounding out of cages,
bellowing freedom,
until
slaves tore at the roots of Rome, and
bare hands and bare feet burst
phalanxes asunder.

Spartacus pounded a path
to the wine-dark sea,
but no ships came;
traders, counting profit and loss,
abandoned him to crucifixion
on the Appian Way.

Blood, buried at the foot of his cross,
exploded out of the pods of time,
scattering seeds like shrapnel;
one fragment, tracing arabesques,
traversed milleniums
to prick Toussaint's heart:
a drop of blood, a flame.

Flowers sprout;
Toussaint shouts,
under a mahoe tree,
holding a rifle high,
'This is your liberty!'

Toussaint died, betrayed,
in the fortress of Joux,
in the cold fortress of Joux.
Christophe and Dessalines were deaf,
but Bolivar heard him;
at Boyaca, he burnt his boats,
a pyre,
five defeats, a spiral in smoke,
mangrove and stars
and giddy garlands of foam,
an altar,
rain-frogs, crying to the moon,
crickets, clicking legs like castanets,
and the wind, winnowing its way
through torn shirts, cooling sweat,
sunrise, burgeoning out a new age.

Bolivar spits
a clinker of Dragons' Teeth
and warriors spring up to free a continent;
Bolivar died betrayed,
and under his feet,
little men crept,
stealthy as serpents,
bailiffs, dispossessing him of dreams;
but Nat Turner heard him say,
'It's easier to plough the sea
than to rob us of our liberty for long.'
Nat Turner left a legacy
for John Brown, Copeland, Kagi,
and Emperor Green;

the arsenal, at Harper's Ferry,
exploded with their dreams.

Marx, Engels, Lenin,
three, who breached the ramparts,
finally led a thousand million working men
down paths of thunder;
even the deaf heard them coming.
Martí, awakening, left a testament for Fidel;
the grass was green,
and green the hills of the Sierra Maestra:
Cuba is free!

Ten years, and
echoes of singing drums
tell of Garvey and Fidel,
Malcolm and Fidel,
Lumumba and Fidel:
ten years.
Come back, Africa!
Free!

The jade archipelago,
green islands,
green mainlands,
Caribbean Sea,
Maracaibo to Patagonia must be
a free continent;
Asia, Egypt to the Yellow Sea,
Japan,
the crippled lands,
cry freedom, where
it's harsh to them,
our enemies;
it all speaks softly to me;
it leaves them naked
but it clothed me, and

makes me stand up straight,
while it hobbles them.
Cuba is free!
Ten years!

The grass is innocent
of vampire dreams, money,
slippery with blood,
stock marketeers,
presidents,
ministers, diplomats, delegates,
greedy for the sun's sweat,
gold; the grass is innocent
of chocolate-coated lies,
advertised,
fifty times a day,
at peak viewing time:
the message slipped between images
of cowboys slaughtering Indians,
Blacks rioting,
police
and dollar-grins wide
as streets,
in chrome.

Revolution is a river;
Lenin cracked it, like a whip,
to sweep the stables clean,
from the Baltic to the Yellow Sea.
Fidel, Camilo
and Che
made their own lariat of it
in Cuba.
Then Tet,
the season of the New Year, came
to Saigon, Hue,
to two hundred cities, hamlets, towns;

Tet is a season of awakening;
Tet is in my blood, today;
Tet is when we greet the New Year,
every day,
with garlands and guns;
Tet is when maidens,
shedding *leis*,
ware a necklace of grenades.

Brothers of the New Year, everywhere,
carry storms
in famished hearts, following
Spartacus, Toussaint, Bolivar,
Marx, Engels, Lenin,
Martí, Fidel, Camilo
and Che.

Do you remember Cuba,
and the seasons of pain,
when black men were denied
the beaches and the sea's foam?
Men and women
walk tall
in the streets
of Cuba, today.
Cuba is free.
Ten years!
For ever!

HAITI

René Depestre   1968

Extract from **The Dance of the Swords of Fear**

(from *Cantata de Octubre*)

> "If we leave the princely heir of Troy alive,
>   the son of the powerful Hector,
>   we shall endure great hardships".
> > Euripides (*The Trojan Women*)

Male Reader:

Look at how restless is
The greenish froth of the gorillas from America!
Look at how they are cheerfully wagging
        their tails
When hearing the news from Vallegrande!
Look at how they are climbing with joy
Up the nefarious trees of death!
Look at their eyes
Redder than their claws and their teeth!

Female Reader:

They are so far from the men of America
That they themselves are not far off being
Wolves, jackals, sharks,
Vultures and other filthy outrages
        from heaven and earth!

Male Reader:

Look at their reddish coat of wild beasts
They are racing each other to be the first to arrive at the Pentagon
Bringing the news fresh and bloody
        at the tip of their claws!

Female Reader:
They are racing each other to be the first to arrive at Wall Street
With their share of entrails and ashes!

Male Reader:
With their share of bones and nerves
Their share of muscles and blood!

Female Reader:
Before the news all of them were
Behind the doors, under the beds
Quivering with lies and cowardice!

Male Reader:
Every night they kept hearing
On the floor of their houses
The warrior steps of Che.
And they cried out to their wives
"Watch out close the doors and windows
It is he that is arriving
It is the incendiary step of Che
The same step as Fidel that was burning
The ground of the Sierra Maestra!
The same step that he shared with Camilo
            at the gates of Santa Clara!
I'm telling you damn it that is his step!
The CIA has recorded it and has broadcast it
            to our 18 general staffs!
The same olive-green step of the Sierra
The same step of jungle blaze
The same step of lion-guerrilla
The same step of tree that walks
And burns the millions of the rich man!"

Female Reader:
"Come on dear
It is nothing but a bad dream

That wraps around your sweaty gorilla
      soul!"

      Male Reader:
"Fuck I'm telling you
That it is his lush rebellious step
Coming from the mountain!
Beware! He is behind the door
He is walking on the roof
He is climbing on the balcony
With a blow of his paw
He'll smash the house!
Let's get under the bed
To pray!"

      Female Reader:
And then under eighteen thousand beds of America
There were eighteen thousand generals
Eighteen thousand petty military hysterias
Eighteen thousand stars face down
Eighteen thousand slithery ruins
Eighteen thousand rats caught in the trap
      blue with fear!
Eighteen thousand swords chattering their teeth
      yellow with fear!

      Male Reader:
There were eighteen thousand little decorated rabbits
      grazing the fantastic wild grass of fear!
Eighteen thousand small rodents
Gnawing at the convulsive buttercups
      of the great fear of the century!

      Female Reader:
Now their eighteen thousand swords
Have found the ferocious teeth of tigers
Eighteen thousand swords surround the wounded
      forest!

Eighteen thousand swords are ready to slice
    the living flesh!
Eighteen thousand swords that dance!
Eighteen thousand swords that jump to attack
    that sole wounded body
Eighteen thousand heroes of the OAS
For that lone heart that still beats
The winged flame in the breath of men!

       Chorus
And look now at how they throw one another
    bloodied flowers!
How they roll themselves on the ground in the blood
    of our Che!
How they devour the cacti leaves
While scrambling for the spoils around the seven
    wounds of Che!

Translated by Alexandra Stanton

Editors' note: Camilo is a reference to Camilo Cienfuegos a leader of the Cuban revolution whom Che Guevara was close to, naming his son Camilo after the revolutionary who died in October 1959. The 18,000 is probably a reference to the size of the Bolivian army during the campaign against Che. The OAS is the Organisation of American States.

JEAN MÉTELLUS   2006

Ernesto Che* Guevara

Celia de la Serna had a vision one day
She will give birth to five children
And among them, Ernesto Guevara
Will be like a forest
Like a plentiful land of grain
Like a boiling river
Like a flame scalding space, burning everything in its way
Or like an image floating on the horizon
Far from men but for men
Near heaven but far from God
Indefatigable like an army of termites
Always fighting
Always standing and smiling
Loving life in all its forms
Loving his brothers, his sisters and his equals
Questioning without end
The sky, the clouds, the rain
The dust lifted by the soles
And the impenetrable master breath that animates us
Energetic and facetious, athletic and courageous
Lover of words, of lyrics, of exchanges
Intrepid
He will remain for a while amongst us
But very soon he will depart
Abandoning all his ties
Despite the love he brings to all
He will become a citizen of the Caribbean, of South America
The only title that befits him
And the only glory he desires
Not for himself, but for others
He will be the pilgrim of the people
A man with a mission all his life

But from where do they come to you, Celia, these premonitions,
                                        asked her husband

The Indian gods have spoken to me
All the divinities of this earth have been suffering for four
centuries the atrocities committed here
Now they demand reparation
Ernesto, our son, has been chosen to demand explanations
He must go far away from all of us
Far from his brothers, Roberto and Juan,
Far from his sisters, Ana María and Celia
The asthma that has been choking him since the age of two
Means that he cannot stand the air of this world
And even the gods have told me: Ernesto will not live long
Ah! You have started to become delirious
Yes, it is possible, if the gods know how to make you delirious
But I have not yet finished talking, or being delirious if you prefer
I have other messages to deliver
I see that inspiration is with us
Ah! I am not inspired, but my head is clear
I see the future
So continue, continue Celia
Our son Ernesto will be admired, given adulation, flattered and
even sanctified
But he will never be loved
For only feeble and sensual men inspire this feeling
He, from the outset will be above men
He will be hard towards himself, towards others, towards
the world
Like Christ who went before him
His smile of a sarcastic angel will show the nobility of his soul
For he will soon grasp the measure of men
Who are not like him but deformed portraits
And yet who all the same believe they are similar to him
He will be a being of flesh since we conceived him
But passionate even in temperance
Exalted even in hope
He will not love himself
But will give his life for men
Whose weaknesses and faults he knows

Another voice

From the splendour,
The adventurers that had come from across Europe plundered
America
A deadly silence ensured the perpetuity of the infamy
But enough is enough

When the army attacks an entire people
For interminable hours
With blows from machine-guns and mortars
Massacred in their hundreds
A night of Saint Joan
The workers of a mine
To strengthen the opulence of the rich
And the prosperity of the lords of tin
The barons of iron, silver, gold and zinc
When the proletarian blood
Runs in the mines of the high Bolivian plateaus
After centuries of violations of human rights
A fundamental fever, the social fever
Declares itself
Settles at four thousand metres of altitude
Among starving men, deprived of everything
Working in the galleries of rarefied air
Yes, at that moment a fundamental fever
The trade union fever, the revolutionary fever
Rises in these exhausted men
Tired of supporting an infernal misery
To guarantee the pleasure of a few

We should follow the course of history
Rediscover the golden age of the Inca
The time where the earth belonged to all
Where paradise was within reach
When men did not have to submit
To cliques, the military caste, colourfully decorated crooks

To the landed and mining oligarchy
To an army in the pay of the U.S.A.

So much poverty endured culminated in an immense wrath
exploding
Miners provided with sticks of dynamite
Marched on La Paz, disconcerted the army
But the movement of these exploited Indians
Reclaimed by narrow-minded and fearful politicians
Lost strength, was weakened

Young doctor Ernesto Guevara was observing the unending
procession of Bolivian people
The indigenous women with infants hanging from their
backs
The old Indians weathered by the sun and coca
The peasants clumsy in their shoes
Others in traditional garb also entangled
All these people were advancing in silence
Waiting patiently for the redistribution of the promised land
by law
But Guevara understood very quickly
That the arrogant rulers were burying this immense hope

So he set out on a voyage of initiation through Ibero-America
Peru, Ecuador, Costa Rica, Honduras, Nicaragua
He visited Cuzco and the Inca country dazzled him
Then he moved on to the land of Miguel Angel Asturias
This country where the indecision of President Jacobo Arbenz
Allowed the success of Eisenhower's plan
The American planes based at Nicaragua
Invaded Guatemala from Honduras
And imposed on the Guatemalan people
Colonel Castillo Armas as President on 3 July 1954
Who subjected the country to terror for three years
Before himself being assassinated and replaced
By General Manuel Ydígoras Fuentes, just as bloodthirsty and
twisted

After the coup d'état
El Che decided to blend his solitude and his despair
With the misfortunes of other lonely and desperate men

So let's play baseball with our Cuban friends
Farewell football, farewell rugby, farewell chess
Said Che, turning away from Argentina for good
It is now necessary to go where spirit and faith are
That is, into the human heart

He descended the Amazon by raft
Conceived and straight away abandoned a project to write a book
on medicine
Wrote poems, dedicated to the sick
Read Marx and Garcia Lorca
Recited *If* by Rudyard Kipling
And *Passion and Death of the Light* by Sara de Ibáñez
Poetry accompanied him everywhere, helping him to breathe
It is then when he encountered Fidel Castro in Mexico and
wedded to the Cuban cause
With the signing of a pact between the students' Revolutionary
Directorate
and the 26 of July Movement
Fidel had welded together the younger generation around a
single motto: Down with tyranny
During this time, Batista made the most of festivities in Havana
Somoza reigned supreme in Nicaragua
And Papa Doc bled Haiti
These flies gorged with money, with madness, with poison
As Pablo Neruda described them
Invented communist plots to repress them in blood

El Che trained to strengthen his breath
To increase his purpose and his power
He practised running, to strengthen himself, to become hard
Caught in a raid, he recited Nazim Hikmet to himself
"I will go to my grave regretting nothing but an
unfinished song"

This combatant still without victory appropriated Mao's maxim:
 "Our principal method is to learn how to make war by
  waging it"
He treated all those around him
Taught with passion the rudiments of hygiene
Learned reading and writing together
While reading in the mountains the life of Goethe
Graham Greene and Faulkner
Proust and Sartre
Whitman and Hemingway
However the guerrilla army went on growing
Batista more and more restless and more and more violent
Proceeded with abusive arrests, with kidnappings
Even the Argentine racing driver Juan Manuel Fangio was
               a victim

More than once Che nearly lost his life
Caught in crossfire at Santa Rosa
He had to run in a zigzag to the thickets
His heart started to beat wildly and his asthma came back
At this point a young lady recruit joined murmuring to him
"Don't worry, commander, I will die with you"
That day, he said, I felt weak at the knees
But the vision on the horizon, the view of the blue line of
             the mountains
Perked up the men
Restored hearts, faces and limbs
And the regrouped revolutionary forces advanced triumphantly
Fulgencio Batista y Zaldívar fled the country on board a plane
           from his private fleet
Sure to find refuge with a dictator friend
He ordered roast chicken, champagne, cognac to be brought along
After a stopover with Trujillo, who profited from his visit
He fled for good to the Spain of Franco
It is then that Che started to smoke cigars
To ease his asthma and to deter the mosquitoes

The war had ended, the revolution was starting

The United States greeted with open arms all
counter-revolutionaries
Starting with Senator Masferrer and his brigades of assassins
The centre of anti-Castro emigration is installed in Miami
>The telephone trust
>United Fruit
>Standard Oil
>Texaco

Pressed to reverse Castro's regime
And El Che became an itinerant ambassador of the new Cuba
Sought support everywhere in the world
In the United Arab Republic with Colonel Gamal Abdel Nasser
In India with Pandit Nehru
In Indonesia with Sukarno
With Japan
He stood in silence before Gandhi's mausoleum
Evoked Gauguin in Bali
Talked at length with Tito, the rebel
And he watched the dawn rise in the homes of the poor
The creativity of liberated peoples was pouring out
Misery was retreating
Life was triumphing
El Che smoked his cigar and drank with delicacies of satay
Recalling his past
Especially the cruel moments where he had nearly lost his life
The tragic, moving stories of willpower, courage, weakness and of
humanity in which he had been actor or witness
He vowed much respect to the writers who vowed it to him
in return
It is at about this time he wrote the story of the "murdered puppy"
And the poetic texts
>*"I am mestizo", cries a painter to his blazing pallet*
>*"I am mestizo" the persecuted creatures cry to me*
>*"i am mestizo" shout the pilgrim poets*
>*"I am mestizo" recalls the man who passes me in the daily pain*
>*of each turn of the road, and as far as the petrified enigma of the*
>*dead race*

stroking a gilded wood virgin:
"He is mestizo this grotesque son of my entrails
I too am mestizo in my own way"...
At the same time doctor and combatant
Knowing only how to choose
Between a rucksack full of medicines
And a case of ammunition

El Che had numerous companions in arms, and lost many
His first book in homage to the prestigious chief of the Rebel Army
To the uncorrupted and generous revolutionary
Camilo Cienfuegos, dead in a mysterious plane accident
Celebrated the natural and fertile union
Between peasants and guerrillas
Between victims of repression and badly equipped but
                                          liberating soldiers
Yes the Monroe doctrine was weakened
Cuba abruptly evaded yankee domination
The Cuban revolution, an example
Guerrilla warfare, a method

The world watched Havana, the intelligentsia applauded
Françoise Sagan, Jean-Paul Sartre, Cesare Zavattini
Admired the vitality of the Cuban revolutionaries, their
                                          enthusiasm was infectious
The Republican Richard Nixon characterised the Cuban regime
                                          as an intolerable cancer
The Democrat J.F. Kennedy swore it necessary to depose
                                          Fidel Castro as soon as possible
The State Department decrees the embargo on exports
                                          destined for Cuba
Diplomatic relations were broken
And a raid by unidentified planes fell upon the recalcitrant island
Leaving many dead on the eve of the Bay of Pigs landing
Che's asthma went into paroxysm
And the revolution was proclaimed a socialist revolution on the
                                          16 April 1961

Che's asthma went into remission
The Americans defended fighting for their own interests
The great landowners and the managers of Havana's brothels
      pretended to want the dawning of true and authentic
      revolutions in Latin America
Yankee academics whipped up the Cuban suvbersion
Because Fidel and Che endangered subjected countries
Like Panama and its precious channel
Nicaragua of the Somoza dynasty
The Dominican Republic and its benefactor, generalissimo
                    Rafael Léonidas Trujillo
And Haiti with François Duvalier and his tontons macoutes

But, El Che, himself, believed in revolutionary contagion,
                in its propagation, in its victory
Beyond the seas
In the frozen or scorching deserts
Everywhere
In Shanghai, Moscow, Berlin
In Geneva, Algeria, Paris
In Dahomey, Tanzania
In Red Square next to Gagarin
In Leipzig, Punta del Este before the OAS
In New-York, before the UN
He spoke
Of the Cuban experience, of agrarian reform
Of nationalisation of oil and banks
Of the pirate planes sowing death
Of the explosion of La Coubre at Havana harbour
Of the isolation of Cuba
Of the social conditions in Latin America
From then on he finished his articles and letters with a
                sibylline formula
    "Receive our ritual salute like a clenched fist or an Ave Maria.
           Fatherland or death"
Already, he deviated from the state structures
Conscious of the excesses of the professionals of power

He launched a struggle against the emerging, cold and corrupted
bureacracy in La Havana
Certain that revolutionary enthusiasm, political education of
the masses
Can alone counterbalance the inertia of public officials
That only the example of sincere and honest leaders can
mobilise the mob
That the destiny of the Cuban revolution is played out in
each state of Latin America
Che spoke of and made incarnate faith in a fairer world, more
fraternal
He separated from Fidel, renounced his posts
He was no longer of this world but still lived for the world
and men
So that the rich don't become richer and the poor poorer
Thus thought Toussaint Louverture
Thus spoke Lenin
Thus lived Che

* Word that signifies something like "Hey! you", typically Argentine interpellation at the
start of a phrase, a nickname given to Ernesto Guevara by Cuban Antonio "Ñico" López

Translated by Georgina Jiménez

Translator's note: Antonio "Ñico" López, was a Cuban exile who first told Che in
Guatemala about Fidel Castro; Carlos Castillo Armas led the CIA-backed coup in
Guatemala in 1954; José Miguel Ramón Ydígoras Fuentes was one of a series of military
rulers of Guatemala and ruled as president from 1958-63; Sara de Ibáñez was a
Uruguayan poet whose poems, including "Pasión y muerte de la luz", reveal among
other things a preoccupation with death; Nazim Hikmet Ran was a Turkish poet and
communist; Juan Manuel Fangio was in fact kidnapped by Castro's forces as propagan-
da to prevent him taking part in a race in order to humiliate the Batista regime, but
released unharmed shortly afterwards; Rolando Masferrer was a senator in the Batista
government and a paramilitary leader who fled to Miami; the story of the murdered
puppy is recounted by Che Guevara in his reminiscences of the Cuban revolutionary war
(see Guevara, 2006, pp. 177-180); Yuri Gagarin's ashes are interred in the Kremlin wall;
the freighter La Coubre, a French vessel carrying Belgian munitions, exploded in Havana
harbour in March 1960 in an incident blamed by the Cubans on the CIA; the tontons
macoutes were Duvalier's notorious militia.

Anthony Phelps   1969

Che's Poem (from *Les dits du fou aux cailloux*)

Sanctuary for birds of prey incubus of vultures
oh land of America in search of a messiah
the friend the comrade Che is dead

Oh Mother!
In the damned distance the storm rumbles
I feel the blood rise to my hair
The blond and black moon
plays hide and seek with my hand
but the strawberry might try to hide under the nail of childhood
I will find the road to the leaves and to the smell of the woods
where fear will disappear through the sun's mouth

Oh Mother!
I live between the parapets of a woman
a pupil witness of the heart of wheat
her scar tracing a fig leaf
she thinks higher than the rainbow
A unique woman struck by passion
weaving love with her hands of dawn
I live in a woman's geometry
a pearl fished in an ancient sea
and in order not to sleep under the stony lamp of men any more
I have set the butterfly of my memory free
Oh Mother!
I live in a woman's space
my life descends no more and takes its source from her hair
I redesign her vertical face on my door
with New Year's string
at each breath her cheek beats on my heart
and the nocturnal hope untangles the birds' liana

Oh Mother!
I speak for my blood

for a tomorrow that will emerge without pause or seam
and for which we alone will be accountable
For whom is the moon for whom is the sun
but for her my lady with hands of wheat
the silver mouth of children's tales

O Mother!
A sketched future a virgin's crown with a heart of straw
but how can I talk about the star in this lady's ear
when the birds peck at our words
Can you hear the noise of the bullets bursting at the heart of spring
as if water were forever to lose
the intimacy of the lips and of the leaves
Can you hear the cries which invent crystal
to announce the death of a man
as if the road had lost its way
Oh Mother! how to tell my Wife this time
that the child-messenger of the May blossom has returned to
its birth
to look after the wings of our heads
How to tell how everyone is doing
with a tongue that's heavier than memory
The source of the stellar heart shines no more
the friend the comrade Che is dead!

But a death that is spoken in all the languages of the world
is not death
Oh Mother!
entrust him to the milky way
to fields of wheat
to swamps
talk about him in windy spheres
in the sugarfields
at the bottom of the mines
go and tell the windmill on the horizon
that we shall never live again as marginalised rejects
because a bullet in my brother's heart

makes his heart grow bigger
Look at his face shining
like the North Star above America

Melodious memory of my Mother with her solar hands
testing the bathwater
in this country of wax and of petrified mouths
a salutary star awaits on the way to the glazier
where Che's blood will return to our veins.

Land of America nourished on Abel's blood
the moon's mender doesn't play with dolls any more
To my wife I give a kiss that grows bigger with the light
and together we will create a little man in the memory of Che
because fear has switched sides
the curse of the lunatic crow
will rectify itself according to a new future
and the Poet who sows exile
will join up the tenses of the active verb.

Translated by Alexandra Stanton

INDIA

K.G. SANKARA PILLAI   1972

Dear Che

Dear Che,
you came to our university campus
in mid sixties
with a comrade and a modernist friend
with visuals of jungles past and present
with the vision of a new battle for justice.

Like a fresh wind of October
you joined us
moved us
renewed us
and smoothed our entry into history
with love, hopes and plans.

You told us about the sleeping rebel powers
of mountains and forests of the new minds;
quite often you talked of the day when
'the Andes would become
the Sierra Maestra of America.'

Our modernist friend said
that you are the red star over the world
tarnished by America;
that you are the future of the world
crippled by America;
that you are the Jesus of the modern age
crucified by America.

But you remained evergreen in us
showed us the exit to the oceans
from the lyrical ponds of our

post Independent Indian youth;
the exit to the storm from the water lily breeze
of our weeping romantic poems.
dear doctor, you redefined us
living with us
living for us
living in us
passing the confidence of torrents into our deserts
weaving sunlit paths into our prodigal nights.

You brought world into our words
and future into our past.
You opened blast-furnaces for our ore.

Translated by A. Lakshmi

IRAN

Siamak Kiarostami   2000

Memory strands

My friend and I are Iranian
Though we are the sons
Of different people and worlds
Last night we were speaking about being
Prisoners to nostalgia
And other feelings
that lead nowhere
Last night my friend and I were talking about Iran.

It is a topic as old as we are,
Saffron colored with age
He sees it as such —
The Revolution was the
Adolescence of a great nation
Interrupted.

He has the memories of his uncles --
He imagines
Half-full bottles of Shams beer left
Still cold on beaches of shomal-e Iran
And an unfinished joint
Hastily stubbed out on
The Paradise that was taking shape
along the shores of the Caspian.

He sees an entire generation left
Cheated,
He asks what happened
to the beginnings of the
brown thighs rock and roll
and Economic Progress.
A clumsy Shah promised?

I do not think our parents lived in the same country
For I was raised with the idea
That the Revolution was the most heroic
Of all Iranian heroics
Perhaps
I have the memories of my father —
I imagine
It was the battle that Che Guevara would have loved to lead
The passion of 20 million in the streets with
An anger the First World could taste
for reasons the rest of the world would understand.
That was the Iranian Revolution.

I too see an entire generation left
Cheated,
I ask myself how it happened
That in the end
Impostors were able to impose themselves
Onto the unfinished dreams
Of untold generations?

The night went on, we continued talking.
We were philosophers,
we invited each other to our ideas.
Perceptions were as sharp as triangles
We sensed that twenty years ago, had we been the same age,
we would not have been able
to have this conversation.
Twenty years is what it took for our parents
To raise their children as they did
Twenty years is all we've had to absorb
Entire histories, for us
Twenty years is how long it has been
Since Time began.

Twenty years have added wrinkles
To a special generation
And Seen the birth of a new one.

This generation of Iranians is
Held hostage
To linguistic limitations
And to memories of
how much bigger fruit grew back home —
Hostage to ill-construed American notions
Of how to look homeward and
To the taste of pre-revolutionary pomegranates
that never will exist in America.

IRELAND

KIERAN FUREY   1995

The Star

A star twinkles in the black beret
Of the Latin American night.
Dark clouds beard the continent,
Partly obscuring its handsome face.
An asthmatic breeze blows from the Caribbean.

Like Christ you lived
(Though you ceased to turn the other cheek):
Bearded, wandering, badly dressed, misunderstood;
Fighting hypocrisy left and right;
Ejecting money-changers from your temples.

Like Christ you died
(Though you fought to the last):
Hunted, betrayed, captured, tortured and killed
By ill-paid servants of a mundane power.

Some say you'll come again.
There are those who wait for you.
And if you do return,
What will happen on Judgement Day?
Will the bodies of your disappeared disciples
Be resurrected then,
Rising from their resting places
In marine deeps,
In the beds of rivers,
In the bellies of ancient sharks,
In the unmarked graves
Hidden in military precincts?
Will atheist souls be reunited with bodies,
Husbands with wives,

Aged mothers with student sons
Murdered on those many shameful nights
When a prudent America
Passed by on the other side,
Eyes unseeing,
Ears unhearing,
Mouth unspeaking?

Like Quijote you dreamt,
Attacking windmills, heartless giants.
You wanted to abolish money;
Fill bellies with food
And heads with learning;
Create the New Man;
Light a big fire under the gangrenous backside
Of a moribund subcontinent;
Infect that most leprous of all your patients
With the giddy virus of revolution;
Sow seeds of sedition in the deserts
Of countryside and city.

Though they hid your body,
You wouldn't stay in the anonymous tomb,
Preferring to roll back the rock of oblivion
With the living force of your faith
In a better future.
You wander abroad with bright dark eyes,
With throaty beard and chesty cough.
Your scattered faithful wait for you,
Attuned to small signs:
A rebel thought; a fiery speech;
A bearded face drawn badly on a wall;
A newspaper article; a radio programme;
A T-shirt worn in a shopping mall;
An old Mexican who remembers;
An Argentinian inflection in a voice;
A scrap of good news from Cuba;

A just complaint about the price of rice;
A magazine photo; a dog-eared book;
A poster on a bedroom door;
A poem written; a pamphlet read;
A child who asks about the poor.

Condor Che, some hunt you still
And fear your twinkle through the cloud.
Others wait, and hope you will
Extend your wings and fan the crowd.

VAL NOLAN   2004

Ché Guevara in a Limerick pub

Elbow-touch by elbow-touch he meets
The old men in old cloth caps, farmers
In their good tweeds or labourers with
Their hands lime-sallow from the sites.

Then a girl is heard to tell him that he
Should dredge his beard for shamrock,
Seeing as he's a Lynch and all beneath
Those tight curls of far-away Americas

And Ché says back something quietly,
Just a few words in the Spanish which
Spur a nodding and a toasting glass —
His ease requires no literal translation.

LIAM Ó COMAIN   1999

Che

*(Che Guevara Ó Loinsig, in part of his writings implied
that we could change economic and social structures
tomorrow but unless we succeed in changing
the hearts of humanity all would be in vain)*

A spirit rides
Across the plains
Flying
O'er the mountains
Che Che in the wind
With the majesty
Of chieftains

In body
He will not come
But the cause
We must follow
Freeing all mankind
And making
A better tomorrow

Fruit of the earth
For everyone
The essence of
His thought
So let's unite and build
A loving socialist planet

ITALY

Francesco Guccini   2000

Seasons

How much time has passed since that Autumn day
well into October, with the sky already dark,
when between exams, days lost in idleness,
youthful trash, the news arrived...

It grabbed us like a fist, it froze us with depression,
to know so bluntly that Guevara was dead:
on that October day, on Bolivian soil,
Ernesto 'Che' Guevara was lost and betrayed...

Books obscured themselves, the room darkened,
because with him had died one of our hopes:
these were the enchanted years of sung myths and of protestations;
these were the days spent in debating and weaving beautiful
illusions.

'Che' Guevara was dead, but all of us believed
that through us his ideas remained in the world...
'Che' Guevara was dead, but all of us believed
that through us his ideas remained in the world...

Seasons passed by, but still we continued
to eat illusions and truth every hour,
years of discoveries, years without mourning:
'Come on, Comrades, be alert, we must go on!'

And on we went always with our flags,
singing all those fancies of ours...
on an October day, on Bolivian soil,
with a hundred shots died Ernesto 'Che' Guevara.

The Third World cries, now everyone sees
that 'Che' Guevara is dead, will never come back,
but something was changing, the days of those emotions
                                           were ending,
and our eternal enemies raised their heads again against
                                        the rebellions...

'Che' Guevara was dead, and everyone comprehended
that a hero has been lost, that something was ending...
'Che' Guevara was dead, and everyone comprehended
that a hero has been lost, that something was ending...

And over the years something ended for real,
smashing against the deceits of daily living:
the Comrades of another day either gone or sold out,
it seems as if one moves among just a few survivors...

Really for this reason I would now like to hear
a voice which would begin again to sing:
on an October day, on Bolivian soil,
with a hundred shots died Ernesto 'Che' Guevara.

The Third World cries, now everyone sees
that 'Che' Guevara is dead, maybe never to return,
but be afraid, all you reactionaries, the revolutions are not over,
and you others who use different words, but the same prisons,

one day, from somewhere, it is not known where,
where you don't expect it, 'Che' will return!
one day, from somewhere, it is not known where,
where you don't expect it, 'Che' will return!

Translated by Francesca Chiarelli

JOVANOTTI (LORENZO CHERUBINI) 1993

Extract from **Positive Thinking**

I believe that in this world
there exists one great church
that goes from CHE GUEVARA
until it arrives at MOTHER TERESA
passing thru' MALCOLM X and across
GANDHI and SAN PATRIGNANO
It reaches a priest in the developing world
who goes forth in spite of the Vatican

I think positive 'cause I live
and as long as I'm alive
nothing and no-one in the world
can stop me saying it

Translated by Georgina Jiménez

Translator's note: San Patrignano is a well-known drug rehabilitation community in Italy where men who have been considered rejected by society can learn to live freely and return to being positive elements in that same society.

ROBERTO VECCHIONI   1997

Celia de La Serna

You don't write anymore, and I no longer hear from you;
I know what you are doing, and, you know, I'm a bit afraid.
The streets in Rosario are without sun;
it makes the heart ache
to have an extraordinary son:
for, knowing that you are there, I am proud and alone,
but to forget you ... that's easy to say ...
My child, grain of salt,
you have always been a bit special,
with your paleness, black with bruises and blows,
and that cough, my love,

which at night never stopped;
and shirtless,
hours and hours in front of the river,
closing your eyes,
hanging on your heart.
O mother, mother,
what an infinite, boundless sky
the world would be, if it resembled you!
Men and dreams like your words,
the earth and the wheat like your hair.
You are my song,
my memory,
there is nothing else
in my tale;
at times, you know, I seem to hear
the 'poderosa' switched on in the courtyard:
and I look out: "Fuser, Fuser has returned!",
and I look out, and there is only the meadow.
O mother, mother,
if you knew what grief!
This is not the world of which you sang to me:
you look out,
you always look out,
and always hope
never to see me;
I will be that son
you truly love,
only if, and as long as,
you don't see me.

Translated by Francesca Chiarelli

Editors' note: Fuser was Che's nickname as a boy; the poderosa ("mighty one") was the
name Che and his friend Alberto Granado gave to the 1939 Norton 500cc motorbike they
travelled across South America on.

JAMAICA

Andrew Salkey   1977

Our Che

We know how much those blue mountains meant to you;
how much *we* meant to you, living in their promise;
how very far you continued to climb to move up to us;
how very far you fell, because you always loved us.

> So, we'll turn the moral light
> all across the material shadow;
> we'll build our island houses,
> in the fold of the mountains!

We know how deep your dream pierced the nightmare;
how deep the sound of love resounded underground;
how very fast it travelled round the plantations;
how very fast the years mount up like mate leaves.

> So, we'll turn...

Things are clearer now, at the top of the range;
the confusing, early mists are all drifting away;
the shape of the slicing peaks is showing through;
the distance of the climb is no longer a mystery.

> So, we'll turn...

From where we stand, at the edge of our foothills,
the steep heights seem much more easily reachable.
Ever since your last journey down into the ravine,
we knew we must climb it, tomorrow, because of you.

> So, we'll turn...

JAPAN

Renji Ono   1972

Ernesto Che Guevara

The nature of asthma is as varied those who suffer it and
the ways of dealing with asthma vary with experience too.

But in the end, I cannot deny the thought that we are linked
                                        originally by asthma.

        "That one has asthma, this one has it too."
Was the game to list the famous people, just to gain a little
                                comfort in seeking other sufferers?
Was it a contest to raise our spirits?
When I mentioned the name of Tochinishiki, the sumo champion,
You replied with a shout,
        "Ernesto Che Guevara".

When I recommended predonine steroids to you who were using
nothing more than adrenalin, inhaler and codeine suppository,
        "That's likely to aggravate TB, and what's more it's too
        expensive for poor people to use."
You told me and glared at me, using so much predonine.
That was in August, the year of the movement against the
                                US-Japan Security Treaty.
You walked out of the treatment centre to join the movement.

Without hesitation, you just did it.
Like Che Guevara who gave up the position of elder statesman of
the revolution and went back to the hardship of a guerrilla's life.

There are only two paths for revolutionaries.
    Victory or death.
We know that the lives of humans are limited.

It doesn't matter, whether it is
"all visible things are in vain" or "vanity is in all visible things"
But facing the realities of daily life,
I tend to cling to my insignificant existence.
Collecting stones, a passion for bonsai, and painting,

Asthma attacks come as if to punish me in my longing for a
                                        comfortable life.

Your glowing eyes like lenses highlight the contrast between my
ideology and my actions transforming my hospital ward into the
                    middle of the mountains in Bolivia in South America.
They turn the pillows into rocks, the gown belts in snakes, and
                            rising waves of the rivers from the sheets.
    Ernesto Che Guevara
    Ernesto Che Guevara

His devotion to these causes, against the US-Japan Security Treaty,
immediate suspension of the Vietnam War and the termination of
the US-Japan Security Treaty shot a cannon ball into your lungs
                    and turned your vision into a map of ruin.

Weren't your eyes glowing with loathing which turned on me
when I patted your back, cared for you, without any sleep, for
                                        you in agony?
    Because of you
    oxygen in the room is stolen!
    A thief who steals the oxygen of society

Even if we form an organisation called 'Asthma Patients' Union',
We are joined by having asthma,
Each person is completely alone.

Your lips and skin of those of you who refused predonine to
the end
Repeated the name of Che Guevara like a chant to the end,
Your closed eyes of those of you whose skin was tattooed with
Che Guevara's name like an epitaph
Became a couple of stars in the sky where my spirit doesn't exist,
My strangers bind those stars and the Asthma uttering
gun together.

Translated by Emiko Hamazaki-Collins

KOREA

KO UN   2002

Memoirs

I was twenty.
For no reason I wearily loathed the apricot-flowered spring days.
I was starving.
I wanted to fall
Clang!
on the bitterly cold snowfields
of Irkutzk in Siberia — forty below.
I wanted to fall, shot, killed like a young Decembrist.

An obtuse age,
all I hoped was a breathless Sturm und Drang.

I felt as if a wizard's hand had been cut off with a straw-cutter.
When a hoe was thrust into the earth's hide
the clods of earth wept wildly.

I was sixty.
I omitted all kinds of disruptions.
Above all I disdained belated excuses.
As ever
lovely clear days were revolting.
Out on plains whose flesh
was being struck by knife-blades of thunder and lightning
through dark, black clouds
I had to go racing on,
unspeakably happy
all the way
all the way to the other side.

Away with every kind of resignation.
Away with every kind of nirvana.

Even on beyond sixty, I still acted childishly.
All I had was a few friends,
only one lung.
For the sake of the absence of the other
I was obliged to go to another place.
Still I bear Che Guevara in mind, that evening star, my retarded
discovery.

The latter half is an explosion of the first.

Translated by Brother Anthony of Taizé and Lee Sang-Wha

MIN YEONG   2001

Before the Grave of the Poet Kim Namju

Namju, here I am, I've come.
But no matter what I say, Kim Namju
the poet lying in his shabby grave here in one corner
of Mangwol-dong Cemetery, makes no reply.

Namju, dreaming of revolution, singing of revolution,
you spoke of driving monopoly capital
and oppression from this land, and of founding
a country of working folk, you, the poet who sang
that you had never thought you would enjoy
the fruits of that revolution, though you fought
like a blazing flame of fire— is that why
you lie buried here all alone like this,
in a patch of ground smaller than a prison cell?

Namju, here I am, I've come.
This cowardly workmate of yours who used to loiter hiding
behind your back, busy just keeping up with you
as you put your life on the line and fought,
I've been unable to sport a flower since you died,
just living for peace at any price, a defeated pawn of capitalism.
It's only now that I've come to visit you.

Before your grave, where a pile of cigarette butts
replaces incense, with empty *soju* bottles rolling around
like on a city garbage-dump, as I gaze at the faded photo,
where you're still smiling that sunny smile,
and smoke a cigarette, I ponder
why Che Guevara died,
why Che Guevara just had to die . . .

Translated by Brother Anthony of Taizé

MEXICO

Efraín Huerta   1968

Cantata for Che Guevara

The yellow death of blind eyes was unleashed,
of blind eyes the yellow death was unleashed.
Bitter blue steps amid the foliage and the mire.
Bitter and dense searching death, mortal whore.
Great death, big and cursèd death, ferocious stalker.
That death of yours was unleashed, that chatter,
those bullets, that worm-like green of the green berets.
Death was unleashed that day of the bullets
and your injured feet and your abused mane
and your voice dried up from damnedly mutilated foliage.
If you said *Let me live. For you
I am worth more alive than dead*, they replied with blasphemies
and the highest leaves of the pine groves flew into the sky,
because you were always guarded by a flight of doves
and your words of love were orchids and butterflies
for the impeccable syntax of our clear future.
It was unleashed like a pack of dogs that death of yours,
Che Guevara. It was unleashed with its leaden steps.
With its leaden steps death was unleashed, Che Guevara.
There was lead in the mouth of the snitch and of the traitor,
and up the ravine rose a river of lead and fear.
The green beret was on the hunt for the wild orchid
and the helicopter was furiously searching for the butterfly.
That greenish-black death was besieging you amid the skirmish
and among your imprisoned and tortured men.
From the snout of the gorilla was coming the black death
and it was your death that the mercenaries were sweating.
The rivers carried on their backs the foam of your death
and there was blood of yours in the frozen reliefs.
You were already dead in our veins as we agonised
and one night the guillotine chopped off our speech and

our dreams.

We knew you were surrounded, isolated, furious and sad
like the last captain of our hope,
Che Guevara. Of that hope of sweet Bolivarian
greens, of Mexican greens and brotherly greens.
The fatherlands small and great shivered
with the irremediable shots that brought your death,
and then, they say, they sliced off your fingers,
and afterwards, the bloodthirsty mayor assures us, they took you
to the unknown to burn your body
and turn it into the infinite ashes of our love,
Che Guevara burdened with the death of the centuries,
Che Guevara father and son of independence,
grandson of all the freedoms of all the world,
forger of poems, maker of futures.
So that death found you, you found her,
and thus the bullets wounded you fatally
and a jungle-like darkness fell upon mountain ranges, hills,
pampas, plains, deserts, forests, seas, rivers…
Oh wounded and dead comandante, oh wept-for comandante
we do not even know, yes we know when and at what time.
At the precise time of your death the chime of our liberty tolled.

Translated by Georgina Jiménez

Translator's note: The phrase "Let me live. For you I am worth more alive than dead"
has been attributed to Che after his capture in some accounts but opinion is divided over
whether he actually said this.

José Tiquet   1968

Remembering Che Guevara

I
My friend Che Guevara:
        A while back,
when you were a living embrace,
I wanted to write to you
in the finest sounding words,
what is said in lines with academic metres;
but you, Che, a man straight to the point,
gave me nothing but the pure image
of a freedom with which I write to you today.

Today I want to remember that image of yours
of beardless student revolution...

When you were an open book in the streets.
A man Che
full of walking agrarian pages.
When you journeyed through Anáhuac
I saw you stop before Morelos:
you were the live flesh of his statue.

That other image so fiery
at all times lightning in your words:
that of the southeastern thunder mounted on a horse
colouring your face with the bronze of Zapata.

And today I want to recall
that trade of yours with so few words,
when with a poor
photographic camera
like a talking sword you said to me:
"If you are a poet with the voice of the people
I'll take a portrait of your whole sonorous body, for free!"

And that other image
when Claudia told you: "If Don Porfirio
were alive, who knows Che what you would be…"
"My steps follow in the path of Carranza…",
sounded the sure shot of your virile reply.

That day you were speaking from your heart
more like a mountain of light to illuminate a people.

Ouch! Bolívar, how America hurts you in Bolivia,
where they priced your young blood in dollars!

II
Shortly afterwards
I looked for you everywhere,
even in the books that we read together;
but in them, Che,
I only found blank pages;
all the history of Juárez,
the Morelos army, Bolívar and Martí,
the heroic deeds of enlightenment,
all of them along with you, Che, all had gone.

Hilda told me nothing nor Lucila either.
No-one could tell me your volcanic whereabouts.
Then,
to find your image more precisely,
I started to read out loud
a new edition of the Quixote with asthma;
only thus could I discover your ideal whereabouts,
an emerald place resembling la Mancha…

One clear morning
rumour walked the streets:
Fidel and you had a heart for the people,
and enlightened followers in the mountains.

Earlier than ever
your name dawned in Santa Clara,
and on the wisest peak
you, commanding star, and in the voices
ever more the hero
that syllable made
great by history...

Ouch! Bolívar, how America hurts you in Bolivia,
where a heinous crime priced your blood in dollars!

III
Never did such a short name
make history so vast,
nor mountain higher, all beret,
he strode through all America...

A star on your forehead was the best news
to tell the world
that an island beside you
was the land of all lands...

With you a new sun was opening doors
wide to another new fatherland,
whose dawning name
welled up from the sierra...

The whole world told itself
that the great Martí was returning to walk
from within the marble of all your statues,
because with you at last,
Comandante Che,
the flag of his clear word was waving.

IV
Vallegrande:
here was born the night for the crime,
this is the black day
in the mouth of all words,
this is the green day vomited by the Earth.

Here they called death
— how sordid the ink that writes it —
to the fallen oarsman of daybreak.
In the mulatto South
sadness incites mutiny in their labours.
In the celestial North
how filthy the blue of the eyes of invasion!

V
My friend Che Guevara:
                In some place
on our poor Earth
where a pure man is fighting,
your name has the hands
of a warrior people,
your indomitable uniform, only empty of the asthma,
goes now with other bodies walking…
You, commanding the dawn.
Everything that is pure, Che, with you rises up.

A happy and victorious song
sings and beats in the open air,
and your boots are put on by
people delirious with hope…

The syllable keeps on growing
in every voice ignited by your words:
it is America with berets
that with your olive uniform
advances,

hitting the target every day
it advances,
advances…

Translated by Gavin O'Toole

Translator's note: Anáhuac is a word in Nahuatl, the language of the Aztecs still spoken in central Mexico, for the Valley of Mexico. Morelos is José María Morelos, a hero of Mexican independence. Zapata is the revolutionary Emiliano Zapata. The reference to the camera describes one of the jobs Che had when in Mexico. Don Porfirio is the Mexican dictator Porfirio Díaz. Carranza is Venustiano Carranza, a leader of the Mexican revolution. Vallegrande is the province in Bolivia where Che died. The "fallen oarsman of daybreak" is probably a reference to the Greek Leander.

MOROCCO

Mohamed Khaïr-Eddine   1971

Tomb of Che Guevara

Freedom is at the edge of a sheet of paper,
at the tip of a rifle without a telescope, at the tip
of a blank cartridge. freedom is a strap
that holds you like a poet or a hare under the
useless gold of the Moon where walk two lonely men
at the time of clicks and condemnations.
at the time of thrones and uncertainties love
protests with a weapon otherwise repressive
that the bullet lost in Africa and that howls
mocks the insistence of the clouds and lifts
the innermost beings of the men rediscovered in this park
that is the magma of precarious insults and aborted orgasms.

at the time in which a soiled asia bitten but not extinct
by the clasp of weapons and their morose teeth
at a time in which the empty cracked wall of the Earth
dishevelled at its nodule where god measured his death,
at a time of interstellar cycles and of wildlife
of harsh *kiff*, of silver herring and nimbus of napalm.

che guevara rearms the ounce of proletarian blood
captured by the yankee in the streets and pulverizes
with his dreams and his berets slugging
the militant misery of the americas
for whom combat is in that ounce of blood
lost like a warhead in the hell of the bystander!

at the time the commoner summoned to obliterate
this prison from which issues the cry of the islanders:
masks chained to the spear and to the rifle
shed the rude life of glairy suns
in African concentration camps:
freedom is at the edge of a sheet of paper.

at the tip of a rifle where black and white
yellowed by a bible forged in cobalt
strike at the enemy in his vaults and gather up
the cancerous remains of liberties denied,
dirtied bruised but laughing at the engineers
of calm death in hallucinated cackles.

Translated by Georgina Jiménez

Translator's note: *Kiff* is Moroccan marijuana

MOZAMBIQUE

Sebastião Alba   2003

Nobel 1

The Nobel Prize for Literature has chosen our dwelling. He will
                                                    have the decisions
well planned. I have only read "The Cat and the Rat" and
                                            "Hitler's Dog" of his.
The one who is happy is Fidel, despite him not having come to
                                            Havana. Once again,
in one of those torrential speeches of his, he could affirm
                                            "The NPL is with Cuba".
When Guevara died everyone hurried to translate "Bolivian
                                    Diary", to dedicate poems
to him. Only his wife could decipher his writing, it was almost
                                    illegible, "a doctor's", as we say.
And it is thanks to this effort (I have no adjective for such effort.
                                            But there is no need
for useless Cervantes's) by "Che" that the island has not yet sunk,
                                            been bombarded.

Translated by Richard Bartlett

NEW ZEALAND

BERNARD GADD   2006

Che Guevara's lyric

optimist, that's the poet I was:
change the links from you to you
and we'd refashion
even our hopes

ah but optimism fatigues
those who hear its niggles,
its hints at what we can change

easier to claim virtue
for what's known,
to say human nature never alters —
we could eye to eye
with Neanderthal —
to insist imagination's
too chancy to rely on

I was like Karl Marx
relentlessly devising
fresh patterns
to aid our understanding

I'm forever now in Cuba
come visit, chat,
and sense how something
of your mate, Che,
works away in you,
si si, the hopeful
Guevara always toting the rifle
of the new

MICHAEL O'LEARY   1997

A Sonnet to Ché Guevara

(For his place in Popular Culture)

'Looks a lot like Ché Guevara,' I heard David Bowie say
Ernesto Guevara de la Serna, otherwise known as Ché
Was tired of witnessing widespread poverty and oppression
Hopped on his bike and headed towards the Revolution

His travels and readings also led him to view liberation
As not for one country, but borderless. His conception
Became disenchantment as the *Realpolitik* in Cuba too
Began to make Castro's ideals seem to ring untrue

Irony is the meat and blood of life and love and pop
Culture also. Lennon's take on Leninism and Mao —
Hate 'Ain't going to make it with anyone, anyhow'
But 'posterboy Ché' and 'Moondog Johny' lives both stop

By a bullet: Ché, murdered on Lennon's birthday, his last words can
Be for both of them, 'Shoot, coward, you are only going to kill a
man'

Note: This sonnet was written in 1997 when Guevara's body was exhumed from its communal grave in Vallegrande and returned to Cuba. The 30th anniversary of his death was celebrated across Cuba. (Ché died on 9 October, 1967, John Lennon's 27th birthday.) Ché was 39 when he was shot, John Lennon was 40 when he was shot in 1980. "Why did they think that by killing him, he would cease to exist as a fighter?" Castro said at the ceremony to mark Ché's reburial. "Today he is in every place, wherever there is a just cause to defend."

MARK PIRIE   2003

City Walk

(for Che Guevara)

Now around the city I go and recurring is an image of Che:
you'll see him out there 'living it up' on stylised pop posters

postcards, and key rings, all the latest funky t shirts,
                                                    commercialised
and re-packaged for the disaffected post-counter culture youth.

A sign of being a rebel, resisting authority, but unlike Jimmy Dean
this man had a cause. Che, you're lauded by some for rising up

and taking arms, a real Revolutionary, and sometimes I wonder
do these trendy pop kids ever understand the pain and injustices
                                                              of war,

living on good incomes in First World countries and sporting
                                                          your face
like you were their brother, their saviour; the ironies

abound even after you took your final bullet; would you
                                                    have guessed
the evolving impact of your feats, your legend and your myth?

Now around the city I go, and recurring is an image of Che:
you'll see him out there, 'living it up', he's a punk on a
                                                    good income.

NICARAGUA

Jorge Eduardo Arellano   1972

In Rivas, Nicaragua

In Rivas
  Nicaragua,
     I saw you
skinny,
  bearded
     stinking
singing tangos
with other travellers.
You were coming from the Andes
exhausting and frozen
and from the Caribbean
your sea.
From a window
us lads watched you
eat rice with chicken
in briefs.
Then off you went
and we did not get
to know
anything
about you
until your name
sparkled
Che Guevara.

Translated by Gavin O'Toole

PANAMA

CHANGMARÍN   1977

The Che feeling

They say through my town he passed
one day, on his way to Guatemala...
and upon his death
there were mourners
in the street where Che
stopped to ask
the way

It is the monument of the legend
well, for the people,
because as with Victoriano Lorenzo,
he is not dead
and you can find his heart in the hand
of each poor man across the world,
in their flag.

And they do well when they paint Che Guevara
on the walls of Alba
(on the curved sky of America
blackened with dollars)
with coal or soil
or the blood of other martyrs.

The enemy will never erase
the global hand
of Che Guevara on the trigger,
unto the last drop of his blood,
and the spittle on the face of the CIA
and even with death upon him;
inevitably upon him
and surrounded by hyenas and bandits.

His expression has the profile
of the Aconcagua,
and of certain Amazons
his wellspring of blood.

What is immortal are his words
unto the very last affirmed
like an irascible bull
unbending and without fear.

He fulfilled in death
what he promised in life
his conscience was clean, like dew
he had a beard full and pure.
Neither life nor death could bind him.
And so it was, according to history
and everything continues without Che
and with Che, it moves onwards.   .

They say that through my town
one day he passed on the way to Guatemala
and I must say,
now that death has trespassed against him,
nonetheless,
I would like him alive.

I would like him alive
lending me a hand
right now
when it's most needed
his human smile,
of canefields and of hope,
and when just there, in the canal,
the beasts bellow
for the new night
of St Bartholomew of the Americas.

But they say he is dead
and I take comfort in his reality
his burning ashes
and light with his embers
a new fire.

Translated by Gavin O'Toole

Translator's note: Victoriano Lorenzo is considered one of the greatest heroes of Panamanian history, dying during the Thousand Days War, shortly after which the country finally gained its independence. Alba is a reference to Panama's financial district. The Cerro Aconcagua in Argentina is the highest mountain in the Americas.

PERU

JUAN CRISTÓBAL   1968

Che, Friend

> *for Juan Pablo Chang*

You could have died in an earthquake
As you were drinking with friends of your barrio
When you were declared unfit for compulsory military service
When you were first disappointed in love
And you went travelling the world like a lost train driver
Or that night
When the lads from school mocked you
Because you did not know how to dance
                              caminito que el tiempo ha borrado
And loneliness grew like a mysterious eel on your lips
Yes, you could have died in the cinema
Or in the tranquility of the rain like any one of us:
Daydreaming or thinking about carlitos gardel
        or about borges as a kid
Or about that girl next door who believed your friendship
                                        was like a tree
        full of mirrors
But no — you did not even die on time
Nor even close your eyes
When they cut off your hands
And fired a shot into your nape and another into your chest
Nor when you were writing in the jungle some brief poems
        at the foot of a mossy trunk
Nor when you used to wake up looking for the sun in the forests
Nor when you told monje (of the Bolivian CP) to go to hell
And you were left alone
Kissing the solitude of the night with your comrades
And not even when the revolution triumphed
And the whelks and *retamas* delivered their sprays of fire

Because you will never die, "contemporary bloodhound" of history
You only died as you wished:
Recalling the history of men and advancing to war cries
          in the rivers of the jungle
And spitting on the heart of your executioner
And making a humble teacher comprehend
The miseries of her fatherland
And the perforated shadows of her life

Translated by Gavin O'Toole

Translator's note: Juan Pablo Chang Navarro-Levano, "El Chino", was a Peruvian member of Che's guerrilla caught and executed alongside him in Bolivia. "Caminito que el tiempo ha borrado" is the opening line of a famous song, El Caminito, written by Gabino Coria Peñaloza. The Argentine Carlos Gardel was considered one of the most important singers and composers of tangos in the first half of the 20th century. The reference to the young Borges alludes to an incident in which, as a boy, Che's father, Ernesto Guevara Lynch, hit his then classmate Jorge Luis Borges, who would become the famous writer. Mario Monje was the leader of Bolivia's Communist Party at the time of Che's campaign. The party did not aid the guerrillas despite having promised to do so. The retama is a leguminous shrub. The humble teacher is a reference to Julia Cortez, the teacher at the La Higuera schoolhouse where Che was executed, to whom he pointed out the poverty of the education being given to local peasant children.

PORTUGAL

EUGÉNIO DE ANDRADE   1971

Elegy to the Black Waters for Che Guevara

Tied to silence, the heart still
heavy with love, death in profile,
listening, so to speak, to the black
waters of our affliction.

Pale voices seek you in the mist;
from hideout to hideout seeking
the liveliest colt, the tallest
palm tree over the lake, the boat perhaps
or the honey coating our happiness.

Eyes wide with fear
awaiting the midday sun at night,
the vibrant face of the sun where you arise,
where you mingle with the branches
of summer's blood or the rumour
of rain's white feet in the soil.

The word, as you said, arrives
humid from the forests: we have to sow it,
arrives humid from the earth: we have to defend it;
arrives with the swallows
who drink it syllable by syllable from your mouth.

Every word of yours is a man standing;
every word of yours
turns the dew into a knife,
turns hatred into an innocent wine
that we can drink with you
in the heart surrounded by fire.

Translated by Richard Bartlett

JORGE DE SENA   1971

Poem

In this vile world that immerses us in fate
because of our grandparents and we ourselves
too occupied with excuses to save it,
there is a difference in revolutions.
Some suffer in the stomach, they write verses,
others get together weekly to discuss
the scripture of the week; others clamour
for peace of mind that they acquire
by clamouring in riots and protests;
and others end up with their backs in jail,
so that there can be protests. there are also
revolutions, some serious, which end
in compromises, and others imagined,
that neither ended nor began. But rare are those
who do not die from an ulcer or a severe beating,
and against whom agencies and computers
are organised to know them in the wilds
trying to get the peasants to revolt.
The peasants do not revolt. And they
are hunted, shot at, presented
in the form of a semi-naked corpse,
from which they afterwards cut off the head, hands
or fingers only (anxious to castrate them
even after they are dead) and business
transforms them later into a romantic poster
for the rooms of youngsters who still dream
rebelliously before being employed
in the punctual assassination of their humanity
and that of others, day by day, by month,
with social security and pushing aside
reform for the ageing idiot.
The world plays and pillages so that the dead live!

Translated by Richard Bartlett

NUNO GUIMARÃES   1971

Darkroom

decomposition.   The taut light, legible over the burnt
face, of the picture. the page, weak,
comes loose from the folio. or is it autumn?
the hole of fury, in the earth itself?

i re-open the portfolio. the blind light of fo-
liage scorches, invades the face, the tangible
areas, vocabularies — the darkroom,
the baths, negative. page

which dissolves, quickly, from the fra-
gile diaphragm to the body, dead.
Vallegrande.   Now the light is expanding. guiding
the body, between the foliage, with arms

of light, sobrieties of fire, air, crackle
in the rigorous space — *rigor mortis* —
the birds, over the ash. it is your flight
between the sobs and the wrinkles, the humidity

unravelled by time, in the retina.
and facing those boards, humus, rain,
which face still lives? blind, sleeping,
in the rigidity of skin, another picture.
recomposition.   The face rises, in flames. the ang-
le wide, between the retables and shadows,
sustain what image, what vio-
lent retina, between escarpments and hardness?

the rural aridity, from that dead
cranium, razed by the wind. i take it out,
then, from the bath. i place it in the *portfolio*,
over the tense foliage: fibres, nerves.

Translated by Richard Bartlett

SOPHIA DE MELLO   1972

Che Guevara

Against you are ranged the prudence of the intelligent and
                                            the audacity of idiots
The indecision of the confused and the arrogance
Of those who confuse revolution with destruction

From poster to poster your image decorates the consumer society
Like Christ in blood decorates the sponsored alienation of churches

However
In front of your face
The adolescent meditates in his room
When he seeks to emerge from a world which is rotting

Translated by Richard Bartlett

RUSSIA

Yevgeny Yevtushenko   1971

Keys of the Comandante

Our horses pad their way to the village
                where they killed you,
                         Comandante.

Near the precipice go, as in politics,
           neither too far to the left,
                nor too wide to the right.

Let go the reins, muchachos,
           give the horses lead

to direct our destinations,
           otherwise we'll vanish in vain.

There is in the sullen cheekbones of the rock face
                   a partisan look

the wind
      has sculpted with longing and pain.

The clouds are heavy, unmoving
           above the forests and swamps,

like exhausted thoughts
        of the scowling Bolivian mountains.

We struggle upward,
       as though evading pursuit.

Better to confront phantoms in the mountains
          than adjust to the marsh's slime

The clip-clop of horseshoes dictates
        the rhythm of these lines,

stumbling on the stones
      of this deadly serpentine trail.

But fear makes bad reins.
        And while not particularly fearful,

I detect with every nerve
      the putrid smell of immortality.

Remembering you, Comandante —
        overwinds the soul,

and the quiet inside
>> pulsates like an earthquake.
Comandante, in trading you,
>> bidding the price ever higher,
they sell your precious name
>> too cheaply.
With my own eyes, Comandante,
>> in Paris I saw
your portrait, your beret with a star,
>> on modern "hot pants."
Your beard, Comandante,
>> on bracelet charms, brooches, and saucers.
In life you were once pure flame,
>> they turn you into smoke.
But you fell, Comandante,
>> in the name of justice, of revolution —
not in order to become an ad
>> for the commerce of the "left"-minded.
You were shot in this school,
>> where my horse suddenly grows still:
>> "Where are the keys to the school?"
The campesinos are unfriendly and silent
>> with guilt in their eyes.
A rusty padlock crowns the door.
>> A glance through the window — it's dark and bare,
and the wall is white like the sail of a ship
>> with no captain.
The ancient village bell slumbers.
>> A drunkard drags on a can of beer.
Horse manure by the doors
>> leaves an odour of posthumous chrysanthemums.
I repeat: "Where are the keys to the school?"
>> "The keys! Do you understand?!" — I yell in Spanish.
"We don't know, señor, we don't know …"
>> The campesinos stand like a wall.
All the same, where are the keys to the school,
>> and to your soul, Comandante?

Time to go back, muchachos.
                    The clouds are pregnant with a storm.
This key is held by a mystery,
                    and just try and get
the real key — not a picklock!
                    You see, breaking in would settle nothing.
I understand
        how through the pain in your hearts, muchachos,
your hands itch for rifles
                    or machine guns.
If they pull you to the right, muchachos —
                    to the left, boys, always to the left,
but not more left than your hearts,
                    otherwise the precipice awaits.
They hacked off your hands, Che,
                    there, in the square of Valle Grande,
in order to remove your fingerprints.
                    (Perhaps, "sewed on" others, in haste.)
But the rebellious hands of the muchachos —
                    are your hands, Comandante,
and no one can chop them off
                    — they'd grow back anew.
Trust your horses, muchachos,
                    and not simply youthful impulse.
The horses have a peasant wisdom —
                    no matter what their age.
A vulture circles in the sky above us,
                    led on by his rapacious beak,
his talons drawn in,
                    but, while waiting for victims,
                                        takes aim.

1971, La Paz

Translated by Albert C. Todd and James Ragan

SAINT LUCIA

ARTHUR RAYMOND   1971

A Revolutionary Core: Che Guevara

One spark
lights the twig;
and the pile of wood blazes;
the sky blazes;
one man
lifts his head;
four eyes see blood;
and, in a million brains,
flames of anger light
the funeral-pyre of fear.

Do not worry,
out of season,
if you are the only one
in the village
with clear eyes
or reason;
the enemy is your helper.

So,
stand strong,
and trust your people,
your poor people;
they will not let you down.

Strike hard,
Brother!

234

DEREK WALCOTT   1969

Che

In this dark-grained news photograph, whose glare
is rigidly composed as Caravaggio's,
the corpse glows candle-white on its cold altar —

its stone Bolivian Indian butcher's slab-
stare till its waxen flesh begins to harden
to marble, to veined, white Andean iron;
from your own fear, *cabrón*, its pallor grows;

it stumbled from your doubt, and for your pardon
burnt in brown trash, far from the embalming snows.

SOUTH AFRICA

JOE A.A [ANTI-APARTHEID]   1968

In tribute to Ernesto Che Guevara

The *baas* thinks
when it comes
napalm tanks
wire dum-dums
shrapnel whips
electric shocks
booby traps
will block us

The *baas* thinks
flesh and blood
sinew flanks
black and red
shall not stand
the war machine
the steel wind
the iron whine

Che, now our fingers are propellors
cities burn where our minds were numb
our arms are the barrels of mortars
our heads are fused like a bomb

You have turned our tribes to brigades
we flow remorseless where rivers ran
our loins are the seed of grenades
our ribs are the armoury of man

After you, we will never yield
we have one thing to give you, a life
and the bullet shall break on our shield
and the vulture shall fall on our knife

The *baas* fears
when it comes
we'll wash our spears
in blood and bones
But Che knows
it comes soon...
the white night grows...
See the black moon!

MASA MBATHA-OPASHA   1995

To Che Guevara with love

Dear brother, warrior and possible friend,
A distant echo brings me these sad notes;
a low slow cry, a deaf pain
and five billion scarlet illusions.
It was for you, brother Che,
that many of us cried at great length
for your early death.
It was for many of us, Guevara,
that you died that violent, merciless death.
Life was truly unjust to you
and perhaps you to life!

You died in my childhood
and thus deprived me completely
of a chance to meet you
in flesh and in blood.
You denied me a chance to know
who, how, and why you were.

I have since met you however,
in books, songs, movies and conversations.
You taught revolution not evolution
you chose liberation but not revelation

which won us freedom without any wisdom.
You were for rebellion and never changed that opinion,
but maybe I'm too young to say you were wrong.

Mankind is still bewildered by your courage,
still stunned by your sacrifice.
You have been crowned a hero, a legend and a myth.
You have been elevated to the holy seat of saints, prophets
                                                    and gods.
Was this really your dream?

There is no peace yet here — only war!
Guns thunder across the scared skies
of Europe, Africa, Asia and the Americas.
Helpless, hungry children run amok
in search of land, life and love.
The grown-ups mourn and curse in their graves.
Senseless violence reigns like a king.
"Bloodbaths of peace" flood the earth
as darkness fills the emptiness of our dreams.
Are we doing the right thing?

Rivers of tears line the face of the universe
since you went away;
there is no more place to watch,
to listen, to pardon.
There is no more place to smile,
to give, to love.
There is no more place to ask,
to receive and to grow.
There is no more place to live!
Is this the "new world" you lived and died for?
Is this the "new man" you so much desired?

Every day I see you perish;
shrivelled and lacerated.
You bleed, I bleed, they bleed.

All your hopes have waned into silence.
God's heart is caught up in the grips of solitude.
Is war really the only price of peace?
If you were to ask me
I would tell you no.

SPAIN

Rafael Alberti   1970

To Ernesto Che Guevara

I met you as a boy
There in that countryside of Argentine Córdoba
playing among the poplars and maize fields,
the cows of the old manors, the peons...
I did not see you again, until I learned one day
that you were the bloodstained light, the north,
that star
that has to be watched at every moment
so as to know where we stand

Rome, October 1970

Translated by Gavin O'Toole

Víctor Manuel Arbeloa   1967

Scary lullabies with Che Guevara in the background

Wake up, my child,
here comes Guevara,
his eyes like fire,
his beard bushy.

Wake up, my child,
here comes Che;
he's very nasty they say
I don't know why.

Wake up, my child,
Ernesto is close,
howling at the poor
that this world is ours.

Wake up, my child,
he's amongst us
a shepherd of the people
scaring off the wolves.

*

Sleep, my child,
it's better not to see
what those wolves
have done to him.

Translated by Georgina Jiménez

GALICIA

Proclamation of the new peasant

Homage to Che Guevara

In the depths
of the resonant cavities
of the Sisargas islands, Ons
and Oncela
we are going to yell
so that our vigour
echoes in the depths
of the world
and in the hearts of the chestnut trees
of the world
and in the root of men's hearts, comrades
of the world.
Because we want to say more than four truths
related to our class.
We are the peasants of Galicia.
We had the cellular condition
of honey;
we gathered in concentric layers
around the fire;
we scratched a homeland
dark and lush;
we lived horrified, cramped, loving,
governed by lard soup;
we left, behind us, at the crossroads of time,
a cold procession of shrivelled grandfathers,
of corn;
our eyes used to turn green or brownish-grey
according to the rains;
the enclosures divided our communal lands

and hearts;
the enemy laws and bars,
clumsy like the flapping of the owl's wings,
continuously vigilant;
our hands knew how to focus on the tools
and how to be stone;
we lived in clusters, at times, in the folds of the mountains
like colonies of mushrooms.
And at the sunset of unlived history
we used to dream sometimes;
and in the dark night, with faraway lights, on the paths,
we didn't declare ourselves
— because we were stubborn as the scrubland —
lost forever.
And falling headlong upon the slow, deep rivers of the eel,
we learnt that all things come to an end.
But today
— gallant Ho Chi Minh, bamboo that bends but doesn't break,
Fidel Castro of sugar and green hope,
Mao pressed from silt and common blood —
we decided that history
is the work of each morning and each day;
that the plough
is guided by the all-powerful hand of man;
that the harvests
resolve themselves after the labour of the sowing.
And today
— brothers, miserable
peasants of the earth —
we will shout over the misty valleys
of the subjugated earth
to speak the name Che Guevara. And we say:
The hoe, the powerful ploughshare,
the horse of the peaks, the wretched
stone, the tile, the flagstone
of our houses, the damp heart of our winter beds
(where we copulate numb with cold),

the human sound of the old clogs,
the din of the spring rising over the country like a hat
the powerful pollens,
the dust and the dryness that wrinkle our faces
in the bitter harvest time,
the livid breath of the cemeteries
where our ancestors contemplate us waiting,
the cow, the bread, the smoke,
the moss that grows over our eyes like a trait,
the blackbird that sleeps on the left side of our chest,
the dull and sad light they allowed into our eyes,
and the earth,
that thing that only can be said in one way: CHE GUEVARA.
In short, our cursèd
substance,
the sad and viscous flesh that makes up
the farmer's heart,
the servitude that made us
men sold and bought many times,
our filthy bodies,
lost, on the wrong track,
today everything lifts a steel fist,
a sickle that expands in the sky like an eagle of fire.
Our class raises over the valleys of terror and the greenery
a new tool
known by the name of liberation.
And a red spiral
unravelling slow and alive,
fluctuating like dough, like a galaxy ablaze,
shows the way of the bread and the good light
for the peasants of Galicia.

And so the most eagerly awaited dawn is arriving,
the singing of all the birds of Galicia
stopped for an instant
on contemplating so much future ahead.

Translated by Nuria Madroño

SWEDEN

INGEMAR LECKIUS   1967

Ramón

Matt. 5:6

A man walks around in outlawed stride,
Yet carrying the passport of brotherhood.

His tenderness is frightening. It resembles
A dove, lashing its wings.

A moon gleam falls on his sparse band
Struggling to keep the future smouldering.

With difficulty, his breath makes its way
Through the ravines and ambushes of the chest.

He moves deeper and deeper into the world
Consumed by this mysterious hunger.

Until suddenly the rifle muzzles thicken
And an invisible flame erupts.

Translated by Niklas Törnlund

Note: Ramón was Che Guevara´s cover name in Bolivia.

TRINIDAD

Claude Lushington   1971

Simon: How many Bolivars?

Simon: How many Bolivars?
Latest of the brood, Che Guevara.
Salute Juarez, Zapata again:
horsemen of the Apocalypse,
Andean scorpions of stone,
volcanoes in their hands,
fingers rooted in time,
splitting mirrors and
assaulting fortresses
with their puma paws.

Patriarchs bearing
granite lamps ride
their horses in the moon,
their light like Orion's,
a source of consolation,
bride to the altar of leaves
in a cathedral of timber.
Were they not also a fragment once?

Their poor hands are familiar,
their old hearts, unremembered,
by hearts of a thousand years
of recondite truth.

Come to birth, now,
in the midst of clay
and flint; light up
forests,
deserts,
cities,

where congregate
sleeping jaguars,
boa constrictors,
birds like condors.

Heirs to greenheart,
pastured in woodlands,
fire the torch-trumpet again;
rock the ship-eagle once more,
crying with your blood
in a silence of hope, a
magnet clinging to struggle and
bequeathing love, until
earth gives up time and
night collapses at the
new day's red knees.

TURKEY

Arif Damar   1967

Che

A voice he was
Distinct among all others
Walk said that voice
War said that voice
Join said that voice.

The loudest voice is no stranger to the mountains
To the mountains belonged his voice

He had hands that flowed like rivers
Could not get used to stopping and caressing
His hands opened from flowers, from waters,
From leaves to pens, to guns
His hands fitted his voice

He would hide the joy of the city in his palms
He would hide a warmth
Reminiscent of the future sun

Hey Hey Hey
So many *Köroğlus* are gone
So many *Dadaloğlus* came down the mountain
So many rivers stopped so many stars slid
And to the ground, so many rifles fell.

The day will come, the day will come
Rain will stop in a village
Children will be happy in the sun
Guevara's road is open

Guevara's road is open
Who would know better than children
He will walk and walk and walk

If only he visited our home
But he has a road to take
If only all sounds and lights stopped

The day will come, the day will come
And it has a road to take.

Translated by Yusuf Eradam

Translator's note: Köroğlu was a rebel, a hero and bard of Anatolia (Asia Minor) Turkey, who stood up against the rule and cruelty of the governor of Bolu in the late 17th century. An Anatolian Robin Hood, he would ride a white horse, aiming to bring justice and poetry to people's lives. Legend says he beheaded the governor with his sword and replaced him. Dadaloğlu was another hero and bard. He lived in the Mediterranean Region of southern Turkey in the 19th century and his name is identified with the Taurus Mountains.

METIN DEMIRTAŞ   1967

Che Guevara

Che Guevara, we too have our mountains
Don't worry if they are still now, still like falcons,
They are weary, have seen wars, hosted partisans,
Yet, they are not traitors, if no rifle is fired,
Their guns lean against the pines and oaks
We too have our mountains Che Guevara.

Che Guevara, we too have our people here
Forsaken in the warm winds of distant fields
Committed to brotherhood with ballads
Like all the peoples of the world
And moving only in storms and thunder
We too have our people here Che Guevara.

Che Guevara, we too have our poets
They too have survived rooms of stone, rooms of no sun
Their hearts beating for peace and love
One half is steel anger, while the other is docile blue

They too have passed through iron gates upright
We too have our beautiful people Che Guevara.

Che Guevara, we too have our young men
Who have made their way out of poverty here
By feeding on only a few olives and bread at universities
Young men hit by girls like sirens, then by alcohol
Wandering along the streets in anger
And who rebel when they realize the truth.

For Vietnam is our Vietnam
Congo is our Congo
Once the sap runs in the branches
Darkness blows up with pains in deep
To reach that beautiful tomorrow
Che Guevara, we too have our mountains.

*Translated by Yusuf Eradam**

*After the authorised revision by the poet

Sennur Sezer   2003

Che was a doctor

Did you see him looking at children
Did you see the joy in his eyes
The passion
How he looks, the cure in his eyes…
Did you see him looking at children
Why he did not stay in Cuba, do you know why he didn't
Ahead, children were dying
Children were hungry. Children.
Just children.
Hope and anger in his eyes he drove his motorbike and his life
to craggy heights.
On his way, children were waiting.
Medicine in his bag, sweets in his bag, and revolution in
his hands…
Then children…
Then children's smiles flipped to bleed on his chest.
He was a doctor…
Now, on top of the Andes children salute him.
He is always there: medicine and sugar in his bag, and
revolution in his hands.
He is always there with children's smiles bleeding on his chest.

Translated by Yusuf Eradam

UKRAINE

Dmitro Pavlichko   1972

Ernesto Che Guevara

I

Like smoke upon the earth Guevara fell,
In bushes of pain his shattered shoulder burst...
So quiet between his fingers blood-streams well,
Like golden clouds between the cliffs dispersed.

Above him, like a ghost, his murderer looms,
And fires point-blank, yet once, and twice, and thrice...
"Well, isn't that enough?" Che at him booms,
And ridicule sparkles in his dark brown eyes.

So take good care, you butchers, all the same.
Because he'll rise from the grave to punish your souls,
And your foulness wipe away with flame.

And see, in oil-cloth now they wrap him fast,
And carry him secretly to the jail, like moles,
And there behind the bars his corpse they cast.

II

Well, burn him then, or give him to the ants,
Or wall him up, in concrete pack him tight,
Or hide him in an atomic bunker, gents,
That dust, as dangerous as dynamite.

Their spite so roared, their fears so furious ran,
That so dead Che should not reach for his gun,
They took an axe, and hacked off both his hands,
Scorched brown by many years of wind and sun.

But, like some fabulous blood-stained bird,
Those hands then came to life, and trembling stirred,
And flew out of the prison cell afar,

And new victorious troops they called and led,
And as a five-pointed early morning star,
They blaze on in American skies overhead!

Translated by Walter May

UNITED KINGDOM (ENGLAND)

ALAN C. BROWN   2005

Patria o muerte — Venceremos

"Wherever death may surprise us, it is welcome,
provided our battle cry reach some receptive ear"   Che Guevara

No one is fated to love; but accidents happen.
Your profile, a Gethsemane confronts us all now
Like great love — a car crash in our lives
That changes us, deflects us from base motives,
To sacrifice self, to a higher cause, for others.

And you took this direction — Revolution,
With toe-hold tenacity, slashed with blood;
A white full moon, distinct as a bare skull;
A mouth, speaking out still like sparks from fired wood;
Light between trees — cold water — the taste of iron.

The gashed bat-black wing of your sparse beard
Confronts us like a hurricane; you're still alive
In words you left. *Hells Creek* where you tended the wounded,
Hungered, thirsted, sweated with those of your kind;
With courageous men and women — diamond-hard.

One man can make a difference; many with equal
Love as yours — a new horizon. Machetes against
Machine-guns, enough if a handful dare to act
As one, outnumbered by better armed opponents,
Who lacked your passion for a just cause.

Theology? Did you have one? Yes, liberation!
Memory, a way for reviving all those who died.
"Take my heart and hold it up to the sun" you cried,
Alongside those of hedge priests and *guajiros* who died.
No one's destined to love — but accidents happen!

KEVIN CADWALLENDER   2001

Chez Guevara

slumped in front of the tv
riddled with bulletins
from the latest armed coup.
Wondering if that razor blade
in the bathroom is sharp enough
for one last close shave.

khaki underwear drying,
faded camouflage for
the play station photo shoot.
a walk on role in Evita
in the west end and then
a poster in the Athena
end of season sale.

feeling less than legendary.
eyes full of bluebottle larvae.

Someone, somewhere
has disconnected the
revolution.

IAN CAWS   1972

The View from Two Murders: Ernesto Che Guevara

Ernesto Che Guevara. Physician, Scholar and Cuban Revolutionary.
Killed by an unknown hand; Bolivia, 1967

Given faith, a cold brain, warm blood,
We can slice the tops off egg-like tyrannies;
Given love, we may understand.

But love is a coat which restricts movement,
The saboteur waiting in a back room,
And order alone defines the ascetic,

Tearing up the poet's manuscript,
Ruling off the academic page.

From my holster comes a belief in metal
Which history dictated
And which the centuries will bend
        in a fairground act of strength.
We confine ourselves to the hour,
Demanding roots for the banner
As it unfurls over our graves.

ALASDAIR CLAYRE   1968

Ballad

Where the dry river runs
the soldiers took their time;
he could not breathe or climb
when they ringed him in their guns

Two soldiers scrubbed
the school where he was shot
for farmers who could not
read might read in blood:

And those who live by the word will die by the sword
and their bodies will be burned either alive or dead
like a new book that must not be read
by people who should never have been taught to read
because the word of law and order is the only book they need.

Mother mother see your son
what do his wounds say
Only he should not have gone
not have gone to play

Out beyond the streets we know
out beyond the town
till the bullets that he sowed
grew up in a thousand guns to cut him down

He could have lived by the word and shunned the sword
and his body would have been cherished alive or dead
He could have written books that would have been read and read
by later children who'd have learned to read
because time to grow is all a child and all a world need

But where could he find rest?
Writing in the east
hunted by the police
tortured till he confessed

Where those who live by the word are tried by the sword
and their bodies are buried either alive or dead
like a new book that must not be read
by a people who oughtn't to be free to read
because the word of law and order is the only book they need

Or here in the easy west,
where he could live at least
writing books in peace
well fed and well dressed

Where those who live by the word are afraid of the word
and their bodies are constricted alive or dead
by a dread they won't be read or won't be fit to be read

Out beyond the streets...

And yet the dead man still
is with his wounds alive
will with his wounds survive
the dictator's will
and the rich man's mind
who when he will not give
to let the poor man live
turns and sees behind
a man with a broken knife

a man not pure or good
a slaughtered man, whose blood
pays for the rich man's life
pays for the rich man's life.

DON COLLIS   1968

Fleet through the forest trees

Fleet through the forest trees
ran Che Guevara
moccassined were his feet
round his cigar a
beard curled in devil's horns
brushed by the clutching thorns
soundless he rushed, a breeze
shaking the mighty seat
of McNamara

Camped in the mountain's heart
with his guerrillas
bold Che Guevara sat
in his stone pillars
taunting the Government
mocking the conscripts sent
to tear his world apart
Somewhere a rifle spat
Che faced his killers

Men from the CIA
knives in their garter
fell on the hero band
Dreaming of Sparta
loosed off a fusillade
Swift through the Everglade
in brown Bolivian clay
Cuba's bright star, outmanned,
died like a martyr

CHRISTOPHER LOGUE   1968

Haiku for Che

December. Late birds shake their wings.
On the snowy windscreen of a car, I write
CHE LIVES!

EDWARD LUCIE-SMITH   1968

The revolutionary

The revolutionary
Believed in revolution —
Even in art. What was real
Was too good for 'realism'. Burn
L'art pompier! Such a smell
As those waxworks flared, and their glass
Eyes dropped from the sockets and rolled
On the floor, gleefully winking.
Only what was alive would do.

Yet he died, and the photograph
His enemies took of him showed
A face that looked like wax. He lay
There on the rough boards — a dummy
Which even resemblance had left.

The thing is, one shouldn't accept
What one's enemies make of one.
They killed you, Che. But your mind lives,
And it speaks as plainly. No wax
For you, no frozen heroic
Poses. Merely a name which now,
When we speak it, honours mankind.

Ewan MacColl   1968

Compañeros

The good ship Granma lies at anchor in the harbour
Waiting for the evening tide to bring high water
It's bound for Cuba she must go across the Gulf of Mexico
And the Caribbean ocean
She's carrying a human cargo,
Eighty-three good compañeros
Each one burning with determination to be free

Against Batista, the Fidelistas
Courage was their only armour
As they fought at Fidel's side
With Che Guevara

Ten days out from Mexico these compañeros
Landed on the Cuban beach Los Colorados
Fidel said, this year will see our country and its people free
Or else we will be martyrs
We've only guns enough for twenty,
The enemy has arms a-plenty
Meet him then defeat him and he'll keep us well supplied

Against Batista, the Fidelistas
Courage was their only armour
As they fought at Fidel's side
With Che Guevara

Five weeks later in the Canyon Del Arroyo
The people's army numbered eighteen compañeros
Hungry, weak, but unafraid,
They're learning Revolution's trade
In the high Sierra Maestra
And in the mountains winds are blowing
Bearing seeds of hope and sowing
Crops in Cuban earth that mark the birth of victory

On compañeros, to El Uvero!
Courage was their only armour
As they fought at Fidel's side
With Che Guevara

They fought their way across the peak of El Turquino
Joined by peasant bands and men from Santiago
They faced Batista's tanks and planes
And drove them down into the plains
From the high Sierra Maestra
They drove the gangsters from Las Villas
Straight across the Cordilleras
Santa Clara fell to Che Guevara and was free

Against Batista, the Fidelistas
Courage was their only armour
As they fought at Fidel's side
With Che Guevara

The fire lit on that Cuban beach by Fidel Castro
Shines all the way to Tierra del Fuego
Its sparks are blown upon the breeze
And men rise up from off their knees
When they see the night is burning
It blazes up in Venezuela, Bolivia and Guatemala
Lights the road that men must go in order to be free

On compañeros, Americanos!
For a peoples' free America
Fidel has shown the way with Che Guevara

JOHN McGRATH   1968

An impersonal note to Che Guevara

I don't know what you were like.
I've looked at the photos,
read what Fidel had to say,
gone through your books, speeches.

I've got a feeling that if I'd met you,
I might have found you arrogant or mad.
So what I say about you is not personal,
nor do I want to be you, now or later.

I just want to say that my mind is richer for your thoughts,
my humanity prouder for your actions,
my life less acceptable for your death,
my death more acceptable for your life.

ADRIAN MITCHELL   1968

How to kill Cuba

You must burn the people first.
Then the grass and trees, then the stones.
You must cut the island out of all the maps,
The history books, out of the old newspapers,
Even the newspapers which hated Cuba,
And burn all these, and burn
The paintings, poems and photographs and films
And when you have burnt all these
You must bury the ashes
You must guard the grave
And even then
Cuba will only be dead like Che Guevara —
Technically dead, that's all,
Technically dead.

ANDREW SINCLAIR   1968

Put a bullet in his head

Put a bullet in his head
Fields are dumb   the earth is dead
Shoot the rebel from behind
Walls are deaf   the roof is blind
Burn his body   pound his flesh
Blood and water dry to ash
Cut his finger from his hand
Print it as his last command

      After Zapata
        Lumumba
      Nadie y nada

Put a bullet in his head
Fields are marching   earth is red
Shoot the rebel from behind
Walls have ears   the roof a mind
Burn his body   pound his flesh
Blood and water flood the ash
Cut his finger from his hand
Print it as his last command

      After Zapata
        Lumumba
        GUEVARA
      Viva la tierra

C‌LIFF W‌EDGBURY   1996

my love sold revolutionary newspapers

i once loved a girl
who sold revolutionary newspapers
in charing cross road

her red
nipple-tight t-shirt
sang the praises
of che guevara
as we linked arms
and marched with thousands
on grosvenor square

she was fearless when the stones flew
brave when the police charged
valiant among the legs of galloping horses

they fined me twenty pounds
for disturbing the peace
and the only peace I wished to disturb
was hers

'i'm going to cuba!' she said

but ended up in catford
with a bangladeshi bus conductor
and a tenth-floor balcony
full of nappies

my love
who sold revolutionary newspapers

TED WILLIS   1968

What can I say to you, Che Guevara?

What can I say to you, Che Guevara?
Only that I feel sorrow
Because I did not know you better.
And shame
Because I did so little to help.

> I am fifty years of age, Che Guevara,
> I will not bother to describe myself
> I am sure you get the picture.
> Even a super-silver stainless blade
> Cannot shave away
> The grey hostages I have given
> To expediency.
> The comfortable compromising
> And the flatulent phrases.
> Such as
> 'The need to be patient'
> And 'to exercise restraint'
> The suggestion that Socialism
> 'Is, perhaps, an old-fashioned notion,
> Rendered obsolete by modern technology'
> Or that
> 'Freedom, after all,
> Is a relative concept'
> Above all,
> That 'the hero has no place
> In Literature.
> Or in Life, for that matter'

You were a real and actual man, Che Guevara
In your dying
There was no myth
No trick to fool the simple.
Your body did not arise on the Third Day.

In practical terms
You are quite dead.

> But you have proved to me, Che Guevara
> That all the vinegar years
> Have not entirely soured the wine of youth.
> Freedom,
> Is still more than just a word to me.

What do you mean to me, Che Guevara?
Of course, you were a hero.
But I think of you as a friend
As a good comrade
Who is still with us.

Of course, your name will be honoured.
My children and their children
Shall say it as easily
As if it were their own.
But more important than all this
I shall try
A little harder
Because of you
To climb the forbidding and inhospitable mountain.

SCOTLAND

<small>ALEXANDER SCOTT</small>   1972

Hero

As lang as Ché Guevara lives
   in harns o hauflin laddies,
there's aye a stallion, willsome, wud,
   in herds o couthie cuddies.

Editors' note: This is written in Scots, and the following words can be found in the glossary of *Scott's Collected Poems* (Mercat Press, 1994):

harns	*brains*
hauflin	*adolescent*
wud	*mad*
couthie	*pleasant*
cuddies	*donkey or domestic horse*

WALES

John Greeves   2005

The Date

He's spent a long time preparing for his date.
Wants to impress her with *Motor Cycle Diaries*,
a Brazilian film with English subtitles.

Knows nothing about Che Guevara,
revolutionary fervour, C.I.A., life in the fifties,
because he wasn't born then.

He's of another generation, trailing his feet in circles,
trying to remember what she said last week.
Digging hands into pockets, hoping she'll arrive soon.

Tried picturing her face,
tugged at battered jeans for reassurance.
Allowed languid laces to lick the floor.

He's sat on concrete bollards, walked back and forth, kicked at air,
contorted his face like a sponge, wrung out droplets of despair,
saw girls pass by.

Lent against a pillar, crouched in uncertainty,
glanced into cabs and buses,
never doubting her, when she arrived forty-two minutes late.

UNITED STATES OF AMERICA

LYMAN ANDREWS   1968

To the memory of Che

beneath the white map
or chaos
of the stars
the moon floats

he stands barefoot
on the cracked
warm earth
nightbirds shriek

swoop
his mineral sweat
make luminous
his fear

he waits to kill
a tank
with an old gun
that his father

killed rabbits with
and a broken-
bladed knife
but no tank appears

so at dawn he turns
to go and two
soldiers
shoot him twice

walk away
not talking

buttoning
their pistol holsters

and when the sun
makes salt
from his sweat
and he lies dying

in the flat field
nursing his
torn belly
he tries to say

JUDY COLLINS   1973

Che

One morning in Bolivia
The leader of the partisans and two of his companions
Were forced to flee the mountains for their lives
Through green and dusty villages they sped along the little roads
The peasants smiled and shouted as they hurried by
Jesus called out to every one "Don't think that we are leaving,
They only tried to frighten us with guns, we shall return,"
Continue with your work, continue with your talk
You have it in your hand to own your life to own your land
The people smiled and shouted and they ran along a little while
The stood and watched, their hands were restless and empty
The body of Jesus was in the jeep that they blew up
Before it reached the plane

The priest was proud to bless him for what there was
of him remaining in the afternoon

Continue with your work, continue with your talk
You have it in your hands to own your life to own your land

There is no one who can show you the road you should be on
They only tell you they can show you and then tomorrow

> they are gone

The smell of oil and incense fill the room in this adobe hut
Where on the table lies the body of a man
His face is pale and young, his beard is dark and curled
Pennies hold his eyelids from the evening light
People from the village those who knew him, those who killed him
Stand inside the door, their hands are restless and empty
They watch the priest make silent crosses in the air
And pray to God inside their hearts for their own souls

Continue with your work, continue with your talk
You have it in your hands to own your life to own your land
There is no one who can show you the road you should be on
They only tell you they can show you and then tomorrow

> they are gone

LAWRENCE FERLINGHETTI 1968

The Mind of Ché Guevara a Day After His Death

AH ACA LA VIDA GONDOLA PUERTA
ESCONDIDA REVOLUTIONARIA ACA PALMITO
ACA CHOCLOS ZAPALLOS YUCAS ACA CHACO
HAMBRE EL ELEVADOR ESCONDIDO AYMARAS
Y CAMBAS ACA ARMADILLO PERDIDO NO
REVOLUCIONARIO ACA TAPERAS PALMITOS
DE COROJO PERDIDAS TRANSPORTES DE
ANIMALES FORRAJES Y SEMILLAS ADONDE
ADONDE ESTAN   ADONDE ESTAN
GUARIJOS   ADONDE ADONDE ESTAN
ADONDE ALEIDA   ERNESTITO   CELIA
TANIA HILDA CELIA   CHICOS Y CHICAS
HERMANOS   ADONDE   EN ESTE CHILCHEO
NADA   NADA   NADA QUE CHANCHOS

TATUS   NADA QUE NADA   CHILCHEO EN
CHUCHIAL Y DONDE DONDE ESTA DONDE
PACHUNGA Y DONDE ESTA BIGOTES Y DONDE
ESTA PAPI Y DONDE ESTANISLAO   NEGRO
ANTONIO JOAQUIN   APOLINAR
RICARDO CHINCHU   JORGE EL LORO
PACHO PACO PACHUNGO   OLO VILO POLO
MORO   MOROGORO   MUNGA
MUGANGA Y EL MEDICO FELIX EL RUBIO
IVAN RENAN Y PEDRO   PAN DIVINO
MAURICIO PAN DIVINO   EL PELAO
CARLOS LUIS CHAPACO   CAMPANEROS
CAMPANEROS   GONDOLO
REVOLUCIONARIO   TATU Y TANIA
Y CELIA   Y ALEIDA   Y ALEIDA
ERNESTITO NADA QUE CHOCLO
HUMINTA BAGRE SED Y HAMBRE   JOCO
CHARQUI   ADONDE   ADONDE
GUARIJOS   ZAPALLOS YUCAS HOCHIS
CARACORES   CARACORES
CARACORES ANTAS   CAMBAS
GUERILLAS   YANQUIS
NADA QUE   BOROS   CHANCOS   Y
CHINCHAS   Y PULGAS   CHINGA MI
MADRE   CHINGA   QUE   QUE
PASA QUE PASA SENOR   QUE
ES   QUE   PASA AQUI
TIENEN SED HAMBRE   ADONDE
ADONDE   CACARES CACARES   CARAJO
NINGUN CACARES AHORA AQUI
AQUI AHORA ADONDE   NO CHANKAKA   NO
CACA NO CARACORE CHINGA
HAMBRE ADONDE CACARES   NADA AQUI
NO SENTINAL RADIO BEMBA ABAJO EN
BARRANCO PIERDAS NO REVOLUCIONARIOS
PERO   PERO   ESTAN   ADONDE   MIS
ABARCAS   ADONDE MIS BOTAS   SI

272

MIS BOTAS   EN ELEVADOR SIEMPRE   ACA
ALLA   ALLI   VAMOS PA'LANTE
GRITA CACARE   MIS ABARCAS
          LLEVALAS

                    PA'LANTE
                              SIEMPRE

MIS BOTAS
                    LLEVALAS
                              SIEMPRE
                    AL TERRITORIO LIBRE

          AL TERRITORIO LIBRE

                              AQUI
                                   ACA

          PA'LANTE
                         Y

                         Y

               GRITA
                    GRITA
                         CACARE

ALLEN GINSBERG   1967

Elegy Ché Guévara

European Trib. boy's face photo'd eyes opened,
        young feminine beardless radiant kid
                lain back smiling looking upward
Calm as if ladies' lips were kissing invisible parts of the body
Aged reposeful angelic boy corpse,
            perceptive Argentine Doctor, petulant Cuba Major
                    pipe mouth'd & faithfully keeping Diary
                        in mosquitos Amazonas
Sleep on a hill, dull Havana Throne renounced
More sexy your neck than sad aging necks of Johnson
                            DeGaulle, Kosygin,
        or the bullet pierced neck of John Kennedy
Eyes more intelligent glanced up to death newspapers
        Than worried living Congress Cameras passing
                dot screens into T.V. shade, glass-eyed
                MacNamara, Dulles in old life …

Women in bowler hats sitting in mud outskirts 11,000 feet
                                    up in Heaven
                with a headache in LaPaz
            selling black potatoes brought down from earth
                                    roof'd huts
                    on mountain-lipped Puno
        would've adored your desire and kissed your Visage
                        new Christ
They'll raise up a red-bulb-eyed war-mask's
            white tusks to scare soldier-ghosts
                who shot thru your lungs

Incredible! one boy turned aside from operating room
        or healing Pampas yellow eye
    To face the stock rooms of ALCOA, Myriad Murderous
                    Board Directors of United Fruit
Smog-Manufacturing Trustees of Chicago U

274

Lawyer Phantoms ranged back to dead
John Foster Dulles' Sullivan & Cromwell Lawfirm
Acheson's mustache, Truman's bony hat
To go mad and hide in jungle on mule & point rifle at OAS
at Rusk's egoic Courtesies, the metal deployments of
Pentagon
derring-do Admen and dumbed intellectuals
from *Time* to the CIA
One boy against the Stock Market all Wall Street ascream
since Norris wrote *The Pit*
afraid of free dollars showering from the Observer's
Balcony
scattered by laughing younger brothers,
Against the Tin Company, against Wire Services,
against infra-red sensor Telepath Capitalism's
money-crazed scientists
against College boy millions watching Wichita Family
Den T.V.

One radiant face driven mad with a rifle
Confronting the electric networks.

November 1967, Venice, Italy

John Haines   1968

Guevara

Somewhere inside me,
perhaps under my left shoulder,
there is a country named
Guevara.

I discovered it one day
in October,
when I fell into a cave
which suddenly opened
in my chest.

I found myself climbing
a hill, steep
and slippery with blood.
The ghost of a newspaper
floated before me
like an ashen kite.

I was a long way from the top
when I halted;
I felt something wrong
with my life, like a man
who has marched for years
under an enemy flag.

I came down from that hill
bearing a secret wound;

though a fever beats there,
I still don't know
what I suffered —
a truce with my own darkness,
or some obscure defeat
on the red slope of my heart.

GREG HEWETT   2006

Extract from **The Eros Conspiracy**

I was the jealous one
watching Che in fatigues as he sucked
on Fidel's cigar that was not
just a cigar but a tool
for revolution. He sucked without regard
for the asthma that haunted him
like a specter. He was
far too impatient to finish his smoke,
wanted to finish the revolution
before it started, a move
Marx would have denounced
the way he denounced the Communards
and their runaway mascot Rimbaud
for their utter lack of theory and discipline.
Before he was Che he went off
on a motorcycle a little too Euro for Brando.
With the sleeve of his Parisian suit
he wiped the fine coat of chartreuse
piñon pollen from the chrome.
He was going up, up, up
the chiaroscuro coast of Argentina,
swatting at iridescent butterflies
with *A Season in Hell* because
their beauty rivaled the true
revolution he was learning
to breathe easily without inhaler.
He never thought he would soon be condemned
as the unpragmatic ideal beauty
of revolution and confined
to the wall of your musky bedroom
of arrested development
or mine, a militant pinup
for global fantasies in the dark.

PATRICK HYLAND (RAVING MADCAP)   2006

Revolution Merchandise

The Broken Star

That Adorns the Che Guevara's Beret
Is broken
because
He is a commercial

Ideals of Revolution
are a joke
when your picture
may as well be
on a fucking cereal box

But

We would all eat Guevara-o's
and it would be a well balanced breakfast

Revolution of the past
is the butt of jokes
on prime-time television

(so it goes.)

The Che
is not dead
if his picture
is not alive

on merchandise

The paraphernalia of truth!
The cheap gift-shop plastic of despotic reign!

The Che is:
Hero
Villain

The lava lamp is a vehicle for a revolutionary cause

The Ouiji board is Cuba

The Che is the explosion.

MAGGIE JAFFE   1992

Death of Che

On the day that Che
Guevara died,
a woman, thirtyish,
from the wealthy
"first circle" of La Paz
exploded her heart with a snub-
nosed .38. Radios played
Morir por Amor / to die for love.
Even his executioner, Barrientos,
that shit, felt a "great loss" at his dying.
Che was betrayed by the CIA
and by the Bolivian workers
he meant to aid, wanted to love.
Che said, "I can't sleep
on a mattress while my soldiers
are shivering up there."
And he divided men into two groups:
those who can sleep
on a mattress while others suffer,
and those who cannot.

LA LOCA   1989

Why I choose black men for my lovers

Acid today
is trendy entertainment
but in 1967
Eating it was eucharistic
            and made us fully visionary

My girlfriend and I used to get cranked up
            and we'd land in
            The Haight
            and oh yeah
            The Black Guys Knew Who We Were
            But the white boys
            were stupid

I started out in San Fernando
            My unmarried mother did not abort me
            because Tijuana was unaffordable
            They stuffed me in a crib of invisibility
            I was bottle-fed germicides and aspirin
            My nannies were cathode tubes
            I reached adolescence, anyway
            Thanks to Bandini and sprinklers

In 1967 I stepped through a windowpane
            and got real
            I saw Mother Earth and Big Brother
            and
            I clipped my roots which choked in the
                    concrete
                    of Sunset Boulevard
            to go with my girlfriend
            from Berkeley to San Francisco
            hitchhiking
            and we discovered

that Spades were groovy
and
White boys were mass-produced and
watered their lawns
 artificially with long green hoses in
 West L.A.

There I was, in Avalon Ballroom
 in vintage pink satin, buckskin and
 patchouli,
 pioneering the sexual
 revolution
I used to be the satyr's moll, half-woman,
and the pink satin hung
 loose about me
 like an intention
I ate lysergic for breakfast, lunch and
 dinner
 I was a dead-end in the off-limits of
 The Establishment
 and morality was open to interpretation

In my neighbourhood, if you fucked around, you were a whore

But I was an émigrée, now
 I watched the planeloads of white boys fly
 up from Hamilton High
 They were the vanguard
 of the Revolution
 They stepped off the plane
 in threadbare work shirts
 with rolled-up sleeves
 and a Shell Oil, a Bankamericard,
 a Mastercharge in their back pocket
 with their father's name on it
 Planeloads of Revolutionaries
 For matins, they quoted Marcuse and Huey Newton

For vespers, they instructed young girls from
    San Fernando to
    Fuck Everybody
To not comply, was fascist
I watched the planeloads of white boys
    fly up from Hamilton High

All the boys from my high school were shipped to
    Vietnam
And I was in Berkeley, screwing little white boys
    who were remonstrating for peace
    In bed, the pusillanimous hands of war protestors
        taught me Marxist philosophy:
    Our neighbourhoods are a life sentence
    This was their balling stage and they
        were politicians
    I was an apparition with orifices
    I knew they were insurance salesmen in their
        hearts
    And they would all die of attacks
    I went down on them anyway, because I had
        consciousness
    Verified by my intake of acid
    I was no peasant!
    I went down on little white boys and
    they filled my head with
        Communism
    They informed me that poor people didn't have
        money and were oppressed
    Some people were Black and Chicano
    Some women even had illegitimate children
    Meanwhile, my thighs were bloodthirsty
        whelps
    and could never get enough of anything
and those little communists were stingy
I was seventeen
    and wanted to see the world

My flowering was chemical
I cut my teeth on promiscuity and medicine
I stepped through more windowpanes
      and it really got oracular
In 1968
One night
The shaman laid some holy shit on me and wow
I knew
in 1985
      The world would still be white, germicidally
          white
      That the ethos of affluence
      was an indelible
      white boy trait
      like blue eyes
      That Volkswagons would be traded in for
          Ferraris
          and would be driven with the same
          snotty pluck that sniveled around
          the doors of Fillmore, looking cool
I knew those guys, I knew them when they had posters of
      Che Guevara over their bed
      They all had posters of Che Guevara over
          their bed
      And I looked into Che's black eyes all
          night while I lay in those beds,
          ignored
Now these guys have names on doors on the 18th floor of
      towers in Encino
      They have ex-wives and dope connections.
Even my girlfriend married a condo-owner in Van Nuys.

In proper white Marxist theoretician nomenclature, I was
      a tramp.
The rich girls were called "liberated."

I was a female from San Fernando

and the San Francisco Black Men and I
had a lot in common
Eyes, for example
dilated
with the opacity of "fuck you"
I saw them and they saw me
We didn't need an opthalmologist to get it on
We laid each other on a foundation of
       visibility
and our fuck
was no hypothesis

Now that I was worldly
     I wanted to correct
     the nervous blue eyes who flew up from
     Brentwood
to see Hendrix
but
when I stared into them
They always lost focus
and got lighter and lighter
and
No wonder Malcolm called them Devils.

ROBERT LOWELL   1969

Che Guevara (from October and November)

Week of Che Guevara, hunted, hurt,
held prisoner one lost day, then gangstered down
for gold, for justice — violence cracking on violence,
rock on rock, the corpse of the last armed prophet
laid out on a sink in a shed, displayed by flashlight —
as the leaves light up, still green, this afternoon,
and burn to frittered reds; as the oak, branch-lopped
to go on living, swells with goiters like a fruit-tree,
as the sides of the high white stone buildings over-
shadow the poor, too new for the new world,
Manhattan, where our clasped, illicit hands
pulse, stop the bloodstream as if it hit rock. . . .
Rest for the outlaw . . . kings once hid in oaks,
with prices on their heads, and watched for game.

MICHAEL MCCLURE   1988

Berkeley Song

POWER — GLORY — SCANDAL — MOVIES
— T.V. — SEX —
that is all the SOCIAL WHIRLING
that is the thrilling box that uses up
OUR HEADS
but I hug you in peyote-colored morning
where Master Mozart is singing doves
and robins back to sleep.
This touching of our hands and feet
is the velvet curtain that we keep
AS
WE
DIVE INTO THE DAY
TO FLARE LIKE STARS

making daily layers
interspersed with dreams.
WHERE THE GRIEF OF EVERY BEGGAR
hurts me in my seams.
I'm getting threadbare in my spirit.

WHAT DOES THIS MEAN?

I'll get myself an uzi and blast bursts at this machine.

WHY ARE ALL THESE PEOPLE STARVING?

Come back, Che Guevara, we didn't mean to kill you!
We were parading in the streets.
There was even tear gas and we weren't hiding
in the silken sheets.

I hug my lover in peyote-colored morning
where Master Mozart is singing doves
and robins back to sleep.

THOMAS MERTON   1968

Letters to Che: Canto bilingüe

Te escribo cartas, Che,
En la sazón de lluvias
Envenenadas

They came without faces
Found you with eyeless rays
The tin grasshoppers
With five-cornered magic
Wanting to feed you
To the man-eating computer

Te escribo cartas, Guerrero,
Vestido de hojas y lunas

But you won and became
The rarest jungle tree
A lost leopard
Out of metal's way

Te escribo cartas
Hermano invisible
Gato de la noche lejana

Cat of far nights
Whisper of a Bolivian kettle
Cry
Of an Inca hill

Te escribo cartas, Niño
De la musica callada.

ANNE DELANA REEVES   1997

The Hands of Che Guevara

The crowds huddle close like harnessed cattle
to see the small black hole above his heart.
A nun receives the Host. The hard white scar
dissolves on her tongue. She recalls how gentle
his eyes were, how the balm embraced the air
when she smoothed his hair and cleaned his feet.
Do you come to anoint me, Magdalene,
here against the day of my burying?
Soon the Generals will cut off the hands,
burn the body because they're afraid.
Kneeling, she kissed his fingers. Warm bands
of gunpowder lashed cupped palms. The taste —
metallic — stained her lips and throat like love.
From his hands water flowed. She couldn't drink enough.

DANIEL SCHECHTER   1968

Was his death in vain?

Was his death in vain?
The inevitable outcome for a romantic
adventurer whose vision substituted
the impatient clatter of machine gun
bullets for the inevitable unfolding
of the dialectic?

Did he have a chance?

A writer reminds us:

Fidel,
Back in December, 1956, you landed near Niquero
in the Oriente of Cuba with 82 men and a few arms.
Your plan was to ignite an insurrection which would
rid Cuba of Batista in a few *weeks*. Instead, you
were to wander through fields and forests in the
dark, without real food or water, living on sugar
cane for five days and five nights.
In the depth of this disaster, you were to
announce to the few men still with you: 'The days
of the dictatorship are numbered.'

'This man is crazy', one of them admits he said
to himself.

That man could have been Che.
This is why we will go on.

PEGGY SEEGER   1968

Che Guevara

The hunt is over, the hounds are weary,
The hunter's home and laid him down;
Wild and free was Che Guevara
Till, torn and spent, they brought him to the ground.

Stars are lost in the fields of darkness,
Hunter's moon stalks the empty night;
Like a farmer walks Che Guevara,
Bearing suns to sow the world with light.

The way is dark and beset with danger,
The road may end in a prison cell;
A guiding hand is Che Guevara,
To lead us past the place at which he fell.

Brave ones show the way, and brave ones follow,
The earth bears heroes when a hero dies;
A hero's hero is Che Guevara,
Meeting death with morning in his eyes.

In jungle earth the hunters laid him,
No stone to mark a lonely grave;
Then, farewell, Comrade Che Guevara,
We will clear the trail that you have blazed.

BRUCE STEPHENS   1968

Tune for Che

Che, your comrades will create
A hymn from you of love and hate

Your body is their instrument
Of faith and courage and dissent

Keys have been made from all your bones
To play the scale of human groans

Your skin is stretched to make a drum
That plays the beat of fights to come

From your throat they've made a flute
That pleads for those who are still mute

From your lips a whistle calls
Every time a just man falls
Your heart's a bell that rings each time
An unjust man commits a crime

A guitar from your rib-cage
Plays the sorrow of our age

Your sinews have become the strings
That weep each time the guitar sings

Each of your words is now a song
Which has the power to right a wrong

Each deed a note, each note a word
Each word a song that can be heard

And the foe learns to his cost
That nothing of you has been lost

Do you see, Che, what love can do
For those you loved who now love you?

URUGUAY

Mario Benedetti   1967

In Grief and Rage

> *On we go,*
> *undeterred by affronts*
> Ernesto "Che" Guevara

So here we are
filled with grief
and rage
even if your death is
one more predictable absurd

I feel guilty looking around at
these paintings
my armchairs
my rugs
grabbing a bottle from the refrigerator
typing the three global letters of your name
on my hard metal typewriter
(its ribbon has never
ever been
so pale)

it seems wrong to feel a chill
huddle by the hearth as usual
get hungry and eat
do something that simple
turn on the phonograph and listen in silence
especially if it's a Mozart quartet

I feel guilty having all this comfort
guilty about my asthma too
as I picture you falling comandante

gunned down
larger than life
vivid
pure

you are our bullet-riddled conscience

they're saying they set you afire
what flames
could burn the good
good news
that edgy tenderness
you carried around
with your cough
and the mud on your boots

they're saying they reduced you to ashes
with all your ideals
except for one finger

but that's enough to point the way
denounce the beast and its fiery cohorts
pull those triggers again

so here we are
full of grief
and rage
of course in time this heavy grief
will give way
leaving only our rage
sharpened
cleansed

you're dead now
alive now
falling
you're cloud now
rain now
star

wherever you are
if you are somewhere
or just arriving

take a moment at last
to breathe easy
to fill your lungs with sky

wherever you are
if you are somewhere
or just arriving
it's a pity there will be no God

but there will be others
there are sure to be others
worthy to welcome you
comandante

Montevideo, October 1967

Translated by Louise B. Popkin

ANÍBAL SAMPAYO   C.1970

Unto victory

I am Ramón
the one who breaks the chains.
Chisel, the solar
faith that lights the bonfires.
Fundamental clamour
the voice of justice
the one who turns the soft breeze
into a hurricane.
I am Ramón
the one who will never die.

May the oppressive despot tremble
that insatiable vulture of evil.
Behind death I am Ramón
unto the final victory.

I am Ramón,
the one light of the oppressed.
The flesh, blood and skin
of the redeemed man.
I am the lion that roams
across the mountain,
through hills and ravines
roaring freedom.
I am Ramón,
the one who lives beyond.

May the oppressive despot tremble...

Note: Ramón was Che's nom de guerre in Bolivia.

Translated by Georgina Jiménez

VENEZUELA

PABLO MORA   2000

Ernesto "Che" Guevara

To know that it is strictly forbidden to cry over the living and even less over the dead.

To embrace us to Peace from the barricades of war. To render unto the Comandante his mountain, his hills, his mortars; his solitude, his ruin, his maps, his trenches, his secrets; his hiding place, his hands and portents; to brandish the guns once again.

To give him his rucksack, his shotgun, his carbine, his beret, his beard, his star, his flag or fury; his revolver, his shirt, his jacket and documents.

His boots, his pistol, his pain, his tenderness, his smile, his anguish and moods; his battle-cry, his rifle and mortars; his strength, his focus, his asthma, his throat and his kerchief.

His kitbag, his memory, his pathways; his nobility, his magic and luck and empathy and poetry and longing; the time he has remaining for a New Era.

Translated by Gavin O'Toole

VIETNAM

Cu Huy Can   1968

Che Guevara

Che Guevara,
many people asked you:
Where is your real home?
And you replied:
My home is where I can fight the revolution.

Your home is where people suffer,
and you can join in their struggle.
Oh, Che, your home is America,
and the footprints you leave on your way to battle
trace the frontiers of your country.
For guerrillas on the march, all day all night,
outline the map of their true nationality.

There, wherever humanity cries out
and its anger catches fire,
and it strikes out at the enemy,
there is your home.
It's true, Che, that you were born
in one specific point in space;
but your heart made you a citizen
of all the horizons of life.

And Cuba, what about Cuba?
Cuba is the home of my heart.
Yet for the sake of the revolution
I gave up my duties, my home and my house.
I even gave up my nationality,
to set off again, taking only the uniform
I had worn in bygone days.
But Cuba will always be mingled

with all of me, each drop of blood;
so how can I really part from Cuba?
Oh, Fidel, Cuba is home!

And Vietnam, what about Vietnam?
Vietnam is a land I never went to,
and yet I have been there. With its selflessness and its sacrifice,
my heart is there in the line of fire.
And what the world needs is at least two or three
or more Vietnams. You once said this,
and *meant* it...
As you blew on the coals of the revolution,
until they grew red and glowed.

And now, Che Guevara,
You have fallen on that path of fire and blood;
while you were forging real homes for people,
you were struck down on the road you had chosen.
And as you fell your long arms stretched out to the whole
of America.
There are millions left to love you,
and hearts everywhere to remember you,
all those who love the people and the truth you loved.
Some names fill us with pride in humanity.
Some fighters can go on giving strength when they have fallen;
which is why you, Oh, Che, are with us right now in the battle-line.

Translated by Marianne Alexandre

ZIMBABWE

COSMAS MAIROSI   2006

Bayete Latin Warrior!

I was born a warrior
I was born a revolutionary leader
I was born an anti-capitalist
I was born a Marxist
I was born an architect of guerrilla warfare
I was born Ernesto Che Guevara de la Serna
I was born a hero!

I dedicated my life all to struggle
To free the oppressed and impoverished
Conquering the infidels with Fidel
Crucifying the colonialists in the Congo
Playing death games in the forests of Bolivia
Spreading the gospel of socialism in Afrika, America
                                        and the Caribbean
When I fell into the hands of my enemies
The capitalists could not forgive me
They could not let me live

Was it not a noble cause I fought for?
Let the story be told then
That Che was a true Latin warrior
In years to come let the children sing
'Bayete Guevara, the Argentinian gunslinger'

Note: Bayete is an Ndebele praise word equivalent to "Hail, o King!"

POET BIOGRAPHIES

Djamel Amrani (1935-2005) was a poet, writer and freedom fighter. On completing his secondary education in Algeria he joined the Armée de Libération Nationale (ALN), participated in the student strike of 19 May 1956 and, during the Battle of Algiers in 1957, was arrested, tortured and jailed. In reprisal, the colonial forces killed his father, brother and brother-in-law. It was the anthropologist Germaine Tillion who advised him to denounce his torture and his first work was entitled *Le Témoin* (*The Witness*) in 1960. Thereafter he published poetry and short stories and, after a stay in Cuba from 1962-64, was employed by the cabinet of president Houari Boumédienne and met Che Guevara. He helped to found the journals *Chaâb* and *Atlas* and produced literary broadcasts for Algerian television. In 2004 he was awarded the Pablo Neruda Medal and the Algerian Booksellers prize.

Bagdad S. Maata (1948-) was born in Oran, Algeria, and his childhood was traumatised by the arrest and torture of his father and teenage brother in the struggle against French colonialism. He dropped out of school for refusing to sing the Marseillaise. He subsequently taught himself medicine. He settled in Saida with his wife where he became active in human rights struggles. A pacifist, he eventually left Algeria amid the fratricidal violence and settled in France. He has been active in campaigns for immigrant and Muslim rights and writes as a poet and contributor for online journals such as caloucaera.net and oulala.net.

Jofre Rocha (Roberto António Víctor Francisco de Almeida, 1941-) was born in Cachimane, Angola, and after school joined the armed struggle against Portuguese colonialism. After independence in 1975 he held various ministerial posts and has been chairman of the country's National Assembly. He has published a number of anthologies of poetry.

Julio Cortázar (1914-84) was an influential writer and intellectual who published experimental novels, poems, plays and short stories. Born to Argentine parents in Belgium, he became a professor of French literature in Mendoza, Argentina, but in 1952, in opposition to the government of Juan Domingo Perón, he emigrated to France where he lived until his death. There he worked for Unesco as a translator and in his later years he became actively engaged with leftwing causes in Latin America as a supporter of the Cuban Revolution and the Sandinista government in Nicaragua.

Gabriel Fernández Capello (Vicentico) (1964-) is a singer and a core member of Los Fabulosos Cadillacs, a Latin rock band from Buenos Aires formed in 1985. He is responsible, along with bassist Flavio Cianciarulo for most of the group's songwriting and lyrics. The band released 15 albums, won several awards including the MTV Latino Video Music Award 1994 and the 1998 Grammy for Best Latin Rock/Alternative Album, and collaborated with major international rock stars. Since 2002 Vicentico has been releasing songs as a solo artist, although the band occasionally gets together to tour.

Juan Gelman (1930-) is considered to be Argentina's most important living poet. The son of Russian-Jewish immigrants, as a young man he was active in literary groups and became a journalist. He knew Che Guevara and was a leftwing political activist until 1975 when he was forced into exile because of his opposition to Argentina's brutal military dictatorship. In 1976 his son Marcelo and his pregnant daughter-in-law María

Claudia, both aged 20, were "disappeared" by the regime and executed. Gelman lived in Europe until 1988 then returned to Argentina and worked for the newspaper *Pagina 12*. In 2000 he was able to find his granddaughter, who had been born before his daughter-in-law's murder and given to a pro-government family, in Uruguay. He has published more than 20 collections since 1956 and in 1997 was awarded Argentina's National Poetry Prize in recognition of his work. He now lives in Mexico.

Leopoldo Marechal (1900-70) was an Argentine poet, novelist, playwright, critic and educator. He published extensively and was known for his philosophically oriented work, which has influenced many contemporary Argentine writers, cineastes, and intellectuals, and has been seen as a national and popular alternative to Jorge Luis Borges. He won a number of literary awards for his poetry and theatrical writing. In 1967 he was invited to Cuba by Julio Cortázar to join the jury for the Casa de las Américas literary awards.

S.K. Kelen (1956-) is an Australian poet whose work, which has a forceful political strain, has been widely published in his country and elsewhere. He has taught creative writing and poetry in several universities and was a Visiting Professor of Writing at the University of South Dakota and the Asialink Writer-in-residence in Vietnam. He has won a number of awards including the *Poetry Australia* Farmers' Poetry Prize for Australians under 18 in 1973, the ACT Chief Minister's Creative Arts Fellowship for 2000 and the 2001 Capital Arts Patrons Award. He has published a number of collections of poetry and his latest book is *Earthly Delights* (2006).

Josef Lesser (1941-) was born in Poland where his parents were members of the communist party, and the family migrated to Australia in 1948 when he was seven. He grew up in Sydney and worked in photography and, later, services for adults with disabilities. He started writing poetry in 2001 when he retired, and his work has since been published in various countries.

Duncan Richardson (1959-) migrated from Britain to Australia in 1970 and has lived mainly in Queensland. He taught in Botswana in 1987-88 and returned to work in Australia as a part-time teacher. He has worked for the Fellowship of Australian Writers and the Queensland Writers' Centre.

Richard Tipping (1949-) is a poet, writer, artist and film-maker. He studied at Flinders University and the University of Technology Sydney. He was the co-editor of *Mok* magazine from 1968-69, and co-founded the Friendly Street readings in 1975, editing the first anthology published in 1977. He is known as a poet through four published collections and his inclusion in major anthologies, and he is also know for his photography, sculptures and documentary films. He lives in New South Wales and lectures in communication at the University of Newcastle.

Kerry Tilbrook (née Upjohn) (1955-) studied English literature at the University of Sydney and completed a PhD in Management at Macquarie University. She has worked as a teacher, editor, community worker, adult educator, and manager in local government and universities. Her poetry has been published in a number of journals and anthologies and in 2004 her work was highly commended in the Bauhinia Literary Awards. She was a former member of the Varuna Writers' Centre and the Sydney University Poetry Society, and is now a member of NSW Writers' Centre and the Poets' Union Inc. She lectures in management at Charles Sturt University.

Frieda Groffy (1936-) has worked as a comic, journalist, theatre director, lecturer and poet. She has been an active member of peace, anti-fascist and anti-racist, anti-apartheid and feminist movements. She was a member of the International Honorary Committee that prepared celebrations to mark the 100th birthday of Pablo Neruda. She has been visiting South Africa for many years to work on writing and artistic projects.

Alfonso Gumucio Dagron (1950-) is a writer, cineaste and photographer who has travelled extensively. He is the son of Alfonso Gumucio Reyes, a leader of Bolivia's Movimiento Nacionalista Revolucionario (MNR), and his own work as a progressive journalist twice forced him into exile in Paris from 1972 to 1978 and later in Mexico from 1980 to 1984. He has worked for or been a consultant to a number of important international organisations such as Unicef, the FAO, UNDP and Unesco and applies his experience in the relationship between communication and development at the Communication for Social Change Consortium in the United States. He has directed documentary films and published extensively.

José Carlos Capinam (1941-) is a poet-lyricist whose work and ideas have inspired leading musicians and composers, particularly those associated with the Tropicalia movement that transformed popular music in Brazil, such as the singer-songwriter Gilberto Gil. As a young man in Salvador, he studied theatre and participated in the Centro Popular de Cultura until the 1964 coup forced him to move to São Paulo where he worked as a publicity agent. His work brought him into collaboration with figures such as Gil, Caetano Veloso and Torquato Neto. As well as poetry and songs, he has composed opera and served as culture secretary for the State of Bahia.

Gilberto Gil (1942-) is a singer, guitarist and songwriter, and Brazil's minister of culture. From early on in his career as a musician, his songs focused on political and social issues, and in 1969, Gil and his colleague Caetano Veloso were arrested by the Brazilian military regime for anti-government activities. On their release, they were exiled and settled in London where Gil played with groups such as Yes and Pink Floyd. In the 1970s, he toured the US and in 1980 introduced reggae to Brazil. In the early 1990s Gil sought elected office in his home town of Salvador and when Luiz Inácio Lula da Silva became president in January 2003 he was appointed culture minister.

Amadeu Thiago de Mello (1926-) is one of the most well-known Amazonian poets whose work has been widely published and translated. As a young man he studied medicine but abandoned his studies to become a poet, and his first collection was published in 1951. In the early 1960s he served as a Brazilian cultural attaché but, when the military seized power, was jailed. Subsequently he was exiled in Chile, where he met and befriended Pablo Neruda. He participated in exiled opposition groups and also spent time in Argentina, Portugal, France and Germany before returning to Brazil in 1978. His collection written from exile *Poesia Comprometida com a Minha e a Tua Vida (1975)* established him as an influential intellectual committed to the struggle for human rights. In 2006 he joined a number of other prominent Latin American poets and writers demanding independence for Puerto Rico.

Ferreira Gullar (José Ribamar Ferreira, 1930-) is a poet, dramatist, essayist, critic and journalist whose work has been widely published and translated. His first book of poetry was published in the 1940s and in 1959 he formed the "Neo-Concretes" group. In the early 1960s he was appointed director of the Fundação Cultural de Brasília and was elected president of the Centro Popular de Cultura (CPC) of the União Nacional dos Estudantes. He joined the Brazilian Communist Party (PCB) and in 1968 was jailed, eventually going into exile in Russia, Chile, Peru and Argentina. His work was smuggled back into Brazil but, on his return in 1977, and despite guarantees from the authorities, he was arrested and interrogated in Rio. He has launched a number of journals and won many prizes in Brazil and abroad. From 1992-95 he served as director of the Instituto Brasileiro de Arte e Cultura, and in 2002 he was proposed for the Nobel Prize for Literature by professors from universities in Brazil, Portugal and the US.

Martha Chaves is a Canadian comic from Montreal and a Nicaraguan poet from Canada. Born during the Sandinista revolution, she has lived and performed in Rome, Montreal, and in Toronto. She has appeared in numerous festivals and humanitarian fund-raising events and has entertained Canadian peacekeeping troops across the world. She has been nominated for the Canadian Comedy Award and the Latin American Achievement Award.

Alfred Purdy (1918-2000) was one of the most popular and important Canadian poets of the 20th century. Purdy studied at Albert College and Trenton Collegiate Institute in Ontario. He published extensively and his awards included the Order of Canada in 1982, the Order of Ontario in 1987, and the Governor General's Award twice in 1965 and 1986. He wrote the introduction to the last book of poetry by his friend Milton Acorn (see Joe Rosenblatt, below). Purdy was also a long-time friend of the American author Charles Bukowski, who once referred to him as a "tough son of a bitch".

Joe Rosenblatt (1933-) dropped out of trade school as a young adult and worked as a railway freight handler. He became interested in writing in the early 1960s through his association with the worker poet Milton Acorn and published his first book of poetry in 1966. He has since written more than 20 books of poetry and several autobiographical works, and he has won major prizes such as the Governor General's award in 1976 and the BC Book Prize in 1986. He has held writer-in-residence positions in Canadian and European universities, and was president of the League of Canadian Poets from 1983-85.

Víctor Jara (1932-73) was a Chilean poet, folk singer, educator and political activist whose songs inspired by traditional folk music and his own left-wing political activism became a symbol of struggle against military repression in Latin America. He actively supported the Unidad Popular (Popular Unity) candidate Salvador Allende in Chile's 1970 elections, and was murdered by the military shortly after Pinochet's 1973 coup.

Pablo Neruda (Ricardo Eliecer Neftalí Reyes Basoalto, 1904-73) was one of the most celebrated and influential poets of the 20th century and a winner of the 1971 Nobel Prize for Literature. His work has been extensively published and translated. He published his first volume of verse in 1927 and worked as a diplomat for the Chilean government, but was radicalised while in Spain by the Civil War, which transformed him into an ardent communist. He spent time in Mexico where he published his lengthy epic *Canto general* then returned to Chile and became active in politics. Repression of the communists by President Gabriel González Videla forced him into exile in Argentina. He came to admire the Soviet Union and was awarded the Stalin Peace Prize in 1953. He returned to Chile and in 1970 was nominated as a candidate for the presidency, but gave his support to the unity candidate Salvador Allende, who once in office appointed him ambassador to France. Poor health forced his return and he was hospitalised with cancer at the time of Pinochet's coup, dying 12 days later.

Floridor Pérez (1937-) is a poet and educator who was working as a teacher of Spanish in rural schools when he was incarcerated in the notorious concentration camp on Quiriquina island following the Chilean coup of 1973. There he wrote *Cartas de prisionero* (*Letters of a Prisoner*), one of his best known works. He is well known for his efforts to conserve Chilean traditions and for compiling folk tales, and has run the poetry workshop at the Neruda Foundation in Santiago.

Jaime Valdivieso (1929-) has published essays, short stories, novels and poetry and has taught and lectured about literature in a number of countries including Cuba and the United States. He was exiled from Chile after the 1973 coup and lived in Mexico, where he wrote a number of important works. He has been an active champion of Mapuche poetry and been involved in a number of initiatives to gain greater recognition for this.

Jiang Fei (1974-) was born in small village near Linyi in Shandong province and, out of a desire to lead a life of "romance and revolution", joined the navy in 1993. The death of his beloved grandmother in 1994 prompted him to write his book *Fifty Poems of Hopelessness and One of Despair*, and he left the armed forces in 1998 to concentrate on his writing. In 2000 he published a poem in an official literary journal for the first time, and has since won many awards.

Jun'er (1968-) was born in rural China in 1968 and attended Shandong University. She works as a journalist in Tianjin with the newspaper *Beifang jingji shibao* (*Northern Economic Times*). She has published two collections, *Chenmo yu xuanhua de shijie* (*Quiet in a tumultuous world*) (2001) and *Dahai yu huayuan* (*Oceans and gardens*) (2005).

Yi Sha (1966-) was born in Chengdu, Sichuan province, during the Cultural Revolution. He won his first poetry prize at the age of 18 and in 1988 published his first collection *Jimo jie* (*Lonely Street*). An assistant professor at the Xi'an International Studies University, he has also edited literary magazines and presented TV programmes. He has published nine books of poetry, and also written novels, short stories, essays and literary criticism.

Zhang Guangtian is a composer, theatre director and playwright, who has written the musical scores for several films. He was the director and composer of the music in *Qie Gewala fanxiang yu zhengming* (*Che Guevara: Responses and Controversies*) the play from which his verses are taken. It was first performed in Beijing in 2000. He wrote and, in 2001 directed, the epic play *Mr Lu Xun* about the great left-wing Chinese writer whose works were banned in Taiwan until the late 1980s.

Nelson Osorio Marín (1941-97) studied law and sociology, but became a poet. He published the first of his three books in 1963 aged 22, and his last, *Al pie de las letras*, in 1976. His poems often addressed social themes such as poverty and were influenced by Nadaism, the Colombian literary movement that developed from 1960-65 and expressed a nihilistic, counter-cultural protest against traditional social institutions. His work incorporated features found in mass media such as newspaper text, song lyrics and lines from movies, and he also wrote protest songs.

Ernesto Con (1961-) was born in Costa Rica to a family whose antecedents included one of the first Chinese immigrants to arrive in the country at the end of the 19th century. In 1981 his family emigrated to Los Angeles and it was there that his first poetry appeared in English. His first collection was published in 1996. "Ode to Ché Guevara" was read during the 100th anniversary of the birth of Pablo Neruda by the Neruda Foundation in Chile.

Gerardo Alfonso Morejón (1958-) is a musician and singer who joined the Nueva Trova musical movement in 1990. His work has often focused on the themes of Cuban youth mixed with Afro-Caribbean rhythms and he is considered an important representative of that generation of musicians who have grown up with the revolution. In 1997 he participated in the inaugural concert of the XIV World Festival of Youth and Students in Cuba, and he has attended protest song festivals in Cuba and abroad. In 2002 he was honoured for his contribution to Cuban culture and awarded the Alejo Carpentier Medal.

Miguel Barnet (1940-) is a is a poet, ethnologist and president of the Fundación Fernando Ortiz. After an early education in the US, he studied sociology at the University of Havana against the backdrop of the Cuban Revolution under Fernando Ortíz, the pioneer of Cuban anthropology whose studies of Afro-Cuban cultures influenced many of Barnet's themes. Barnet's *Biografía de un cimarrón* in which he tells the story of Esteban Montejo, a 105-year-old Cuban man of African descent, became a pioneering work of testimonial narrative. He has published ten collections of poetry as well as novels, essays and ethnographies.

Vicente Feliú (1947-) is a songwriter and musician whose work has been extensively recorded and who has collaborated with popular musicians across the world. He began playing the guitar as a child and writing songs at the age of 17 and was a key figure in the establishment of the Nueva Trova musical movement alongside such figures as Pablo Milanés and Silvio Rodríguez. He has been a radio and television musical director in Cuba and has composed music for works of theatre. He has written and recorded a number of works about Che Guevara.

Antonio Guerrero Rodríguez (1958-) is an engineer and poet best known for his bilingual collection *Desde mi altura* (*From my Altitude*). He was born in Miami to Cuban parents and the family returned home when he was one month old. He completed his university studies in civil engineering in the Ukraine, and gained a master's degree in aerodrome construction. In Cuba he was the principal engineer in the construction of the International Airport in Santiago de Cuba. In the early 1990s he went to live in the US and in 1998 he was arrested by the FBI and subsequently charged and convicted of conspiracy to commit espionage and other related crimes as one of the so-called "Miami Five" in a case that has become an international *cause célèbre*. He was sentenced to life imprisonment plus ten years and is now imprisoned in a US penitentiary in Florence, Colorado, where he continues to write poetry. (See www.freethefive.org)

Nicolás Guillén (1902-89) was an Afro-Cuban poet, sometimes referred to as revolutionary Cuba's poet laureate, whose work was widely published and was highly influential. He studied law in Havana but gave this up to work as a journalist, publishing his first poems in the 1920s. In 1936 he was jailed briefly in a climate of repression, and the following year he joined the Communist Party and attended the congress of writers and artists in Spain during the Civil War. He stood as a communist candidate in Cuban local elections in 1940, and travelled widely over the next 20 years. In 1953 he was prevented by the Batista regime from re-entering Cuba, and in 1954 he was awarded the Lenin Peace Prize. He was welcomed back to Cuba following the revolution and appointed president of the Unión Nacional de Escritores y Artistas de Cuba (UNEAC). His poetry often highlighted poor social conditions and he is the best-known representative of the "poesía negra" ("black poetry") that tried to synthesise black and white cultural elements.

Pedro Pérez Sarduy (1943-) is an Afro-Cuban poet, novelist, journalist, broadcaster and academic now living in London. He worked in Cuba for national radio (1965-79) and for the Latin American section of the BBC World Service (1981-1994) and has also co-produced documentary films. He has published a number of collections of poetry and novels including *Las Criadas de la Habana* (*The Maids of Havana*), considered to be the first novel by a contemporary Afro-Cuban writer on family life in Cuba. He was also a pioneering writer and co-editor of books and collections about race and identity in contemporary Cuba. He has won several literary awards and, among other residencies, has been Ford Foundation Writer in Residence at Columbia University and a Rockefeller Visiting Scholar at the University of Florida.

Carlos Puebla (1917-89) was a self-taught composer who recorded more than a thousand musical works and is internationally known for his most famous song, "Hasta siempre comandante" included in this collection. He first began recording in the 1950s with his group Los Tradicionales and gained popularity for singing about the difficult living conditions of the Cuban people under Batista. His political activities made him a supporter of Fidel Castro before the 1959 Cuban Revolution, and subsequently he performed at concerts all over the world as a form of musical ambassador for revolutionary Cuba.

Klaus Høeck (1938-) made his debut as a poet in 1966 and has since published more than 30 books of poetry. *Hjem* (*Home*) (1985) is considered one of the most outstanding works of Danish literature of the 1980s. He is particularly well-known for the two collections *Fairy-Tales* and *1001 digt* (*1001 poems*). In 1985 he was awarded the Danish Art Foundation's Lifetime Grant, and he has been a member of the Danish Academy since 1989.

Jorge Enrique Adoum (1926-) is a major exponent of Latin American poetry whose work, often reflecting social concerns, has been extensively published. He was the personal secretary of Pablo Neruda who, in 1952, said of him: "Ecuador has the greatest poet in America". He has been nominated for the Cervantes Prize and in 1989 the Ecuadorean government awarded him the "Eugenio Espejo" National Culture Prize in recognition of his work.

Salama el Tawil is an Egyptian poet. His poem about Che first appeared in translation in Meri Lao's collection *Al Che: Poesie e canzoni dal mondo* (1995). He has performed his work at a number of international festivals in Italy, including the Theatrón International Festival of Mediterranean Theatre (2002) in Salerno and the 2006 Milagro Acustico multiethnic concert in Rome.

Roque Dalton (1935-75) was one of Latin America's most compelling and influential poets, a journalist and communist activist. He was exiled sporadically from El Salvador where he was arrested and escaped execution, mostly by good fortune, several times. He spent time in Mexico and revolutionary Cuba and eventually joined El Salvador's Ejército Revolucionario del Pueblo (ERP, People's Revolutionary Army) guerrilla organisation. He was tortured then executed by a militaristic faction of his own organisation.

Anselm Hollo (1934-) is a poet, translator and lecturer who has lived for much of his life in the United States. He has published more than 40 poetry titles in a style influenced by the American beat poets, his work has appeared in many anthologies, and he has won many awards. In 2001, poets and critics associated with the State University of New York elected him as "anti-laureate" in protest at the appointment of Billy Collins as Poet Laureate Consultant in Poetry to the Library of Congress. He is a professor at Naropa University in Colorado.

Pentti Saarikoski (1937-83) was a central figure in Finnish literature and a visible intellectual in the 1960s and 70s. Something of a bohemian enfant terrible, he struggled with heavy drinking and marital conflict. In the 1960s he joined the Finnish Communist Party, and as editor of the magazine *Aikalainen* published Mao Tse-tung's poems. He was a prolific poet and translator, translating Allen Ginsberg's work among others, and was fascinated by Che Guevara.

André Benedetto (1934-) is a theatre director, poet, playwright and performer and is the director of the Théâtre des Carmes in Avignon. In the 1960s he staged plays derived from the poems of the Beat Generation and his work assumed a political character with productions such as *Napalm* about Vietnam. In 1968 he wrote and staged *Zone Rouge, feux interdits* whose protagonist was a bearded character modelled on Che Guevara. More recent works have looked at the voices of great progressives such as Nelson Mandela, the malaise of France's inner cities and social issues such as pollution and gender. He has published several collections of poems since 1966 and his work *Les Poubelles du Vent* (1971) contained seven poems about Guevara.

Francis Combes (1953-) is a poet, journalist, editor, translator, essayist and literary critic whose work has been widely published. He was a member of the editorial board of the review *Europe* and literary director of the publisher Messidor. He has published at least eight collections of poetry, including *Cause commune* (2003) about revolutionary figures and politics. He helped to found and is literary director of Le Temps des Cerises publishing house, and he is active in poetry events and initiatives throughout France and abroad.

Jean Ferrat (Jean Tenenbaum, 1930-) is a French author, poet and singer. He dropped out of school to help support his family after his father was deported to Auschwitz, where he died, during the second world war. His long musical career began in the 1950s. His poetry and protest songs often contain militant messages and at times during his career he faced difficulties with censorship owing to his links with the French Communist Party. He has won a number of awards including that of the French Authors' and Composers' Society (SACEM).

Colette Magny (1926-97) was a French singer-songwriter whose protest songs contained critiques of contemporary social and political problems. Her work, often inspired by the Blues, was extensively recorded. Her album *Vietnam 67* (released in 1968) had Che Guevara and Ho Chi Minh on its cover and developed themes of revolution and about the Third World.

Auguste Macouba (Auguste Armet, 1939-) is a poet, dramatist, essayist and anti-colonial activist. He gained a doctorate in sociology in Paris and also studied at l'Ecole Nationale de Santé de Rennes. He has held various government positions in Martinique including health and social affairs inspector, and was a co-founder of the Comité Martiniquais de Prévention de l'Alccolisme. In 1978 he joined the communist Parti Progressiste Martiniquais (PPM) but left this in 1993 to found the Mouvement Populaire Pilotin (MPP). He has published a number of books and has contributed to socio-historical studies such as *Esclaves noirs, Maitres blancs* (*Black Slaves, White Masters*, 2006).

Volker Braun (1939-) is a writer, poet and playwright whose career initially developed within the former socialist German Democratic Republic (East Germany). As a school student his political comments brought him into conflict at an early age with the authorities and prevented him going straight to university. He worked in various factory jobs then studied philosophy in Leipzig where he compiled his first volume of poetry. He later became involved in the Berliner Ensemble theatre founded by Brecht. His many awards include the prestigious Büchner Prize (2000).

Hans Magnus Enzensberger (1929-) is an author, poet, translator and editor whose work has been extensively published and who has also worked in theatre, film, opera and radio. He studied literature and philosophy in Germany and at the Sorbonne in Paris and participated in the influential Gruppe 47 literary association. He lived in revolutionary

Cuba for several years and many of his poems feature themes of civil unrest over economic and class-based issues. He edited the magazine *Kursbuch*, founded the monthly *TransAtlantik*, and since 1985 has been the editor of the *Die Andere Bibliothek* book series. His work has been translated into more than 40 languages and he has won a number of prestigious awards.

Peter Schütt (1939-) studied German and history in Goettingen, Bonn and Hamburg and completed his studies with a thesis on the baroque poet Andreas Gryphius. His role in student activism in 1968 cost him his university position and, from 1971 to 1988 he was a member of the executive committee of the German communist party. He was excluded from the party because of his commitment to the reforms undertaken by Mikhail Gorbachev in the Soviet Union. He has published nine volumes of poetry, has written several plays, and is known for his literary travel reports. He is also a contributor to the magazine *Courage* and works for *FAZ*, the *world*, *Rheini Merkur* and *Deutschlandfunk*.

Peter Weiss (1916-82) was a German-born writer, dramatist and artist who eventually adopted Swedish nationality. He studied in Berlin, London and Prague before settling in Stockholm. He is most well known as a playwright and novelist but also wrote poetry and made films. He was an active member of the Communist Party and in 1967 participated in the International War Crimes Tribunal held in Stockholm that had been convoked by the British philosopher Bertrand Russell to evaluate US military intervention in Vietnam.

Manos Loïzos (1937-82) was one of the most important Greek composers yet relatively unknown outside Greece. He composed many well-known songs and collaborated with many composers, singers and lyricists, in particular Lefteris Papadopoulos who wrote the lyrics of many of his hits.

Otto-Raúl González (1921-) is a Guatemalan writer, poet, and lawyer who, as a communist, served as an agrarian reform minister in the administration of Jacobo Arbenz. He met Che Guevara in Guatemala in this period and gave him some work, but with the downfall of Arbenz, went into exile in Ecuador then Mexico — where he obtained a law degree from the National Autonomous University (UNAM). He was eventually allowed back to Guatemala by President Vinicio Cerezo. He is a prolific writer who has published more than 60 books, many of which have been translated. He has won many prestigious literary prizes including Mexico's Premio Nacional de Poesía Jaime Sabines and Guatemala's National Literature Prize.

Jan Carew (1920-) is a novelist, playwright, poet and teacher whose works have been widely published. He has travelled extensively and has been a lecturer, professor or programme director at Princeton, Rutgers, George Mason, Hampshire, Lincoln and London universities. An authority in fields ranging from Third World studies to Caribbean literature, he is considered a pioneer in the Pan-African Studies. He is Professor Emeritus at Northwestern University.

René Depestre (1926-) is a poet whose work has been widely published and translated. He published his first collection of poetry, *Etincelles (Sparks)*, in 1945 at the age of 19 and in the early 1950s became active in anti-colonial movements and was expelled from French territory and later a number of European countries. Invited to Cuba by Nicolás Guillén, Depestre was expelled by the Batista regime, ending up in Chile where he collaborated with Pablo Neruda. Depestre went to Paris in 1956, where he took part in the first Panafrican congress, before returning to Haiti where he was arrested. He was again exiled before being invited to Cuba in 1959 by Che Guevara, who believed he would spearhead a revolution in Haiti. Depestre was active in the establishment of revolutionary Cuba's cultural institutions. In 1978 he returned to Paris to work with Unesco, and continued writing. His poetry and prose has won many prizes in France and abroad, and in 1988 he was awarded the Prix Renaudot for his work *Hadriana dans Tous mes Rêves*. He is the uncle of Michaëlle Jean, current Governor-General of Canada.

Jean Métellus (1937-) is a poet, novelist, dramatist and essayist. He worked as a teacher until being forced into exile by the Duvalier dictatorship in 1959 and settling in Paris, where he studied linguistics and medicine. He specialised in neurology and problems of language, and pursued a career as a doctor while writing poetry and novels. He has published widely and has developed a distinctive personal oeuvre within the French language. Among the many awards he has received for his poetry and novels was the Grand Prix International in 2006.

Anthony Phelps (1928-) is a poet, novelist, dramatist and journalist whose work has been widely published and translated. He was a founding member of the 1960 group Haïti-Littéraire, most of whose members were forced into exile during the Duvalier dictatorship, helped to establish the review *Semences,* and was co-founder of Radio Cacique. Imprisoned by Duvalier, he then went into exile and in 1964 settled in Montréal, where he still resides. He began a distinguished career in broadcasting as a journalist for Radio-Canada. He has written and edited a large number of works of poetry and prose, performed on and produced many recordings, made many films, and performed at a large number of festivals internationally. He has been instrumental in the promotion of Haitian authors for 40 years through his company, *Les Productions Caliban*.

K.G. Sankara Pillai (1948-) is one of the finest poets in Kerala and has published several collections in Malayalam as well as translating poems from Africa, Bengal and Karnataka into the language. He taught in various colleges until his retirement in 2002 as principal of Government Maharaja's College, Ernakulam. He has edited literary journals and an important anthology of women's poetry and feminist criticism. He is closely associated with the human rights movement and has been chair of the Jananeethi organisation.

Siamak Kiarostami (1978-) is an Iranian writer and scholar currently residing in New York City. He has written poems, short stories, and articles under his own name and others for several publications. Born against the backdrop of the Iranian Revolution to Marxist activists, Siamak has long been inspired by Ernesto Guevara, and has explored much of Latin America in search of Che's legacy.

Kieran Furey (1953-) is a poet and writer. He has travelled extensively outside his native Ireland and has lived in Cuba and Ecuador as well as London, India, Africa and the US. His only son, Ernesto, is named after Che Guevara. He has published several books and booklets of poetry, short stories, satire and travel stories, and also writes in Spanish. In 2006 he won the Féile Filíochta Poem of Europe Award for his poem in Spanish, "El Tren".

Val Nolan (1982-) teaches twentieth-century poetry in the Department of English at the National University of Ireland, Galway. His poetry and criticism has been widely published. Most recently he was selected to participate in the 2007 Poetry Ireland Introductions reading series in Dublin and the Document writer/artist collaboration exhibited at Galway's Cúirt International Festival of Literature.

Liam Ó Comain (1940-) is retired and lives in Derry. He has been a revolutionary Irish republican since the age of 14. In the early 1960s he became a full-time organiser for the republican movement and held that position untill after it split in the 1970s. As an organiser, he was a member of the Sinn Fein's Ard Comhairle (ruling executive) and the headquarters staff of the IRA. Committed to a resurrected republic based upon the socialist ideas of James Connolly, he became dissatisfied with the Official movement and resigned. He is no longer a member of any political grouping and studied to postgraduate level as a mature student.

Francesco Guccini (1940-) is a singer-songwriter, novelist and comic writer whose songs have been widely recorded. As a young man he worked as a journalist and in the 1960s he achieved success writing popular songs and collaborating with other musicians. Later work explored personal themes and links with the US. He has appeared on television, compiled soundtracks for several films and has stood, very unsuccessfully, as an Italian presidential candidate. He has won a number of awards including the Librex-Guggenheim award in 1992.

Jovanotti (Lorenzo Cherubini, 1966-) is a singer-songwriter, rapper and occasional television presenter whose work has many echoes of the Italian *cantautore* tradition. He has released a number of albums and his songs have also appeared on international compilations. He is prominent in the campaign for the cancellation of the public debt owed by Third World countries.

Roberto Vecchioni (1943-) is a singer-songwriter and writer who graduated in ancient literatures, lectured on the history of religion and then became a literature and history teacher at a Milanese high school. In the late 1960s he achieved success as a songwriter for popular artists and his first solo album, *Parabola*, came out in 1971. He has since recorded widely and also been a music promoter. His most recent album was *Il contastorie* (*The Storyteller*, 2005). In the 1990s he also began to publish prose, most recently the novel *Il libraio di Selinunte* (*The Bookseller of Selinunte*, 2004).

Andrew Salkey (1928-95) was a poet, novelist and journalist who was born in Panama but raised in Jamaica. In the 1960s he was a key figure in the West Indian Students Union at the University of London of which John La Rose (see below) was also a member. Salkey wrote or edited a large number of books, was a BBC radio interviewer, and taught as a professor in writing at Hampshire College in Amherst.

Renji Ono (1918-78) was a poet and literary critic whose work was widely published in his native Japan. Born in Hakodate, Hokkaido, he was hospitalised with tuberculosis while studying at business school and suffered the consequences of this illness for the rest of his life. He was a prolific "people's poet" whose work was aimed at ordinary people and whose collections included *Noutan Danzoku* (*Light and shade intermission*). He was influenced by the Japan Romantic School (Nihon Romanha) and his poetry often reflected on the suffering of those with physical afflictions.

Ko Un (1933-) is one of Korea's greatest poets and has been shortlisted for the Nobel prize for literature several times. Traumatised by the suffering of his family and friends in the Korean war, he became a Buddhist monk, only returning to secular life in 1962 as a poet. He suffered emotional problems and attempted suicide several times. He was a leading activist in South Korea's democracy, human rights and labour movements and was jailed four times after 1974 as well as suffering house arrest and torture. His obvious deafness is due in part to beatings inflicted by the police when he was arrested in 1979.

In 1980, during a coup d'état, he was accused of treason and sentenced to 20 years' imprisonment but was released in 1982 as part of a general amnesty. He has published some 140 volumes, including verse and fiction. His works have been translated into 15 languages, he has won many awards and he has been a leading light in efforts to improve relations with North Korea.

Min Yeong (1934-) is a poet, writer and democracy activist who is best known as one of the poets who resisted South Korean dictatorship in the 1970s and 1980s alongside Ko Un, Shin Kyong-Nim, and Kim Nam-Ju. He was born in Cholwon, to the north-east of Seoul, but in 1937 his parents fled the poverty of Korea, which had been under Japanese rule since 1910, to seek a better life, before the family returned to Korea after Liberation in 1945. His first published collection of poetry was *Danjang* (*Fragments*, 1972) and at least four other collections have followed, his most recent being *Haejigi chon ui sarang* (*Love before Sunset*, 2001). He has also written a number of books for children.

Efraín Huerta (1914-82) was one of Mexico's most recognised poets who, from 1938 to 1941, participated in the Taller literary group with university colleagues who included Octavio Paz. He was also a journalist, working on Mexico's most prominent newspapers, and film critic. He travelled extensively and won many awards, including the French Palmas Académicas in 1945 and Mexico's National Poetry Prize in 1976. His collected poems were published by Mexico's Fondo de Cultura Económica (FCE) in 1988.

José Tiquet (1928-2006) trained as a school teacher and later left his native Tabasco for Mexico City to study law, philosophy and literature. His first collection of poetry was published in 1951 and his last, *Buscando en Dios la Rosa*, in July 2006 just a few days after his death. Tiquet knew and maintained correspondence with Che Guevara, whom he first interviewed in Cuba as a journalist in the early days of the revolution, and he was a friend of Hilda Gadea, Che's first wife.

Mohamed Khaïr-Eddine (1941-95) was a leading post-independence Moroccan poet and novelist. He completed his studies in Casablanca and then worked for the government in Agadir, helping to restore order after an earthquake. As a young writer he joined the Amitiés littéraires et artistiques literary circle in Casablanca and in 1964 founded the Poésie Toute movement. In 1965 he was exiled to France where he spent several years working in factories. He resumed publishing and wrote for *Lettres nouvelles* and *Présence africaine*. In 1966 he launched the artistic journal *Souffles*. He returned to Morocco in 1979 and continued to write, and won a number of prizes including the Enfants Terribles and l'Amitié Franco-Arabe prizes.

Sebastião Alba (1940-2000) was born in Portugal but grew up in Mozambique and became a secondary school teacher in Quelimane. He was a prolific poet and also worked as a journalist. He moved to Portugal in 1984, where he died in 2000. A posthumous collection of his work, *Albas*, was published in Portugal in 2003.

Bernard Gadd (1935-) is a retired high-school English teacher and polytechnic tutor. He was a pioneer in the development of teaching material for working-class multi-ethnic schools. He has published several collections of poetry and his work has appeared in magazines, on-line, and in international anthologies. He has also published short stories, novels and plays and writes a satirical column for a leftwing newspaper. He has edited several collections of poetry and other literature, and is an occasional small press publisher.

Michael O'Leary (1950-) is a publisher, poet, novelist, performer and bookshop proprietor whose work has been extensively published. His poetry and novels explore his Maori (Te Arawa)–Irish Catholic heritage, and include the collections *Toku Tinihanga (Self Deception)* (2003) and *Make Love and War* (2005). Under his Earl of Seacliff Art Workshop imprint he has published his own prolific output as well as various other alternative and mainstream writers.

Mark Pirie (1974-) is an internationally known poet, editor and reviewer who has published extensively in his native New Zealand and abroad. His poetry has been published in many collections and journals, he is the managing editor of HeadworX, a small press publisher, the editor of *JAAM* (New Zealand) and, among other roles, serves on the committee of the Wellington International Poetry Festival. In 1998 the University of Otago Press published his anthology of Generation X writing, *The NeXt Wave*.

Jorge Eduardo Arellano (1946-) is an historian and poet whose work on art, Nicaraguan culture and Sandino has been extensively published. He undertook doctoral and post-doctoral research in Europe, and was Nicaragua's ambassador to Chile from 1997-99. He is an editor, has been honoured by the Academia Chilena de la Lengua for his work, and has won many prizes for his academic writing and poetry, including the 2003 Premio Nacional Rubén Darío.

Changmarín (Carlos F. Changmarín, 1922-) is of mixed Chinese and creole heritage and one of Panama's most important cultural figures. He became politically active as a young teacher in the 1940s and, as a writer, artist, musician and journalist his extensively published work has been notable for its portrayals of class struggle. He met Che Guevara in Havana at a meeting of Latin American communist parties, where he was representing the Partido Comunista de Panamá (Partido del Pueblo). He was jailed several times in Panama and exiled to Chile in 1968, where he became active in Salvador Allende's political campaign. Upon his return, he gained national recognition for his role in the struggle to win back control of the Panama Canal from the US.

Juan Cristóbal (José Pardo del Arco, 1941-) is a poet, academic and journalist. He studied medicine in Spain but abandoned this for literature. His poem about Guevara is dedicated to Juan Pablo Chang — a comrade in arms of Che who was executed alongside him in Bolivia — whom Cristóbal met in Lima. Cristóbal's work has been extensively published and in 2001 he brought out an anthology, *En los bosques de cervezas azules* (*In the forests of blue beers*). He formerly taught literature and communication at several universities, as well as running a poetry workshop at the Instituto Cultural José Carlos Mariátegui. He has won many awards for his poetry, including Peru's Premio Nacional de Poesía (1971).

Eugénio de Andrade (José Fontinhas, 1923 -2005) was one of Portugal's leading contemporary poets whose work was widely published and translated. Born into a peasant family, he abandoned the idea of studying philosophy in order to dedicate himself to poetry. In 1947 he joined the socio-medical services inspectorate in Lisbon and was later transferred to Porto, where he settled. He was often associated wih the generation of '27 in Spain but contributed to many reviews and magazines with a diverse focus. He published a large number of collections, and also wrote prose, including children's stories. He won all of Portugal's most important literary awards including the Camões Prize as well as the French Prix Jean Malrieu and the 1996 European Prize for Poetry.

Jorge de Sena (1919-78) was a poet, dramatist, novelist, critic, translator and university lecturer. He studied civil engineering but developed a career as a writer. An outspoken cultural activist during the Salazar dictatorship, he went into exile in Brazil in 1959, and in 1965 moved to the United States. He was a prolific writer and an influential intellectual, whose many works included an autobiographical novel, *Sinais de Fogo* (*Fire Signals* 1979), which was adapted to cinema in 1995. He won a number of major prizes and was honoured with the Ordem do Infante D. Henrique for his services to Portuguese culture. He was also instrumental in the diffusion of the work of many English-language authors through studies, conferences and translations. In 1980, the Jorge de Sena Center for Portuguese Studies was inaugurated at the University of California in Santa Barbara.

José Nuno Guimarães Guedes dos Santos (1942-73) learned the guitar as a teenager and was introduced to cantigas by a friend. In the 1960s he studied philology at the Universidade de Coimbra and began composing serenatas. His work was noticed by the main broadcaster, Emissora Nacional, and he began to record as well as writing poetry and contributing to and editing a number of poetry journals. At the end of the 1960s he served briefly in the colonial war in Angola, where he later taught in a preparatory school. On his return to Portugal he was offered a post at the Liceu D. João II but died soon afterwards. His collected works were published in a single volume in 1995.

Sophia de Mello Breyner Andresen (1919-2004) was one of the most important contemporary Portuguese poets and also wrote stories, children's books and essays. Her work has been widely published and translated, and she was also an important translator, bringing works by Dante and Shakespeare among others into Portuguese. She was active in the democratic struggle against the Salazar regime and gave poetic voice to her thoughts about freedom. She was awarded all the major Portuguese literary prizes as well as a number of international prizes for her work.

Yevgeny Yevtushenko (1933-) is a Russian poet whose work spanned the Cold war and has been widely published and translated. Born in Siberia, he moved to Moscow, studied at the Maxim Gorky Literature Institute and published his first poem in 1956. He was active in the effort under Khrushchev to confront the legacy of Stalin, and became known for his criticism of Soviet bureaucracy. He visited Cuba, initially as a correspondent for Pravda, where he met Che Guevara, and was recruited to co-write the screenplay for a now celebrated film, *Soy Cuba* (*I am Cuba*, 1964). From 1963-65, Yevtushenko was banned from travelling outside the Soviet Union. In the post-Soviet era, he has been vocal about environmental issues and Russian nationalist writers, and has campaigned for the preservation of the memory of victims of Stalin's gulag. He settled in the US and has taught poetry and cinema at several universities.

Arthur Raymond (1947-) was raised in St. Lucia and went to England in 1966 to study law. He published his poem about Che Guevara in Andrew Salkey's pioneering anthology of Caribbean poetry *Breaklight* (1971), although little is known about his life and subsequent works published.

Derek Walcott (1930-) is one of the greatest poets in English of the 20th century who won the Nobel Prize for Literature in 1992. He is also a playwright and has published more than 20 plays, many dealing either directly or indirectly with the West Indies' postcolonial condition. He founded the Trinidad Theatre Workshop and also the Boston Playwrights' Theatre at Boston University. He has published extensively and travelled widely lecturing and reading throughout the world.

Joe A.A (Anti-Apartheid) is the *nom de guerre* of a South African popular poet whose "In Tribute to Ernesto Che Guevara" appeared in the first collection of homages to Guevara published in London in 1968, ¡Viva Che! as well as in the collection of Meri Lao (1995), although little is known about his life and published work since.

Masa Mbatha-Opasha (1961-) is a tenor opera singer, composer and poet originally from South Africa who now lives in Rome. He began performing at a young age in religious choirs, sang with the Amazwi kaZulu Choir and the Durban Philharmonic Orchestra among others, and studied with leading teachers from the Natal and Pretoria Technikon schools. In 1989 he went to Rome on an Italian government scholarship and in 1990 collaborated in a performance about apartheid. He performed in major concerts and on television, as well as at events to mark the achievement of democracy in his homeland, and has been prominent in Rome in campaigns against racism and to encourage intercultural dialogue. In 1995 he was honoured for his work by the Università La Sapienza di Roma. He has also appeared in film, and founded the Voices of Glory choir.

Rafael Alberti (1902-99) published his first poetry collection in the 1920s and was a member of the influential Generación del '27 avant-garde forum. The declaration of the Spanish republic in 1931 was a turning point and Alberti joined the Communist Party and his work became overtly political. During the Spanish Civil War he rallied the Loyalist cause but after Franco's victory in 1939 fled to Argentina. There, he met the Guevara family and Che as a child. He published extensively and travelled the world, but eventually relocated in Europe. In 1965 he was awarded the Lenin Prize for Peace. He returned to Spain in 1977 after Franco's death and, soon afterwards, was elected as a Communist Party deputy in the first legislature.

Víctor Manuel Arbeloa (1936-) studied theology in Spain and was ordained a priest. In the last years of the Franco dictatorship he was one of the founders of the Partido Socialista Obrero Español (PSOE) in Navarra, and was the first president of its regional assembly in 1979. He served as a PSOE senator and was a Member of the European Parliament (MEP) from 1987-94. He is the author of more than 30 books of poetry, history and essays, has taught at the Universidad Pontifica de Salamanca, and belongs to the Society of Basque Studies and Ateneo Navarro.

Xosé Luís Méndez Ferrín (1938-) is a Galician poet and writer of narrative and essays whose work has been widely published, and is considered to be the highest representative of contemporary Galician literature. He was a founding member of the nationalist-communist Unión do Pobo Galego (Galician People's Union) seeking Galician independence as a socialist state, and is also a member of the socialist Frente Popular Galega (Galician People's Front). He is a member of the Galician Royal Academy, was awarded an honorary doctorate by the University of Vigo and, as well as writing and editing, teaches literature.

Ingemar Leckius (1928-) is a poet, writer and translator whose first collection of poems came out in 1951 and who has published widely since. His *Ljus AV Ljus* (*Light from Light*, 1989) won Sweden's most prestigious poetry award, The Bellman Prize of the Swedish Academy. His poetry has dealt with many religious themes, underlying which is a strong universal message.

Claude Lushington was a painter and writer who served in the Royal Air Force during the second world war then as a housing official in Trinidad. In 1955 he went to England to study law and remained to write; one of a number of West Indian writers to come to Britain at that time. His collection of poetry, *The Mystic Rose*, was published in 1969 and he contributed to other collections and journals.

Arif Damar (1925-) was orphaned at an early age and, after dropping out of high school, started writing. He joined the editorial board of several literary magazines and in 1959 won Turkey's prestigious Yeditepe Poetry Award. He made his name as one of the major contemporary Turkish poets, especially of the 1940s socialist generation in Turkish literature with his committedly leftwing verse. In 1968, he was prosecuted for his poem "Che" in this anthology, although he was acquitted. In 1969, he founded *Yeryüzü* Publications.

Metin Demirtaş (1938-) studied machine engineering and became a factory worker in Ankara before joining the science faculty at Ankara University where he worked until disability prevented him from continuing. In 1968 he was prosecuted over the poem in this anthology. He has published about four collections of poetry and essays and books for children. His work has been translated into many languages, including Russian.

Sennur Sezer (1943-) dropped out of the Istanbul High School for girls in 1959 to work at the Taskizak Dockyard. Her first poetry collection was published in 1964 and since 1965 she has worked as an editor and writer for a number of media. She has published books of poetry, essays and stories and has won many awards, including the Yunus Nadi Poetry Award.

Dimitri Pavlichko (1929-) is a poet, literary critic, scriptwriter, translator and essayist whose work has been widely published. He developed a professional career as a diplomat and held a number of key posts, was actively involved on behalf of Ukraine in the negotiations over the disarmament of nuclear weapons following the dissolution of the Soviet Union, and was Ukraine's ambassador to Poland. Among his many works of poetry, he edited Unesco's 1986 anthology, the *Poetry of Soviet Ukraine's New World*. He has won many awards including the Nikolai Ostrovsky and Taras Shevchenko prizes. His latest collection, *Sonetos blancos*, was published in Cuba in 2005.

Alan C. Brown (1922-) is a poet from Newcastle upon Tyne who, for many years, was a member of the Communist Party. He has published several poetry books and travelled widely in Europe, including the former Soviet Union, and America reciting his work. His poem about Che was written for a group of visiting Cubans, and he meets regularly with the Tyneside Poets at the Old George pub in Cloth Market, Newcastle.

Kevin Cadwallender (1958-) was born in Hartlepool and has long been active in poetry circles in the north-east of England. He has published several books and pamphlets, produced plays, and has been a writer in residence many times. He edits the *Sand* poetry review. His most recent collection is *Baz Uber Alles* (2004).

Ian Caws (1945-) has published 12 collections of poetry since 1975 and has won a number of awards for his writing including the Gregory Award and placings in the National Poetry Competition. His most recent collection is *The Canterbury Road* (2007). He has published widely in magazines, newspapers and journals in the UK, as well as in the US, Canada, Australia, India and Hong Kong.

Alasdair Clayre (1935-84) was a writer, broadcaster, singer-songwriter, and academic. He studied at Oxford where he was a Prize Fellow of All Souls College, wrote several books and produced a number of documentary films about the slave trade, Ezra Pound's poetry, and China. He recorded two albums of songs, which included many of his own compositions, and appeared on other compilations. His translation of Jacques Brel's *La Colombe* (*The Dove*) was recorded by Judy Collins and Joan Baez. He reportedly took his own life.

Don Collis' "Fleet through the Forest Trees" appeared in the first collection of homages to Guevara published in London in 1968, ¡*Viva Che!* as well as in the collection of Meri Lao, *Al Che: Poesie e canzoni dal mondo* (1995), although little is known about his life and published work since.

Christopher Logue (1926-) is a poet, playwright, scriptwriter and actor. As a private in the Black Watch, he spent 16 months in an army prison. He published his first volume of poems in 1953 and was associated with the British Poetry Revival in the 1960s and 70s. He won the 2005 Whitbread Poetry Award for his collection *Cold Calls*. As well as writing for literary journals, he was a long-term contributor to the satirical magazine *Private Eye*, and published an autobiography (*Prince Charming*, 1999). He appeared in Ken Russell's *Dante's Inferno* and *The Devils* in addition to writing the screenplay for Russell's *Savage Messiah*.

Edward Lucie-Smith (1933-) is a Jamaican-born writer, poet, art critic and curator whose work has been extensively published. He studied at Merton College, Oxford and was an education officer in the Royal Air Force and an advertising copywriter before becoming a freelance writer and broadcaster. He succeeded Philip Hobsbaum as organiser of The Group, a movement of poets who met in London from the mid 1950s to the mid 1960s. He has written many books on art and related subjects, has been a curator for many exhibitions, and has lectured all over the world.

Ewan MacColl (Jimmie Miller, 1915-89) was a folk singer, songwriter, poet, playwright and actor, and the father of Kirsty MacColl (1959-2000), a singer who herself had close links with Cuba. As a youth he joined the Young Communist League and began his career as a writer contributing to party newspapers. In 1932 MI5 opened a file on him and would ultimately be responsible for a BBC ban on some of his songs. MacColl enlisted in the army in 1940 but deserted, and after the war helped form the Theatre Workshop as well as developing a career in folk music. He recorded more than 100 albums and his well-known songs include "The First Time Ever I Saw Your Face", written for his partner Peggy Seeger (see below), and "Dirty Old Town" about his home town of Salford.

John McGrath (1935-2002) was a Liverpudlian-Irish dramatist, producer, and director for theatre and films, and the founder of the 7:84 Theatre Company (so named because he had read that just 7 per cent of Britain's population owned 84 per cent of its wealth). McGrath studied at St. John's College, Oxford, and was set to become a teacher when he was invited to write for the Royal Court Theatre. Thereafter he worked in film and television writing, producing and directing plays while pursuing an interest in radical politics. His most well known play was *The Cheviot, the Stag, and the Black, Black Oil* (1974), a title referring to the Highland clearances in Scotland and reflecting his commitment to the cause of Scottish independence.

Adrian Mitchell (1932-) is poet, novelist, journalist, playwright and scriptwriter whose work has been widely published. He wrote his first play at the age of ten, became chairman of the Oxford University Poetry Society and developed a career in newspapers but quit journalism in the mid-1960s to concentrate on poetry, plays and stories. A pacifist, he came to public attention as a poet during protests against the Vietnam War, and has more recently written about the invasion of Iraq. He was anointed by *Red Pepper* magazine the "shadow poet laureate" for the social conscience demonstrated in his work. He is a Fellow of the Royal Society of Literature, has held a number of academic fellowships, and has won or been shortlisted for a number of awards.

Andrew Sinclair (1935-) is an historian, novelist and dramatist whose work has been extensively published. He studied history at Cambridge, where he later taught, and was a Harkness fellow at Harvard and Columbia universities. He has directed several films, including *Under Milk Wood* (1972) and was managing director of Lorrimer Publishing that produced ¡*Viva Che!* (1968). He has won a number of awards and is a Fellow of the Royal Society of Literature and Society of American Historians.

Cliff Wedgbury (1946-) is a London-born poet, playwright, performing artist and broadcaster based in Cork, Ireland. His formative years were spent in the folk and jazz clubs and bookshops of London's Charing Cross Road. He has contributed as a musician to a number of albums, and has released four collections of folk and jazz songs. He has published four collections of poetry, the latest being, *Kiss* (2004), and in the US his work was compared to that of the French poet Jacques Prévert. He was a Cloverdale competition prize winner in 1993.

Ted Willis (1918-92) was a dramatist and leftwing political activist. A member of the Labour movement from his youth, in 1941 he became secretary general of the Young Communist League. During the second world war he advocated opening a second front in order to help the Red Army. He wrote plays for the Unity Theatre in London, films, and is perhaps best known for writing the popular British television series *Dixon of Dock Green*. He was chairman of the Writers' Guild of Great Britain from 1958-64, and was awarded a life peerage as Lord Ted Willis of Chislehurst on a Labour Party nomination.

Alexander Scott (1920-89) was one of the 20th century's greatest Scots makars, a dramatist and a pioneering teacher of Scottish literature at the University of Glasgow. He was a leading figure in the late second wave of Hugh MacDiarmid's Scottish Renaissance literary movement of the early to mid-20th century. His *Collected Poems* was published in 1989 by Hyperion.

John Greeves (1947-) is a poet, short story and feature writer. He has 30 years' experience teaching at various levels in Wales, from Maindee Primary School in Newport to Cardiff University, where he is a creative writing tutor. He has published two books of poetry, *Unlocked* (2005) and *Almost a Doppelganger* (2006), has contributed to several collections, and has written web stories and run workshops for the BBC.

Lyman Andrews (1938-) was born in Colorado and attended the University of California, Berkeley, and King's College London. He has published four volumes of poetry and settled in the UK where he worked for the Times newspaper and became poetry critic for the Sunday Times (1968-78) and a lecturer in American studies at the University of Leicester. He was a friend of Allen Ginsberg and Robert Lowell and also knew William Burroughs. He was witness for the defence in the 1967 trial of his publishers John Calder and Marion Boyars over the publication of the controversial novel *Last Exit to Brooklyn*.

Judy Collins (1939-) is a folk singer, songwriter, novelist and social activist. She released her first album in 1961 aged 22 and developed a broad musical repertoire from traditional folk songs to protest songs and more orchestrated material, winning Grammy awards in 1968 and 1975. She collaborated with some of the major musicians of the era and recorded songs by the Canadian poet Leonard Cohen. After the suicide in 1992 of her son following a long period of depression and substance abuse, she became an advocate of suicide prevention, and chronicled her recovery from his death in her book *Sanity & Grace* (2003). She has also represented Unicef and campaigned for the abolition of landmines.

Lawrence Ferlinghetti (1919-) is a poet known as the co-owner of the City Lights

Bookstore and publishing house which published early literary works of the Beat poets including Jack Kerouac and Allen Ginsberg. The elder statesman of American poetry, he was appointed by San Francisco as the city's first Poet Laureate in 1998.

Allen Ginsberg (1926-97) was an American Beat poet known for his willingness to confront controversial themes and as an early champion of gay rights. He talked openly about his connections with communism and in 1965 he was deported from Cuba for publicly protesting against, among other things, the persecution of homosexuals, but also allegedly for referring to Che Guevara as "cute".

John Haines (1924-) is a poet, essayist and academic whose work has been widely published. He studied at the National Art School, the American University, and the Hans Hoffmann School of Fine Art. He spent many years homesteading in Alaska, and has taught at Ohio, George Washington and Cincinnati universities. He has published more than ten collections of poetry as well as essays and a memoir. He has won many awards for his work including two Guggenheim Fellowships, a National Endowment for the Arts Fellowship and a Lifetime Achievement Award from the Library of Congress. He was named a Fellow by The Academy of American Poets in 1997.

Greg Hewett (1958-) is a poet and academic. He studied in New York and California and has been a Fulbright Fellow and Professor and a Fellow at the Camargo Foundation in Cassis, France. He has lived in California, France, Japan, Denmark, and Norway, and has published three books of poems, the most recent being *The Eros Conspiracy* (2006). He has taught American literature and creative writing with a special interest in poetry and poetics, and is assistant professor of English at Carleton College in Northfield, Minnesota.

Patrick Hyland (1993-) is a teenager in New York and the youngest contributor in this collection at the very start of his career as a poet who has written for the website LitKicks.com, under the monicker "Raving Madcap". His work is influenced by the ideas of dadaism, the Beat Generation poets and the lyrics of contemporary musicians, but he is also interested in traditional poetry, from Dante to Whitman.

Maggie Jaffe (1948-) is a poet, editor and educator. She studied at Vermont College and San Diego State University. Her work has been published in many journals and anthologies and she is the author of six books of poetry. Her most recent works, *7th Circle* and *The Prisons*, were nominated for the San Diego Book Award for Poetry. She became radicalised while travelling and living in Latin America and the Caribbean during the 1970s and her poetry is intrinsically political. She is the publisher of *Roque Dalton Redux: An Anthology of Poetry and Prose* (2005) and an editor of Fiction International. She was awarded a California Arts Council Grant, was twice nominated for a Pushcart Prize, and lectures in English at San Diego State University.

La Loca (Pamela Karol, 1950-) is a poet whose works often recapture the spirit of the Berkeley 60s and adventures with sex and drugs in Haight-Ashbury. In 1987 she read her work as one of the three representatives of the US at the 1988 Winter Olympics Arts Festival in Calgary, Canada.

Robert Lowell (1917-77) was one of the most important poets in English of the twentieth century. He studied poetry at university and won a Pulitzer Prize for his second book, *Lord Weary's Castle* (1946). During the second world war he was imprisoned for being a conscientious objector, and he was later active in protests against the Vietnam war. He was repeatedly hospitalised for severe manic depression and his personal life was distinguished by marital turmoil and erratic behaviour. He published extensively and served as a Chancellor of The Academy of American Poets from 1962 until 1977.

Michael McClure (1932-) is a poet, playwright and novelist who was a key member of the Beat Generation and an important figure in the 60s' Hippie counterculture. His controversial play, *The Beard*, became a theatrical *cause célèbre* in the 1960s after police in San Francisco and Los Angeles raided theatres performing it. He was a close friend of the Doors lead singer Jim Morrison and is acknowledged as having been responsible for promoting Morrison as a poet. McClure has published extensively and won many awards.

Thomas Merton (1915-68) was a Roman Catholic monk acclaimed as one of the most influential American spiritual writers of the twentieth century. Born in France, he completed his education in the US and from 1941 until his death he was a member of an ascetic Cistercian order in Kentucky. He was active in the peace movement of the 1960s, a strong supporter of the civil rights movement and a pioneer of East-West dialogue. He had travelled in Cuba and maintained correspondence with Cuban writers until his death.

Anne Delana Reeves is a Nashville poet and songwriter who won a scholarship to the Indiana Writers' Conference and two *Billboard Magazine* songwriting awards. Her poems have appeared in the *Antioch Review, Image* and other journals.

Daniel Schechter (1943-) is a journalist, editor, radio and television producer, media critic and activist. He studied at the London School of Economics, was a fellow at Harvard and received an honorary doctorate from Fitchburg College. He has been an activist in progressive causes since the 1960s and his journalism has challenged establishment practices and government policy in a wide range of US media. He spent many years in radio news reporting and creating television news and public affairs programmes and independent documentaries. He was news director at the WBCN-FM radio station in Boston where he won awards for his daily news programme from 1970 to 1977. Known in the Boston area as the "News Dissector", he is the executive producer of Global Vision, Inc. His latest book *When News Lies* (2006) looks at media complicity in the Iraq war.

Peggy Seeger (1935-) is a folk singer, political activist and feminist. Born in New York, she lived for many years in Britain, and her work has been extensively recorded. During the 1950s she visited communist China and, in a climate of McCarthyism, had her US passport withdrawn. She travelled Europe and became the partner of the folk singer Ewan MacColl (see above), with whom she recorded many albums. Her citizenship was eventually restored and she returned to the US in 1994. Many of her songs were about the women's movement. She visited the women's camp protesting against US cruise missiles at Greenham Common in the UK and wrote the song "Carry Greenham Home".

Bruce Stephens' "Tune for Che" appeared in the first collection of homages to Guevara published in London in 1968, *¡Viva Che!* as well as in the collections of José Batlló and A. Fornet et al., *Poemas al Che* (1969), and Meri Lao (1995), *Al Che: Poesie e canzoni dal mondo,* although little is known about his life and published work since.

Mario Benedetti (1920-) is a journalist, novelist, and poet considered to be one of Latin America's most important living writers. From 1973 to 1985, when Uruguay was under a military dictatorship, he lived in exile. His first book of poetry was published in 1945, and recent works include *Little Stones At My Window* (*Piedritas en la ventana*, 2003) and *Defensa propia* (*Self-defence*, 2004). He has won major awards, including the Premio Menéndez Pelayo, and has been granted honorary doctorates by both the Universidad de la República in Uruguay and the Universidad de Alicante in Spain.

Aníbal Sampayo (1926-) was born in Uruguay but began his musical career as a singer-songwriter in Paraguay with songs reflecting his leftwing sympathies. He joined the Movimiento de Liberación Nacional (Tupamaros) guerrilla organisation and in 1972 was arrested and jailed until 1980. He spent a period in exile in Sweden, although he travelled and performed extensively, and in recent years has been recognised as one of Latin America's greatest folk-singers.

Pablo Mora (1942-) graduated from the Andrés Bello Catholic University in Venezuela before undertaking doctoral studies in Italy. He taught as an academic for many years and is a prominent figure in Venezuelan literary circles. He has published six collections of poetry under the name Almácigo.

Cu Huy Can (1919-2005) was a poet and revolutionary. His early works in the 1930s earned him a reputation in the country's new poetry movement. A communist and prominent figure in the Viet Minh, he was elected to the National Liberation Committee and witnessed the abdication of Emperor Bao Dai to Ho Chi Minh's government in 1945. He devoted much of his time thereafter to the Vietnamese revolution in the North and returned to poetry after reunification in 1975. He published about 30 collections of poems as well as books and essays.

Cosmas Mairosi (1977-) is a primary school-teacher who has worked with a number of organisations and workshops promoting young writers, including the Budding Writers Association of Zimbabwe and the Zimbabwe Writers Union. He has published several poems and has won a number of local awards for his work, which has often focused on pan-African themes as well as children's rights, gender equality and HIV/Aids.

TRANSLATOR BIOGRAPHIES

Brother Anthony of Taizé was born in England and studied medieval and modern languages at Queen's College, Oxford. He joined the ecumenical monastic community of Taizé in France in 1969, lived in the Philippines from 1977-80, and was invited by Cardinal Kim to Korea in 1980. In 1985 he became a professor in the department of English language and literature at Sogang University in Seoul. He has written books and articles about English literature, and has published more than 20 volumes of translated Korean literature, both poetry and fiction. He naturalised as a Korean citizen in 1994 with the name An Sonjae and is now Emeritus Professor at Sogang.

Marianne Alexandre edited ¡Viva Che! (1968), the first collection of homages and poetry to Guevara to appear in book form. She also translated several titles about art and film as well as the script of the surrealist film *Un chien andalou* by Luis Buñuel and Salvador Dalí.

Sally Azzam is a Palestinian living in Nazareth who works with abused women and on raising awareness of women's issues in schools. She also moderates encounters between Israel's Arab and Jewish populations.

Richard Bartlett is a journalist, translator and publisher. He completed an MA in Southern African literatures from the University of KwaZulu Natal (formerly Durban-Westville). He has translated from the Portuguese works by Mozambican and Angolan writers including Lilia Momplé, Ondjaki, Ungulani ba ka Khosa and Pepetela, and edited *Halala Madiba: Nelson Mandela in Poetry* (2006). He is the editor of the *African Review of Books*, and the co-founder of Aflame Books. He works for the *Financial Times* newspaper and lives in London.

Francesca Chiarelli studied at the University of Florence and completed her doctoral studies at Royal Holloway college, University of London, with an examination of Claudio Monteverdi's madrigals. She has published papers in a number of Italian and English-language journals, co-edited *The Influence of Italian Entertainments on Sixteenth-and Seventeenth-Century Music Theatre in France, Savoy and England* (2000), and contributed to *The Oxford Companion to Italian Literature* (2002). She is currently Graduate School Administrator at Royal Holloway.

David J. Constantine is a British writer, poet and translator. He is a noted translator of German poetry and, among other awards, has twice won the European Poetry Translation Prize. His *Collected Poems* was published in 2004. *Under the Dam*, a collection of short stories, was published in 2005. He is a Fellow of Queen's College, Oxford.

Mererid Puw Davies is a lecturer at University College London where she teaches German language, modern literature and film. She studied at Magdalen College and St John's College, Oxford, and has held scholarships in Germany. Her research interests range from the study of violence and gender in German literature to literary, artistic and political responses to the Vietnam war. She has published two volumes of poetry in Welsh and is also interested in the translation of poetry from and into Welsh and other languages.

Yusuf Eradam is a poet, short-story and song writer, essayist, drama critic, translator and photographer. He graduated from Darüşşafaka, a boarding school for orphans, in Istanbul and Hacettepe University in Ankara, and in 1986 completed his doctorate on "The Haunted Individual in David Mercer's Stage Plays". Later, he received his M.A. TESOL from Moray House College of Education in Edinburgh. He has taught English language and American culture and literature at Hacettepe and Ankara universities, has written ten books, translated and edited many more, is well known for his translations of Sylvia Plath's poems, and has held three photography exhibitions. He has won many awards and lives in Istanbul.

Emiko Hamazaki-Collins was born in Chiba-ken, Japan in 1958 and completed her education in Tokyo. She lives in Wiltshire, England, where she popularises Japanese language and cuisine, and teaches Japanese.

R. Frank Hardy worked as a translator for the Instituto del Libro in Havana before and at the time of Che's death, and translated the work of a number of prominent young poets including Miguel Barnet, Félix Pita Rodríguez, Fayad Jamis and Guillermo Rodríguez Rivera.

John Irons studied languages at Cambridge University before specialising in Dutch poetry for his PhD. He also holds a Scandinavian degree in English and German. He has lived in Scandinavia since 1968 and has translated a considerable amount of poetry, mainly from Danish, Swedish, Norwegian, Dutch and Flemish into English.

Joan Jara is the British-born widow of the Chilean poet, folk singer and political activist Víctor Jara. When she learned of his arrest by Pinochet's military forces in 1973, she went to the British embassy for help — but this was not forthcoming. After his execution at the hands of Pinochet's military forces she retrieved his body and confirmed the harm he had suffered as the result of brutal torture. After her husband's funeral, she fled Chile and, although the military regime destroyed the master recordings of Jara's music, she was able to smuggle recordings out which were later copied and distributed worldwide. She published a moving account of her husband's life and music, *Víctor: An Unfinished*

Song (1983), and runs the Víctor Jara Foundation in Chile.

Georgina Jiménez R. was born in Mexico City. She graduated in journalism and media at the Universidad Nacional Autonoma de Mexico and worked as a journalist in Mexico City before moving to London, where she works as a civil servant and freelance writer. She has translated and written for several British newspapers, including the *Guardian Education* supplement, and writes book and film reviews for the *Latin American Review of Books*.

A.Lakshmi studied chemistry as an undergraduate and English literature for her Master's degree. She now works as a high school teacher in H.S. Poomala, near Thrisur, Kerala. She is the wife of the poet K.G. Sankara Pillai, and maintains a keen interest in literature, particularly poetry.

John La Rose (1927-2006) was a Trinidadian-born poet, writer, publisher and a prominent activist for black rights. Originally a teacher, he helped to form trades unions and became a leader of the West Indian Independence Party. He came to Britain in 1961 and in 1966 founded New Beacon Books and co-founded the Caribbean Artists Movement. He became involved in the Black Education Movement and in 1969 founded the George Padmore Supplementary School. Over the next 20 years he was the founder, co-founder or chairman of a significant number of initiatives and organisations including: the Institute of Race Relations, the Caribbean Education and Community Workers Association, the Black Parents Movement, Africa Solidarity, European Action for Racial Equality and Social Justice and the George Padmore Institute. He was joint director of the International Book Fair of Radical Black and Third World Books (1982-1995), edited a number of journals, and published two collections of poetry. His journalistic writing was widely published and he scripted and produced documentary films.

Lee Sang-Wha is a professor of English Literature at ChoongAng University. Her specialty is utopias in literature and she has published a study of British utopian novels in the 20th century. She has also translated six literary works from English into Korean.

Georgia Loukina helps unemployed Greek and foreign trainees in their search for work in Athens. She studied sociology and personnel management at London Guildhall and Kingston universities in London. She has worked as a personnel manager, office manager and promotions manager as well as a Greek interpreter and teacher. For several years she was a co-ordinator at the National Labour Institute (EIE) in Athens, and now heads the Employment Guidance Office at the Ergon Kek vocational training centre.

Nuria Madroño Calvo took a master's degree in psychology from Salamanca university in Spain and later trained in international conflict mediation, which took her to hotspots in Sri Lanka, Ecuador and Northern Ireland. She is fluent in five languages and has promoted multi-cultural awareness through programmes in Spain, Hungary, Belgium and the UK. While living in the Republic of Ireland, she acted as an interpreter for the French consulate and multinational companies. She currently lives in London, where she is the workforce development manager at Westminster City Council.

Walter May (1913-2006) was a translator and poet who specialised in Russian, Ukrainian and Kyrgyz. He lived for many years in Moscow and translated a large number of poems and anthologies including *Fair Land of Byelorussia* (1976), Maksim Tank's *The Horse and the Lion* (1975), Oleksandr Pidsukha's *Liryka* (1979) and Alykul Osmonov' *Waves of the Lake* (1995).

Joachim Neugroschel was born in Vienna and grew up in New York. He graduated from

Columbia University in English and comparative literature then lived in Paris and Berlin before returning to New York. He has translated at least 200 titles including the works of literary masters such as Maupassant, Proust and Kafka, and is well known for his translation of works of Yiddish literature. He translated *The Shadows of Berlin* (2005), a collection of stories by Dovid Bergelson, considered to be one of the 20th century's finest Soviet Yiddish writers. He is the winner of three PEN Translation Awards and the 1994 French-American Translation Prize.

Jonathan Noble is a visiting assistant professor in the Department of East Asian Languages and Literatures of the University of Notre Dame's Centre for Asian Studies. He has translated and written introductions to a number of theatrical works including *New Youth* by Hang Cheng and *Che Guevara* by Shen Lin, Huang Jisu and Zhang Guangtian. He has written about contemporary Chinese culture for academic journals such as *Modern Chinese Literature and Culture (MCLC)*.

Gavin O'Toole is a journalist, academic and translator. He studied in Liverpool and London, and completed his doctorate on Mexican nationalism at Queen Mary, where he taught Latin American politics and democratic theory. He has worked for a number of national newspapers in the UK including the *Guardian, Observer* and, currently, the *Financial Times*. His latest book is *Politics Latin America* (2007) and he is the editor of the *Latin American Review of Books*.

Isabel O'Toole is a student in London with Mexican and Irish antecedents. She has contributed reviews to the *Latin American Review of Books* and writes poetry. She is also a photographer, known for her close-focus and textured studies of cemeteries, and has made several experimental short films.

Simon Patton is a freelance literary translator specialising in contemporary Chinese literature, and earns a living teaching Chinese language and translation part-time at the University of Queensland. He also co-edits the China domain of Poetry International Web with the poet Yu Jian at china.poetryinternationalweb.org.

Louise B. Popkin divides her time between Boston, where she teaches at Harvard University's Division of Continuing Education, and Montevideo, Uruguay. Her translations of Latin American poetry, theatre and fiction have appeared in numerous literary journals and anthologies. Her most recent book-length publication is Mauricio Rosencof, *The Letters that Never Came* (2004). She has translated a number of short stories by Mario Benedetti (cf., Mario Benedetti, *Blood Pact and Other Stories* [1997]), as well as a selection of 15 of his poems, scheduled to appear in the Fall 2007 issue of *Beacons* (American Translators Association).

James Ragan is an award-winning poet, playwright and screenwriter whose work has been widely published and translated. Born in Pittsburgh to Czechoslovak parents, he has earned many accolades, is a Fulbright Professor, and often returns to the Czech Republic to teach at Charles University. In 1985 he was one of three Americans, along with Robert Bly and Bob Dylan, to be invited to perform at the First International Poetry Festival in Moscow. He is director of the Graduate Professional Writing Programme at the University of Southern California.

Margaret Randall is a writer, photographer and political activist. She pursued a writing career and participated in the beatnik movement, and from 1960-69 lived in Mexico where she co-edited the literary magazine *El Corno Emplumado* and became a Mexican citizen. Repression against supporters of the Mexican student movement with which she was identified forced her to go underground. She moved to Cuba, where she lived from 1969-80 and worked for the Cuban Book Institute, and then on to Nicaragua. She returned to the US in 1984 and began teaching but in 1985 was denied permanent resident status under the McCarran-Walter Act, which was used to exclude people from the US based on perceived adherence to ideologies considered subversive. Supporters formed defence committees across the country and in 1989 the US immigration services yielded.

Alexandra Stanton took European studies and history at Queen Mary and Westfield college, University of London, where she went on to undertake her PhD exploring Italian feminist theory and where she also taught about political ideas. She works for Royal Holloway college, University of London, as a Senior Educational Support Officer.

Albert C. Todd co-edited and was the chief translator of Yevgeny Yevtushenko's *Collected Poems 1952-1990* (1991). A professor of Slavic and East European languages at Queens College, New York, he was a longstanding friend of the poet whom he met in 1961 while undertaking post-doctoral research at Harvard University. Yevtushenko dedicated several poems to Dr Todd and was a godfather to one of his children.

Niklas Törnlund is a Swedish poet. Born in 1950, he lives in Lund. He has published translations of Gary Snyder and Kenneth Rexroth, as well as 11 collections of his own poetry. *All Things Measure Time*, a selection, was published in the US in 1992.

ACKNOWLEDGEMENTS

The following individuals and organisations in the UK deserve mention for their support and help: Richard Bartlett, Monica Seeber and Luzette Strauss of Aflame Books; Jonathan Cook, Rowena Dewar, James Fitzgerald, Richard Flood, Claudia Gerhardt, Felicity Goodall, Pushpinder Khaneka, Jai Kharbanda, Sue Larkin, Simon Pirani, Paul Plant, Paul Roberts, Eileen, Chris and Patrick Stanton, Dave Vallis, Susan Wood, Oscar Luna, Chris McCabe of The Poetry Library (London), Almut Liebler of the Goethe-Institut Library (London) and *Poetry News*. We are grateful to the staff of the following libraries for their professional assistance: the British Library, Bristol University Arts and Social Sciences Library, Cambridge University Library, Senate House Library (University of London), the School of African and Oriental Studies library (London), Institute for the Study of the Americas library (London), the Scottish Poetry Library, and the Robarts Library (University of Toronto).

Last, but by no means least, we are grateful to all the following individuals and organisations for helping us in our effort to bring the poems of countries across the world into this collection, regardless of whether this effort came to fruition or not: Algeria: Alexandra Gueydan-Turek, Yale University; Sabine Dubois, ADAMI, Paris; M. Taousar Hakim, Directeur Général, Office national du droit d'auteur et des droits voisins (ONDA); Hege Roel Rousson, Actes Sud; Rabeh Toubal, Cultural Counsellor, Algerian Embassy in London; Robert Parks, Director, Centre d'Etudes Maghrébines en Algérie (CEMA). Argentina: Ana Paz, Agencia Literaria Carmen Balcells; Carmen Pérez de Arenaza, Directora de la Biblioteca, Fundación Juan March; Jennifer Sarkissian, Nacional Records/Cookman International; Marcello Marcolini, Agenda Cultural, Bahía Blanca; *Página 12*. Australia: Jutta Sieverding and the Poets Union; Rosanna Licari, Editor, *Stylus Poetry Journal*. Belgium: Hugo Franssen, EPO. Bolivia: Antonio Peredo; Jackie Bivens, Communication For Social Change (CFSC) Consortium. Canada: Susan Dubrofsky, *Serai*; The Comedy Network; Cass Bayley and Sara Gundy, The Bayley Group; Rene Garcia, TorontoHispano.com; McClelland & Stewart, Toronto. Chile: Quena Arrieta, Fundación Víctor Jara; Fundación Pablo Neruda; Memoria Chilena; Juan Camilo; Fernando Rendón; José Osorio, Letras de Chile; Ana Maria Salinas. China: Enid Tsui; Alice Grünfelder, Lektorat & Literaturvermittlung; Mani Rao; Kirk A. Denton, Ohio State University; Poetry International Web; Yu Jian; Audrey Heijns, Assistant Editor, *Renditions*; Kirk A. Denton, Ohio State University. Colombia: Martha Lucía Usaquén Ramos, Museo del Oro Quimbaya; David Felipe Álvarez Amézquita, Dirección Nacional de Derecho de Autor (DNDA); Alicia Alfaro , Cultural Attaché , Colombian Embassy, London; Harold Alvarado Tenorio, Fundación Arquitrave; Wilson Rafael Ríos Ruiz, Centro Colombiano del Derecho de Autor (CECOLDA); www.hastasiempre.it. Congo: Dr Valentine Y.

Mudimbe, Duke University. Cuba: Roberto Fernández Retamar, Jorge Fornet and Blanca Hernández, Casa de las Américas, Havana; Aurelio Alonso, *Casa de las Américas* magazine; Ernesto Vila, Director, Editora Musical de Cuba; Alena Zamora Delgado, Centro Nacional de Derecho de Autor (CENDA); Marianela Morales, Cuban Embassy in London; Élsida González, Directora de Música, EGREM; Fundación Fernando Ortiz, Cuba; Minerva Mallo Mesa, Commercial Manager, Soycubano; Jorge Garrido, CubaNow; Alba Alvarez Augier, Fundación Nicolás Guillén; María Eugenia Guerrero; Monica López, British Embassy in Havana; Professor Tony Kapcia, Head of the Hispanic and Latin American Studies Department; University of Nottingham; Professor Jean Stubbs, Caribbean Studies Centre, London Metropolitan University; Professor Jenny Hocking, Monash University; Leslie Mitchner and Marlie Wasserman, Rutgers University Press; Florence Turbet-Delof, Reporteros Sin Fronteras, Sección Española; Rita Pomade, MexicoConnect. Czech Republic: James Naughton, Oxford University; Dr Martin Pilar, Ostrava University. Denmark: Helle Kristjansen; Carole and Clete Mathurin; Annette Bach, Editor, *Danish Literary Magazine*, Danish Literature Centre; Søren Beltoft, konsulent, Litteraturcentret/Kunststyrelsen. Ecuador: Déborah Salgado Campaña, Embassy of Ecuador in the UK; Magno Coronel Calle, Casa de la Cultura Ecuatoriana. Egypt: Jonathan Cook; Cathy Costain, British Council, Cairo. El Salvador: Alberto Cerritos; Jaime Amate. Finland: Lola Rogers and T. Ilkka, FILI-Finnish Literature Information Centre; Hanna Kjellberg and Eila Mellin, Otava Group Agency. France: Julia Grawemeyer, Céline Hérmon and Jean-Pierre Siméon of the Printemps des poètes, Paris. Germany: Professor Leonard Olschner, Queen Mary, University of London. Greece: Marianna Anastasiou, "Lilian Voudouri" Music Library of Greece; Irene Mega, Athenaum; Miranda Spicer. Guatemala: Silvia Molina, Directora, INBA, Mexico. Hungary: Miklos Vajda, *The Hungarian Quarterly*; Olga Zaslavskaya, International Samizdat Research Association. India: Krishna Kimbahune, Sahitya Akademi; George Pulikuthiyil, Jananeethi; R. P. Nair, Editor, *Kavya Bharati*, SCILET American College; Anna Weston, *New Internationalist*. Iran: Jahanshah Javid. Ireland: *Poetry Ireland News*; Dearbhla Mooney, National University of Ireland Galway; *Ireland's Own*; *The Blanket*. Italy: Roberto Massari, Erre Emme (Massari Editore); Edy Campo, Trident Management. Japan: Takeshi Toyoizumi, The Museum of Contemporary Japanese Poetry, Tanka, and Haiku, Iwate; the Library of the Japanese Embassy in London. Korea: Philip Gowman, London Korean Links; Hyun Yoo; Sogang University, Seoul. Mexico: Carlos Pellicer López; Silvia Molina, Coordinadora Nacional de Literatura, Instituto Nacional de Bellas Artes; Raquel Huerta-Nava; Héctor de Paz, Instituto Estatal de Cultura del Estado de Tabasco. Netherlands: Elodie Chavrot, Prince Claus Fund for Culture and Development; Katja Nootenboom, Stichting Poetry International; Thomas Möhlmann, Poetry, Foundation for the Production and Translation of Dutch Literature (NLPVF). New Zealand: Laurice Gilbert, New

Zealand Poetry Society; Vaughan Gunson. Nicaragua: Dieter Stadler. Panama: Rita Changmarín; *Camino Alternativo*. Peru: Margherita Cristiani, Edizioni Fahrenheit 451; Educared Estudiantes; Lorenzo Chang-Navarro L.; Antonio Figueroa Tapia, Director Ejecutivo, IPROGA. Poland: Krystyna Krzyzak; Ania Cannon. Portugal: Paula Borges Fernandes of Literarische Agentur Dr. Ray-Güde Mertin. Romania: Professor Dennis Deletant, University College London. Russia: Dean Starr and Susan H. Kamei, University of Southern California; Igor Mikhailusenko; Andrew Wachtel and Ilya Kutik, Northwestern University; Henry Holt. Saint Lucia: University of the West Indies; Judy Raymond; Victoria Fox, Farrar Straus and Giroux. Serbia: Zoran Milutinovic. South Africa: Morakabe Seakhoa; Andries Oliphant. Spain: Marianne Brull, Editions Ruedo ibérico; Concha Fernández Candau, Biblioteca, Fundación Rafael Alberti; Jean-Louis Cougnon, European Parliament, General Directorate for Information; Luis Pastor; Delegación Socialista Española, Parlamento Europeo; Partido Socialista de Navarra (PSN-PSOE); Almudena Roncero Villa, Sociedad General de Autores y Editores, Spain; Pilar Juanas, Alianza Editorial; Karen Efford, International PEN; Carlos Arias, Xunta de Galicia. Galicia: Celia Torres Bouzas, Directora de Promoción e Prensa, Edicións Xerais de Galicia; Real Academia Galega. Sweden: The Swedish Academy. Thailand: John and Patcharin Hayes; Jira Nan Pit Preecha. Turkey: Professor Suat Karantay, Bogazici University; Tulin Damar. Ukraine: Vladyslav Rohovyi, Cultural Attache, Embassy of Ukraine; John Sherahilo. England: Paul Cronin; Luke Marson, MCPS Licensing, Felix Taylor; Dick Gaughan; Tom Erhardt, Casarotto Ramsay & Associates; Helen Bradbury, Sutton Publishing; Sophie Hoult; David Godwin Associates. Scotland: Lizzie MacGregor, Scottish Poetry Library; Mercat Press. USA: Wylie Agency; Levi Asher, Literary Kicks; Kasli Tai; Victoria Fox; Paul Pearson, Merton Centre. Uruguay: Jose Ibarburu, *Brecha*; Ariel Silva; Graduate School of Arts and Sciences, Harvard University; Martín Rosich and Nelly Mozzo, Dirección de Cultura MEC, Uruguay; Pedro Mendiola, Biblioteca Virtual Miguel de Cervantes; José Carlos Rovira and Carmen Alemany, Universidad de Alicante; Bárbara Graham, Guillermo Schavelzon & Asociados; Cosme David Doti Genta, Sonia Rua, La Cámara de Representantes. Venezuela: J.L. Da Silva; Marianela Vargas, Agencia Literaria Venezolana, Instituto Autónomo Centro Nacional del Libro (CENAL). Vietnam: David Constantine. Zimbabwe: Ignatius T. Mabasa, British Council, Zimbabwe; Victor Mavedzenge, Pamberi Trust; Budding Writers Association of Zimbabwe.

PUBLISHER ACKNOWLEDGEMENTS

The editors and publishers have made considerable effort to contact all rights holders of poems, song lyrics and translations in this book, whether they be poets, songwriters, heirs, agents or publishers and, where there is confusion over rights, to establish who is the correct and legitimate rights holder. This has been difficult in some cases: poets or songwriters are deceased and their heirs are untraceable; publishing houses or music companies have ceased to exist or have merged; the whereabouts of poets or songwriters is unknown. The editor and publishers wish sincerely to thank all those poets, songwriters and translators, or their heirs, who granted permission, in many cases generously without a fee and out of a sense of conviction. In cases where we have been unable to trace a poet, songwriter, heir, publisher or music company, we welcome any further information about their whereabouts.

Our thanks for permission to reproduce these poems and songs go:
For "Che.. Che.. Here's to you!", by Bagdad Maata: to the poet; Paul Mombelli, editor of Caloucaera.
For "I had a brother" by Julio Cortázar: to Agencia Literaria Carmen Balcells, Barcelona. Grateful acknowledgment is made to the *Casa de las Américas* magazine, Havana.
For "Red cockerel" by Gabriel Fernández Capello (Vicentico), Los Fabulosos Cadillacs: to Tomas Cookman of El Leon Music; the songwriter; Gustavo Menendez, Warner Chappell.
For "Conversations" by Juan Gelman: to the poet. Grateful acknowledgment is made to the *Casa de las Américas* magazine, Havana.
For "Words to Che" by Leopoldo Marechal: to María de los Ángeles y María Magdalena Marechal. Grateful acknowledgment is made to the *Casa de las Américas* magazine, Havana.
For "Koki Market" by S. K. Kelen: to the poet.
For "What did you make of it?" by Josef Lesser: to the poet.
For "Che Guevara's Last Bodyguard" by Duncan Richardson: to Duncan Richardson; first published in *Stylus Poetry Journal*, October 2002.
For "Soft Riots / TV News", by Richard Tipping: to the poet.
For "Che Guevara" by Kerry Upjohn: to the poet.
For "To Che" by Frieda Groffy: to the poet.
For "Che" by Alfonso Gumucio Dagron: to the poet. Grateful acknowledgment is made to the *Casa de las Américas* magazine, Havana
For "I'm crazy for you, America" by José Carlos Capinam and Gilberto Gil: © Copyright 1967 by Gilberto Gil & Jose Carlos Capinam. With thanks to Preta Music and Grupo Editorial Musical Arlequim.
For "Blood and dew" by Thiago de Mello: to the poet. Grateful acknowledgment is made to the *Casa de las Américas* magazine, Havana
For "Ernesto Guevara Chez Everywhere" by Martha Chaves: to the poet. © Martha Chaves. Grateful acknowledgment is made to Montreal *Serai* e-zine
For "Hombre" by Al Purdy: to Howard White, Harbour Publishing.
For "The Bee Hive" by Joe Rosenblatt: to the poet.
For "Apparition" by Víctor Jara: to Joan Jara, Fundación Víctor Jara.

Acknowledgements

For "Sadness at the Death of a Hero" by Pablo Neruda: to Agencia Literaria Carmen Balcells, Barcelona.

For "The hands" by Floridor Pérez: to the poet. Grateful acknowledgment is made to the *Casa de las Américas* magazine, Havana.

For "Spectre of the warrior" by Jaime Valdivieso: to the poet. Grateful acknowledgment is made to the *Casa de las Américas* magazine, Havana

For "Che Guevara" by Jiang Fei: to the poet.

For "Yi Sha and Che Guevara" by Jun'er: to the poet.

For "Urban Landscape" by Yi Sha: to the poet.

For "Che Guevara" by Zhang Guangtian translated by Jonathan Noble: to *Modern Chinese Literature and Culture* (MCLC) and MCLC Resource Center; Jonathan Noble.

For "The giant" by Nelson Osorio Marín: to Sergio Osorio Velasquez.

For "Ode to Ernesto 'Che' Guevara" by Ernesto Con: to the poet; Resurgam-Anggraini Publishing.

For "Still it is the dreams" by Gerardo Alfonso: to the songwriter.

For "Ché" by Miguel Barnet: to the poet.

For "A necessary song" by Vicente Feliú: to the songwriter.

For "Che's example" by Antonio Guerrero Rodríguez: to the poet.

For "Che Comandante" by Nicolás Guillén: to Nicolás Augusto Hernández Guillén, Fundación Nicolás Guillén

For "Che" by Pedro Pérez Sarduy: to the poet.

For "Till forever, Comandante" by Carlos Puebla: to Editora Musical de Cuba. Grateful acknowledgment is made to the *Casa de las Américas* magazine, Havana

For "Extract from Act III of Topia or Che Guevara" by Klaus Høeck: to the poet. © Copyright Klaus Høeck and Gyldendal, 1978.

For "Che: the fleetingness of his death" by Jorge Enrique Adoum: to the poet.

For "The creed according to Ché" by Roque Dalton: to Juan José Dalton.

For "walking the beach with my daughter's eyes & the news in my head" by Anselm Hollo: to the poet.

For "On a hot sunny day" by Pentti Saarikoski: to Otava Group Agency. "Helteisenä päivänä" by Pentti Saarikoski (from the collection *Katselen Stalinin pään yli ulos*). First published by Otava Publishing Company Ltd. in 1969.

For "The Stranger Left on the Terraces of Baalbeck" by André Benedetto: to the poet. First published in Benedetto, André. 1971. *Les Poubelles du Vent*. France: P.J.Oswald.

For "Elegy for El Che" by Francis Combes: to the poet; Le Temps des Cerises.

For "Hope is Speaking" by Auguste Macouba, grateful acknowledgment is made to the *Casa de las Américas* magazine, Havana

For "After the Massacre of Illusions" by Volker Braun: to Suhrkamp Verlag, poem "After the Massacre of Illusions" ("Nach dem Massaker der Illusionen") taken from: Volker Braun. 1998. *Tumulus*. Frankfurt am Main: Suhrkamp Verlag. Translation © David Constantine and *Modern Poetry in Translation*.

For "E.G. de la S. (1928-1967)" by Hans Magnus Enzensberger: to Suhrkamp Verlag, poem "E.G. de la S. (1928-1967)" taken from: Enzensberger, Hans Magnus. 1975. *Mausoleum. Siebenunddreissig Balladen aus der Geschichte des Fortschritts*. Frankfurt am Main: Suhrkamp Verlag.

For "Saluting Che Guevara" by Peter Schütt: to the poet.

For extracts from "Concert for Machine-gun: Cantigas for Ché Guevara" by Otto-Raúl González: to the poet.

For "Ten Years: 1959-1969" by Jan Carew: to the poet.

For the extract from "The Dance of the Swords of Fear" by René Depestre, grateful acknowledgment is made to the *Casa de las Américas* magazine, Havana.

For "Ernesto Che Guevara" by Jean Métellus: to the poet. Grateful acknowledgment is made to: Editions le Temps des Cerises.

For "Che's Poem" by Anthony Phelps: to the poet. Grateful acknowledgment is made to the *Casa de las Américas* magazine, Havana.

For "Dear Che" by K.G. Sankara Pillai: to the poet.

For "Memory strands" by Siamak Kiarostami: to the poet. Grateful acknowledgment is made to: Iranian.com.

For "The Star" by Kieran Furey: to the poet.

For "Che Guevara in a Limerick pub" by Val Nolan: to the poet.

For "Che" by Liam Ó Comain: to the poet.

For "Our Che" by Andrew Salkey: to Patricia Salkey. Grateful acknowledgment is made to the *Casa de las Américas* magazine, Havana

For "Seasons" by Francesco Guccini: to the artist. Copyright © Francesco Guccini. Used by permission EMI Music Publishing

For "Positive Thinking" by Jovanotti: "Penso Positivo" lyrics by Lorenzo Cherubini © 1993 Soleluna Srl, D.J's Gang Srl, Universal Music Italia Srl.

For "Celia de La Serna" by Roberto Vecchioni: to the artist. Copyright © Roberto Vecchioni. Used by permission EMI Music Publishing

For "Ernesto Che Guevara" by Renji Ono: to Tamotsu Ono.

For "Memoirs" by Ko Un: to the poet; Changbi Publishers.

For "Before the Grave of the Poet Kim Namju" by Min Yeong: to the poet.

For "Cantata for Che Guevara" by Efraín Huerta: to Herederos de Efraín Huerta.

For "Remembering Che Guevara" by José Tiquet: to Claudia Tiquet Soto on behalf of Estela Soto and the Tiquet family.

For "Nobel 1" by Sebastão Alba: Copyright © Quasi Edições, taken from *Albas*, Quasi Edições, Portugal, 2007.

For "Che Guevara's lyric" by Bernard Gadd: to the poet.

For "A Sonnet to Ché Guevara (For his place in Popular Culture)" by Michael O'Leary: to the poet.

For "City Walk" by Mark Pirie: to the poet.

For "In Rivas, Nicaragua" by Jorge Eduardo Arellano: to the poet.

For "The Che feeling" by Changmarín: to the poet. Grateful acknowledgment is made to the *Casa de las Américas* magazine, Havana.

For "Che, Friend" by Juan Cristóbal: to the poet.

For "Elegy to the Black Waters for Che Guevara" by Eugénio de Andrade: to the Fundação Eugénio de Andrade.

For "Poem" by Jorge de Sena: to the estate of Jorge de Sena. Copyright © Mécia de Sena.

For "Che Guevara" by Sophia de Mello from *Obra Poética III*, Editorial Caminho. © Estate of Sophia de Mello Breyner Andresen.

For "Keys of the Comandante" by Yevgeny Yevtushenko: to the poet.

For "Che" by Derek Walcott: taken from *The Gulf and Other Poems* by Derek Walcott. Copyright © 1970, renewed 1998 by Derek Walcott. Reprinted by permission of Farrar, Straus and Giroux, LLC on behalf of Derek Walcott.

For "To Che Guevara with love" by Masa Mbatha-Opasha: to the poet.

For "To Ernesto Che Guevara" by Rafael Alberti: to Agencia Literaria Carmen Balcells,

Barcelona.

For "Scary lullabies with Che Guevara in the background" by Víctor Manuel Arbeloa: to the poet.

For "Proclamation of the new peasant" by Xosé Luis Méndez Ferrín: to the poet.

For "Ramón" by Ingemar Leckius: to the poet. Grateful acknowledgment is made to the *Casa de las Américas* magazine, Havana.

For "Che" by Arif Damar: to the poet.

For "Che Guevara" by Metin Demirtaş: to the poet.

For "Che was a doctor" by Sennur Sezer: to the poet.

For "Patria o muerte — Venceremos" by Alan C. Brown: to the poet.

For "Chez Guevara" by Kevin Cadwallender: to the poet.

For "The View from Two Murders: Ernesto Che Guevara" by Ian Caws: to the poet.

For "Haiku for Che" by Christopher Logue: Copyright © Christopher Logue

For "The revolutionary" by Edward Lucie-Smith: to the poet.

For "Compañeros" by Ewan MacColl: Copyright © Harmony Music Ltd. Used by permission.

For "An impersonal note to Che Guevara" by John McGrath: to Mrs John McGrath.

For "HOW TO KILL CUBA" by Adrian Mitchell from HEART ON THE LEFT © Adrian Mitchell 1997 is reproduced by permission of PFD (www.pfd.co.uk) on behalf of Adrian Mitchell.

For "Put a bullet in his head" by Andrew Sinclair: to the poet.

For "my love sold revolutionary newspapers" by Cliff Wedgbury: to the poet.

For "What can I say to you, Che Guevara?" by Ted Willis: to John Willis © Ted Willis (1968).

For "The Date" by John Greeves: to the poet.

For "To the memory of Che" by Lyman Andrews: to the poet.

For "Che" by Judy Collins: Copyright © Harmony Music Ltd. Used by permission.

For "The Mind of Ché Guevara a Day After His Death". By Lawrence Ferlinghetti, from THE MEXICAN NIGHT, copyright © 1970 by Lawrence Ferlinghetti. Reprinted by permission of New Directions Publishing Corp.

For "Elegy Ché Guévara" by Allen Ginsberg: taken from *Collected Poems 1947-1980* by Allen Ginsberg. Copyright © 1984 by Allen Ginsberg. Reprinted by permission of HarperCollins Publishers.

For "Guevara" by John Haines: taken from *The Stone Harp* (Wesleyan University Press, 1971). Copyright © 1971 by John Haines and reprinted by permission of Wesleyan University Press.

For 'I was the jealous one', an extract from *The Eros Conspiracy"* by Greg Hewett. Copyright © 2006 by Greg Hewett. Reprinted with the permission of Coffee House Press, Minneapolis, Minnesota, www.coffeehousepress.org

For "Revolution Merchandise" Patrick Hyland: to the poet.

For "Death of Che" by Maggie Jaffe: to the poet.

For "Che Guevara" by Robert Lowell, from *Collected Poems* by Robert Lowell. Copyright © 2003 by Harriet Lowell and Sheridan Lowell. Reprinted by permission of Farrar, Straus and Giroux, LLC.

For "Berkeley Song" by Michael McClure, from Rebel Lions, copyright © 1978 by Michael McClure. Reprinted by permission of New Directions Publishing Corp; and reproduced by permission of Pollinger Limited and the proprietor.

For "Letters to Che: Canto bilingüe" by Thomas Merton: taken from *The Collected Poems of Thomas Merton*, copyright © 1977 by Trustees of the Merton Legacy Trust. Reprinted by permission of New Directions Publishing Corp; and reproduced by permission of Pollinger Limited and the proprietor.

For "The Hands of Che Guevara" by Anne Delana Reeves: Copyright © 1997 by the *Antioch Review*, Inc. First appeared in the *Antioch Review*, Vol. 55, No. 1. Reprinted by permission of the Editors.

For "Was his death in vain?" by Daniel Schechter: to the poet.

For "Che Guevara" by Peggy Seeger: first published in Volume 2 of the New City Songster. Copyright © Harmony Music Ltd. Used by permission.

For "In Grief and Rage" by Mario Benedetti: to Guillermo Schavelzon & Asociados, Barcelona, on behalf of the poet. Grateful acknowledgment is made to the *Casa de las Américas* magazine, Havana.

For "Unto victory" by Aníbal Sampayo: to Estela Quinteros de Sampayo on behalf of Aníbal Sampayo.

For "Ernesto "Che" Guevara" by Pablo Mora: to Agencia Literaria Venezolana (CENAL) on behalf of Pablo Mora.

For "Bayete Latin Warrior!" by Cosmas Mairosi: to the poet.

Grateful acknowledgment is made to Andrew Sinclair and Lorrimer, which first published in English some of the material included in this book, and to Lyudmila Serostanova and Sarah White for permission to use translations. Acknowledgment is given to the following publishers, journals and editors of books, magazines and broadsides, music companies and organisations, past or present, responsible for or believed to have been responsible for previously publishing some of the material in this volume: University of Queensland Press; Editorial Merlín; Hale & Iremonger; Palabra ence; Eskeletra Editorial; Trigram Press; Urizen Books; Quer-Verlag, Hamburg; Editorial Praxis; Si wa Sihaksa; Ediciones Americanas; Campo das Letras; Editora Caminho; Erre Emme; Editori Riuniti; Institute del Libro, Cuba; Utgivningsår; Cem Yayinevi; Can Yayinlari; Evrensel Basim Yayin; Dnipro; Three Spires Press; Viet Nam Generation Inc. and Burning Cities Press; City Lights Books; New Directions Publishing; Biblioteca de Autores y Temas Tachirenses; *MOK; Poetry Australia; The Union Recorder; Víspera; Trilce; Prasakthi; Cuadernos Americanos; Ecuador 0° 0' 0''; Alif,* Tunis; *La Prensa Literaria; Revista España Republicana; Lines Review; Brittle Star;* LitKicks.com; EMI Music Publishing (Greece, Italy); Asociación Cultural "Alma Matinal"; Fundación Pablo Neruda.

INDEX BY POET